Travel Guide

WHERE TO
EAT
NEW YORK

FROM MOBIL FIVE-STARS TO STREET BITES

Ethnic Eateries Food Festivals Star Chefs Bars Maps

Acknowledgements

We gratefully acknowledge the help of our representatives for their efficient and perceptive inspections of the dining establishments listed; the establishments' proprietors for their cooperation in showing their facilities and providing information about them; and the many users of Mobil Travel Guide's products who have taken the time to share their experiences. We are also grateful to all the highly talented writers who contributed entries to this book.

Vice President, Publications: Kevin Bristow

Director, Editorial Content: Pam Mourouzis

Director of Publishing Production Services: Ellen Tobler

Editors: Brenda McLean, Nancy Swope

Publishing Coordinator: Shawn McNichols

Restaurant Research and Compilation: Meira Chiesa

Concept Design: Chris Mulligan

Cover Design: Kellie Bottrell/The Brochure Factory

Maps: © MapQuest.com, Inc. This product contains proprietary property of MapQuest.com, Inc. Unauthorized use, including copying, of this product is expressly prohibited.

Printing Acknowledgment: North American Corporation of Illinois

www.mobiltravelguide.com

Although every effort has been made to verify the information contained herein, restaurants can close or change without warning. Before making your plans, please call the restaurant to verify that it is still open and to confirm the cuisine type, meals served, and other particulars of importance to you. Some restaurants that appear on the maps in this book may not appear in the final listing. The publisher assumes no responsibility for inconsistencies or inaccuracies in the data and assumes no liability for any damages of any type arising from errors or omissions.

ISBN: 0-7627-3596-1

Manufactured in the United States of America.

10 9 8 7 6 5 4 3 2 1

Contents

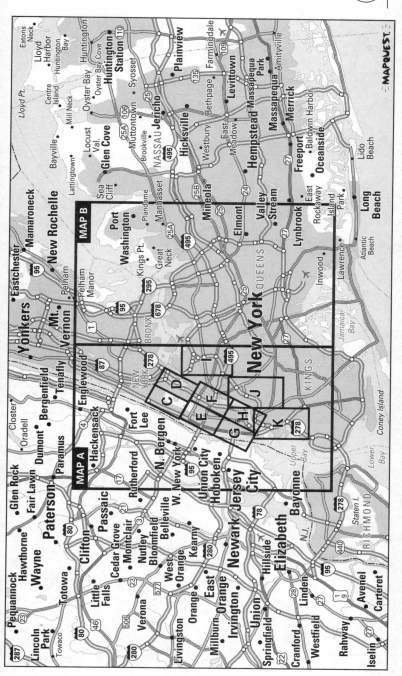

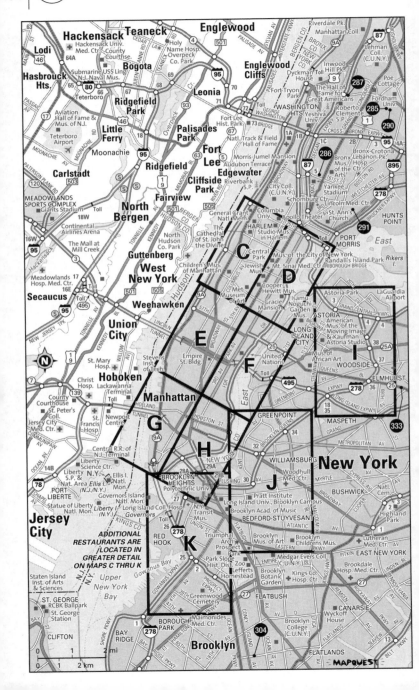

304 **DiFara's Pizzeria**
1424 Ave J
Brooklyn, NY 11230

285 **Emilia's**
2331 Arthur Ave
Bronx, NY 10458

286 **Feeding Tree**
892 Gerard Ave
Bronx, NY 10452

287 **Jimmy's Bronx Cafe**
281 W Fordham Rd
Bronx, NY 10468

333 **Ping's Seafood**
8302 Queens Blvd
Elmhurst, NY 11373

290 **Roberto's Trattoria**
632 Crescent Ave
Bronx, NY 10458

291 **Venice Restaurant and Pizzeria**
772 E 149th St
Bronx, NY 10455

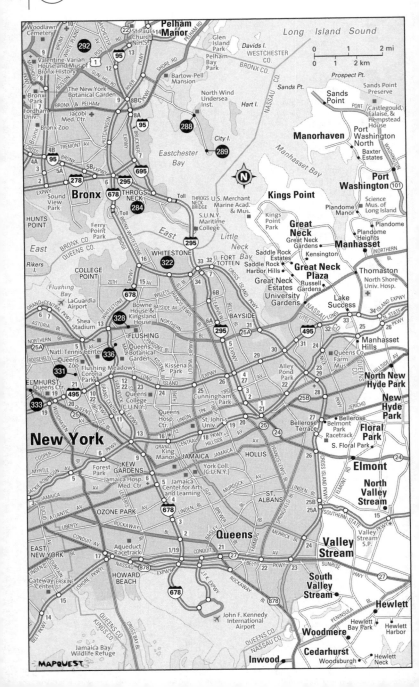

284 Charlie's Inn
2711 Harding Ave
Bronx, NY 10465

322 Cooking With Jazz
12-01 154th St
Whitestone, NY 11357

328 Kum Gang San
138-28 Northern Blvd
Flushing, NY 11354

288 Le Refuge Inn
620 City Island Ave
Bronx, NY 10464

289 Lobster Box
34 City Island Ave
Bronx, NY 10464

331 Park Side
107-01 Corona Ave
Corona, NY 11368

336 Sichuan Dynasty
135-32 40th Rd
Flushing, NY 11354

292 Vernon's New Jerk House
987 E 223rd St
Bronx, NY 10466

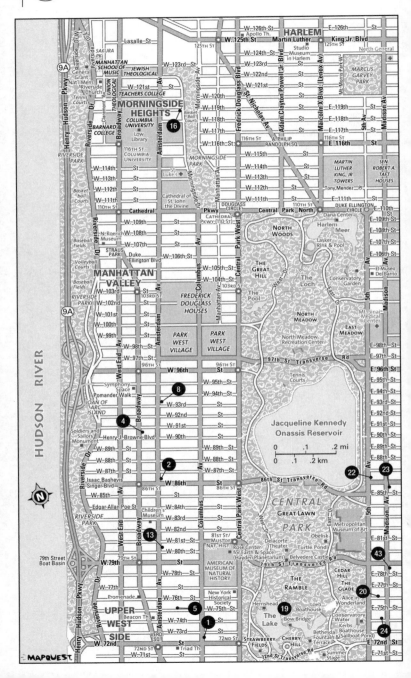

Map C · xi

1 @SQC
270 Columbus Ave
New York, NY 10023

2 Barney Greengrass
541 Amsterdam Ave
New York, NY 10024

19 Boathouse Cafe
72nd St in Central Park
New York, NY 10028

20 Café Boulud
20 E 76th St
New York, NY 10021

22 Café Sabarsky
1048 5th Ave
New York, NY 10028

4 Carmine's
2450 Broadway
New York, NY 10024

23 Centolire
1167 Madison Ave
Manhattan, NY 10028

5 Cesca
164 W 75th St
New York, NY 10023

24 Coco Pazzo
23 E 74th St
New York, NY 10021

8 Gabriela's
685 Amsterdam Ave
New York, NY 10025

13 Sarabeth's West
423 Amsterdam Ave
New York, NY 10024

43 Serafina Fabulous Pizza
1022 Madison Ave
New York, NY 10021

16 Terrace in the Sky
400 W 119th St
New York, NY 10027

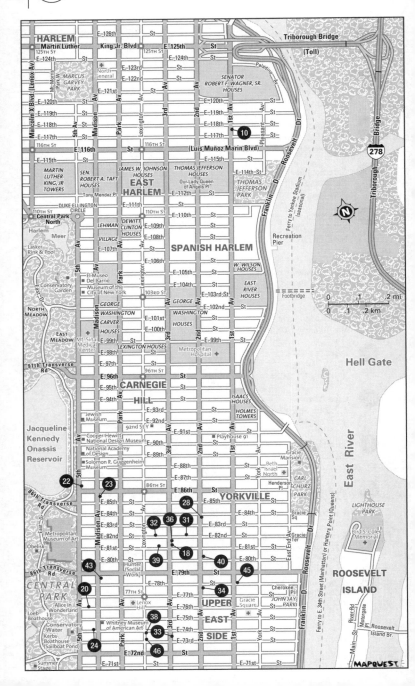

18 Beyoglu
1431 3rd Ave
New York, NY 10028

20 Café Boulud
20 E 76th St
New York, NY 10021

22 Café Sabarsky
1048 5th Ave
New York, NY 10028

23 Centolire
1167 Madison Ave
Manhattan, NY 10028

23 Coco Pazzo
23 E 74th St
New York, NY 10021

28 Jackson Hole
1611 Second Ave
New York, NY 10028

31 Kings' Carriage House
251 E 82nd St
New York, NY 10028

32 Le Refuge
166 E 82nd St
New York, NY 10021

33 Lenox Room
1278 Third Ave
New York, NY 10021

34 Lusardi's
1494 Second Ave
New York, NY 10021

36 Our Place
1444 Third Ave
New York, NY 10028

10 Patsy's Pizzeria
2287 1st Ave
New York, NY 10035

38 Payard Patisserie and Bistro
1032 Lexington Ave
New York, NY 10021

39 Pearson's Texas Barbecue
170 E 81st St
New York, NY 10028

40 Pig Heaven
1540 Second Ave
New York, NY 10028

43 Serafina Fabulous Pizza
1022 Madison Ave
New York, NY 10021

45 Sushi of Gari
402 E 78th St
New York, NY 10021

46 Willow
1022 Lexington Ave
New York, NY 10021

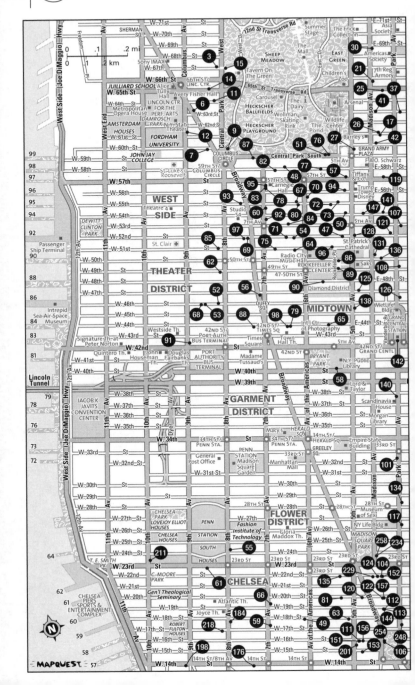

47 21 Club
21 W 52nd St
New York, NY 10019

48 Alain Ducasse
155 W 58th St
New York, NY 10019

49 Amuse
108 W 18th St
New York, NY 10011

50 Aquavit
13 W 54th St
New York, NY 10019

101 Artisinal
2 Park Ave
New York, NY 10016

51 Atelier
50 Central Park S
New York, NY 10019

17 Aureole
34 E 61st St
New York, NY 10021

52 Barbetta
321 W 46th St
New York, NY 10036

53 Becco
355 W 46th St
New York, NY 10036

54 Ben Benson's Steakhouse
123 W 52nd St
New York, NY 10019

104 Beppe
45 E 22nd St
New York, NY 10010

55 The Biltmore Room
290 8th Ave
New York, NY 10001

56 Blue Fin
1567 Broadway
New York, NY 10036

106 Blue Water Grill
31 Union Sq W
New York, NY 10003

229 Bolo
23 E 22nd St
New York, NY 10010

107 Brasserie
100 E 53rd St
New York, NY 10022

57 Brasserie 8 ½
9 W 57th St
New York, NY 10019

58 Bryant Park Grill
25 W 40th St
New York, NY 10018

108 Bull and Bear Steakhouse
301 Park Ave
New York, NY 10022

3 Café des Artistes
1 W 67th St
New York, NY 10023

21 Café Nosidam
768 Madison Ave
New York, NY 10021

59 Cafeteria
119 Seventh Ave
New York, NY 10011

60 Carnegie Deli
854 Seventh Ave
New York, NY 10019

111 Chat'n'Chew
10 E 16th St
New York, NY 10003

61 Chelsea Bistro and Bar
358 W 23rd St
New York, NY 10011

62 Churrascaria Plataforma
316 W 49th St
New York, NY 10019

64 Cite
120 W 51st St
New York, NY 10020

63 City Bakery
3 W 18th St
New York, NY 10003

112 Craft
43 E 19th St
New York, NY 10003

113 craftbar
43 E 19th St
New York, NY 10003

176 Crispo
240 W 14th St
New York, NY 10011

25 Daniel
60 E 65th St
New York, NY 10021

65 DB Bistro Moderne
55 W 44th St
New York, NY 10036

117 Dos Caminos
373 Park Ave S
New York, NY 10016

234 Eleven Madison Park
11 Madison Ave
New York, NY 10010

66 Elmo
156 Seventh Ave
New York, NY 10011

67 Estiatorio Milos
125 W 55th St
New York, NY 10019

119 Fifty Seven Fifty Seven
57 E 57th St
New York, NY 10022

6 Fiorello's Roman Cafe
1900 Broadway
New York, NY 10023

68 Firebird
365 W 46th St
New York, NY 10036

120 Fleur de Sel
5 E 20th St
New York, NY 10003

121 The Four Seasons Restaurant
99 E 52nd St
New York, NY 10022

7 Gabriel's
11 W 60th St
New York, NY 10023

69 Gallagher's
228 W 52nd St
New York, NY 10019

184 Gascogne
158 8th Ave
New York, NY 10011

26 Geisha
33 E 61st St
New York, NY 10021

122 Gramercy Tavern
42 E 20th St
New York, NY 10003

70 Harley-Davidson Cafe
1370 Ave of the Americas
New York, NY 10019

27 Harry Ciprirani
781 Fifth Ave
New York, NY 10022

9 Jean Georges
1 Central Park W
New York, NY 10023

71 Judson Grill
152 W 52nd St
New York, NY 10019

30 Kai
822 Madison Ave
New York, NY 10021

124 Kitchen 22
36 E 22nd St
New York, NY 10010

125 Kuruma Zushi
7 E 47th St
New York, NY 10017

126 L'Express
249 Park Ave
New York, NY 10003

72 La Bonne Soupe
48 W 55th St
New York, NY 10019

128 La Grenouille
3 E 52nd St
New York, NY 10022

75 Le Bernardin
155 W 51st St
New York, NY 10019

131 Le Cirque 2000
455 Madison Ave
New York, NY 10022

134 Les Halles
411 Park Ave S
New York, NY 10016

135 Lola
30 W 22nd St
New York, NY 10010

136 Maloney & Porcelli
37 E 50th St
New York, NY 10022

198 Markt
401 W 14th St
New York, NY 10014

201 Mesa Grill
102 Fifth Ave
New York, NY 10011

76 Mickey Mantle's
42 Central Park S
New York, NY 10019

77 Mix New York
68 W 58th St
New York, NY 10019

78 Molyvos
871 7th Ave
New York, NY 10019

138 Morton's of Chicago
551 Fifth Ave
New York, NY 10017

140 Nadaman Hakubai
66 Park Ave
New York, NY 10016

141 Oceana
55 E 54th St
New York, NY 10022

248 Olives
201 Park Ave S
New York, NY 10003

79 Osteria al Doge
142 W 44th St
New York, NY 10036

80 Osterio del Circo
120 W 55th St
New York, NY 10019

142 Oyster Bar
Grand Central Terminal
New York, NY 10017

37 Park Avenue Cafe
100 E 63rd St
New York, NY 10021

42 RM
33 E 60th St
New York, NY 10022

81 Periyali
35 W 20th St
New York, NY 10011

86 Rock Center Cafe
20 W 50th St
New York, NY 10020

82 Petrossian
182 W 58th St
New York, NY 10019

12 Rosa Mexicano
61 Columbus Ave
New York, NY 10023

11 Picholine
35 W 64th St
New York, NY 10023

87 San Domenico
240 Central Park S
New York, NY 10019

144 Pipa
38 E 19th St
New York, NY 10003

147 San Pietro
18 E 54th St
New York, NY 10022

41 The Post House
28 E 63rd St
New York, NY 10021

88 Sardi's
234 W 44th St
New York, NY 10036

211 The Red Cat
227 Tenth Ave
New York, NY 10011

89 The Sea Grill
19 W 49th St
New York, NY 10020

83 Redeye Grill
890 Seventh Ave
New York, NY 10019

90 Shaan
57 W 48th St
New York, NY 10020

84 Remi
145 W 53rd St
New York, NY 10019

14 Shun Lee Cafe
43 W 65th St
New York, NY 10023

85 Rene Pujol
321 W 51st St
New York, NY 10019

91 Siam Grill
586 Ninth Ave
New York, NY 10036

254 Republic
37 Union Sq W
New York, NY 10003

92 Stage Deli
834 Seventh Ave
New York, NY 10019

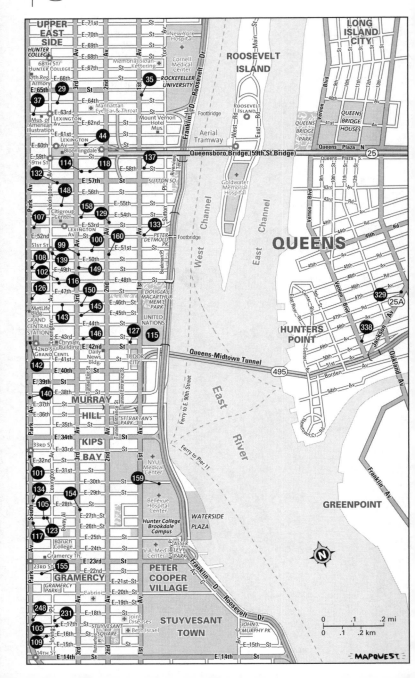

99 Al Bustan
827 Third Ave
New York, NY 10022

100 Amma
246 E 51st St
New York, NY 10022

101 Artisinal
2 Park Ave
New York, NY 10016

102 Avra
141 E 48th St
New York, NY 10017

103 Bar Jamon
125 E 17th St
New York, NY 10003

105 Blue Smoke
116 E 27th St
New York, NY 10016

107 Brasserie
100 E 53rd St
New York, NY 10022

108 Bull and Bear Steakhouse
301 Park Ave
New York, NY 10022

109 Candela Restaurant
116 E 16th St
New York, NY 10003

231 Casa Mono
52 Irving Pl
New York, NY 10003

114 Dawat
210 E 58th St
New York, NY 10022

115 Delegates Dining Room
UN General Assembly Bldg
New York, NY 10017

116 Diwan
148 E 48th St
New York, NY 10017

117 Dos Caminos
373 Park Ave S
New York, NY 10016

118 Felidia
243 E 58th St
New York, NY 10022

123 i Trulli
122 E 27th St
New York, NY 10016

29 Jo Jo
160 E 64th St
New York, NY 10021

126 L'Express
249 Park Ave
New York, NY 10003

127 L'Impero
45 Tudor City Pl
New York, NY 10017

129 La Mangeoire
1008 Second Ave
New York, NY 10022

132 Le Colonial
149 E 57th St
New York, NY 10022

133 Le Perigord
405 E 52nd St
New York, NY 10022

134 Les Halles
411 Park Ave S
New York, NY 10016

329 Manducati's
13-27 Jackson Ave
Long Island City, NY 11101

137 March
405 E 58th St
New York, NY 10022

35 Maya
1191 First Ave
New York, NY 10021

139 Mr. K's
570 Lexington Ave
New York, NY 10022

140 Nadaman Hakubai
66 Park Ave
New York, NY 10016

248 Olives
201 Park Ave S
New York, NY 10003

142 Oyster Bar
Grand Central Terminal
New York, NY 10017

37 Park Avenue Cafe
100 E 63rd St
New York, NY 10021

143 Patroon
160 E 46th St
New York, NY 10017

145 Riingo
205 E 45th St
New York, NY 10017

146 Sakagura
211 E 43rd St
New York, NY 10017

44 Serendipity 3
225 E 60th St
New York, NY 10022

148 Shun Lee Palace
155 E 55th St
New York, NY 10022

149 Smith & Wollensky
797 Third Ave
New York, NY 10022

150 Sparks Steak House
210 E 46th St
New York, NY 10017

338 Tournesol
50-12 Vernon Blvd
Long Island City, NY 11109

154 Turkish Kitchen
386 Third Ave
New York, NY 10016

155 Union Pacific
111 E 22nd St
New York, NY 10010

158 Vong
200 E 54th St
New York, NY 10022

159 The Water Club
500 E 30th St
New York, NY 10016

160 Zarela
953 Second Ave
New York, NY 10022

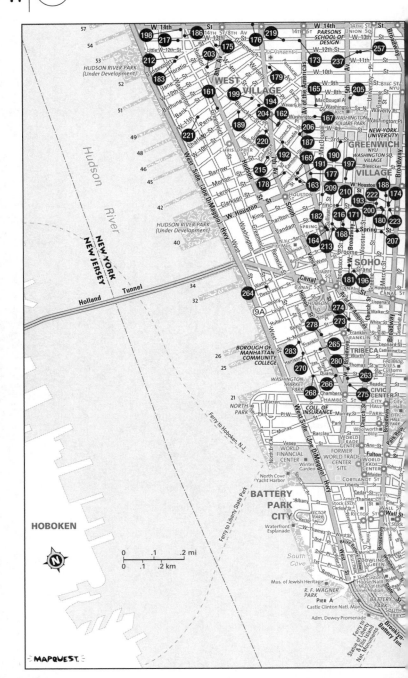

MAPQUEST

161 Alfama
551 Hudson St
New York, NY 10014

162 Annisa
13 Barrow St
New York, NY 10014

163 AOC Bedford
14 Bedford St
New York, NY 10014

164 Aquagrill
210 Spring St
New York, NY 10012

165 Babbo
110 Waverly Pl
New York, NY 10011

167 Blue Hill
75 Washington Pl
New York, NY 10011

168 Blue Ribbon
97 Sullivan St
New York, NY 10012

169 Blue Ribbon Bakery
33 Downing St
New York, NY 10014

171 Boom
152 Spring St
New York, NY 10012

263 Bouley
120 W Broadway
New York, NY 10013

173 Café Loup
105 W 13th St
New York, NY 10011

174 Canteen
142 Mercer St
New York, NY 10012

264 Capsouto Freres
451 Washington St
New York, NY 10013

265 Chanterelle French Restaurant
2 Harrison St
New York, NY 10013

175 Corner Bistro
331 W 4th St
New York, NY 10014

176 Crispo
240 W 14th St
New York, NY 10011

266 Danube
30 Hudson St
New York, NY 10013

177 Da Silvano
260 6th Ave
New York, NY 10014

178 Do Hwa
55 Carmine St
New York, NY 10014

179 Elephant and Castle
68 Greenwich Ave
New York, NY 10011

180 Fanelli's Café
94 Prince St
New York, NY 10012

181 Felix
340 W Broadway
New York, NY 10013

182 Fiamma Osteria
206 Spring St
New York, NY 10012

183 Florent
69 Gansevoort St
New York, NY 10014

268 Gigino Trattoria
323 Greenwich St
New York, NY 10013

237 Gotham Bar and Grill
12 E 12th St
New York, NY 10003

270 The Harrison
355 Greenwich St
New York, NY 10013

186 The Hog Pit
22 9th Ave
New York, NY 10014

187 Home
20 Cornelia St
New York, NY 10014

188 Honmura An
170 Mercer St
New York, NY 10012

189 Hue
91 Charles St
New York, NY 10014

190 Il Mulino
86 W Third St
New York, NY 10012

191 ino
21 Bedford St
New York, NY 10014

192 John's Pizzeria
278 Bleecker St
New York, NY 10014

193 Kelley & Ping
127 Greene St
New York, NY 10012

194 La Metairie
189 W 10th St
New York, NY 10014

273 Layla
211 W Broadway
New York, NY 10013

196 Lucky Strike
59 Grand St
New York, NY 10013

197 Lupa
170 Thompson St
New York, NY 10012

198 Markt
401 W 14th St
New York, NY 10014

199 Mary's Fish Camp
64 Charles St (W 4th St)
New York, NY 10014

200 Mercer Kitchen
99 Prince St
New York, NY 10012

203 Mi Cocina
57 Jane St
New York, NY 10014

274 Montrachet
239 W Broadway
New York, NY 10013

275 Nam
110 Reade St
New York, NY 10013

278 Nobu
105 Hudson St
New York, NY 10013

280 Odeon
145 W Broadway
New York, NY 10013

204 One if by Land, Two if by Sea
17 Barrow St
New York, NY 10014

205 Otto
1 Fifth Ave
New York, NY 10003

206 Pearl Oyster Bar
18 Cornelia St
New York, NY 10014

207 Penang Malaysian
109 Spring St
New York, NY 10012

209 Provence
38 MacDougal St
New York, NY 10012

210 Raoul's
180 Prince St
New York, NY 10012

212 Rhone
63 Ganesvoort St
New York, NY 10014

213   Savore
200 Spring St
New York, NY 10012

215   Snack Taverna
63 Bedford St
New York, NY 10014

216   SoHo Steak
90 Thompson St
New York, NY 10012

217   Spice Market
403 W 13th St
New York, NY 10014

257   Strip House
13 E 12th St
New York, NY 10003

218   Suenos
311 W 17th St
New York, NY 10011

219   Sumile
154 W 13th St
New York, NY 10011

220   Surya
302 Bleeker St
New York, NY 10014

283   Tribeca Grill
375 Greenwich St
New York, NY 10013

221   Wallse
344 W 11th St
New York, NY 10014

222   Woo Lae Oak
148 Mercer St
New York, NY 10012

223   Zoe
90 Prince St
New York, NY 10012

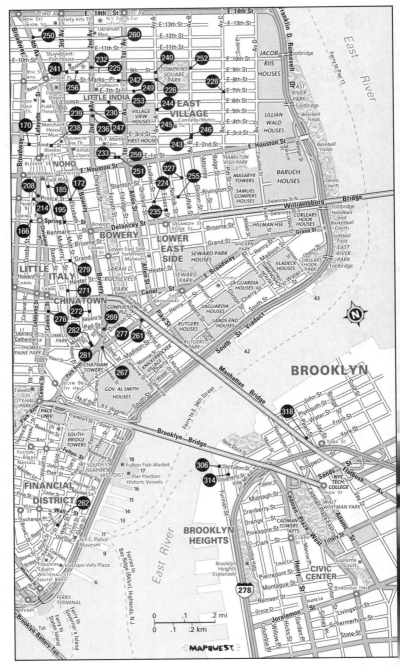

225 2nd Avenue Deli
156 Second Ave
New York, NY 10003

261 88 Palace
88 E Broadway
New York, NY 10002

226 Alphabet Kitchen
171 Ave A
New York, NY 10009

227 Azul Bistro
152 Stanton St
New York, NY 10002

166 Balthazar
80 Spring St
New York, NY 10012

228 Bao 111
111 Avenue C
New York, NY 10009

262 Bayard's
1 Hanover Sq
New York, NY 10004

170 Bond Street
6 Bond St
New York, NY 10012

230 Brick Lane Curry House
342 E 6th St
New York, NY 10003

172 Café Habana
17 Prince St
New York, NY 10012

232 Chikalicious
203 E 10th St
New York, NY 10003

267 Dim Sum Go Go
5 E Broadway
New York, NY 10038

233 The Elephant
58 E 1st St
New York, NY 10003

235 Essex Restaurant
120 Essex St
New York, NY 10002

236 Frank
88 2nd Ave
New York, NY 10003

185 Ghenet Restaurant
284 Mulberry St
New York, NY 10012

269 Great NY Noodletown
28 ½ Bowery
New York, NY 10013

306 Grimaldi's Pizzeria
19 Old Fulton St
Brooklyn, NY 11201

238 Il Buco
47 Bond St
New York, NY 10012

271 Il Cortile
125 Mulberry St
New York, NY 10013

224 'inoteca
98 Rivington St
New York, NY 10002

239 Jewel Bako
239 E 5th St
New York, NY 10003

272 Jing Fong
20 Elizabeth St
New York, NY 10013

240 Komodo
186 Ave A
New York, NY 10009

241 La Paella
214 E Ninth St
New York, NY 10003

242 La Palapa
77 St. Marks Pl
New York, NY 10003

243 Le Souk
47 Ave B
New York, NY 10009

244 Leshko's
111 Ave A
New York, NY 10009

195 Lombardi's
32 Spring St
New York, NY 10012

245 Mamlouk
211 E Fourth St
New York, NY 10009

246 Max
51 Ave B
New York, NY 10009

247 Mermaid Inn
96 Second Ave
New York, NY 10003

276 Nha Trang Centre
148 Centre St
New York, NY 10013

277 Nice
35 E Broadway
New York, NY 10002

279 Nyonya
194 Grand St
New York, NY 10013

249 Pat Pong
97 E 7th St
New York, NY 10009

250 Pie by the Pound
124 Fourth Ave
New York, NY 10003

281 Ping's
22 Mott St
New York, NY 10013

208 Pravda
281 Lafayette St
New York, NY 10012

251 Prune
54 E 1st St
New York, NY 10003

252 Radio Perfecto
190 Ave B
New York, NY 10009

253 Raga
433 E 6th St
New York, NY 10009

314 River Café
1 Water St
Brooklyn, NY 11201

214 Savoy
70 Prince St
New York, NY 10012

255 Schiller's Liquor Bar
131 Rivington St
New York, NY 10002

256 Soba–Ya
229 E 9th St
New York, NY 10003

318 Superfine
126 Front St
Brooklyn, NY 11201

282 Sweet and Tart
20 Mott St
New York, NY 10013

259 The Tasting Room
77 E 1st St
New York, NY 10003

260 United Noodles
349 E 12th St
New York, NY 10003

MAP I

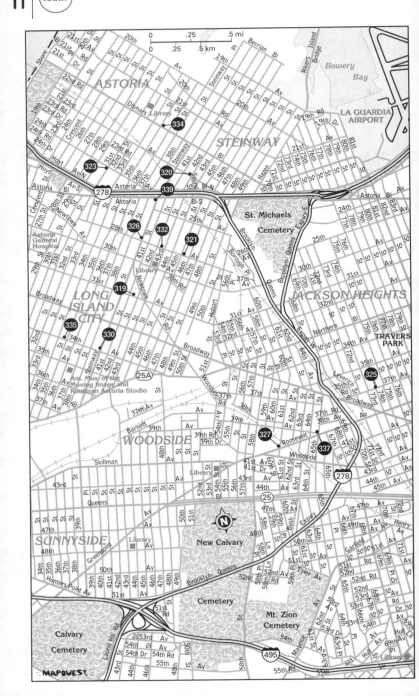

MAP I xxxiii

319 Cavo
4218 31st Ave
Astoria, NY 11103

320 Christos Hasapo-Taverna
41-08 23rd Ave
Astoria, NY 11105

321 Cina
45-17 28th Ave
Astoria, NY 11103

323 Elias Corner
24-02 31st St
Astoria, NY 11102

325 Jackson Diner
37-47 74th St
Jackson Heights, NY 11372

326 Kabab Café
25-12 Steinway St
Astoria, NY 11103

327 Khao Homm
39-28 61st St
Woodside, NY 11377

330 Mombar
2522 Steinway St
Astoria, NY 11103

332 Piccola Venezia
42-01 28th Ave
Astoria, NY 11103

334 Restaurant 718
35-01 Ditmars Blvd
Astoria, NY 11105

335 S'Agapo Taverna
34-21 34th Ave
Astoria, NY 11106

337 Sripraphai
64-13 39th Ave
Woodside, NY 11377

339 Ubol's Kitchen
24-42 Steinway St
Astoria, NY 11103

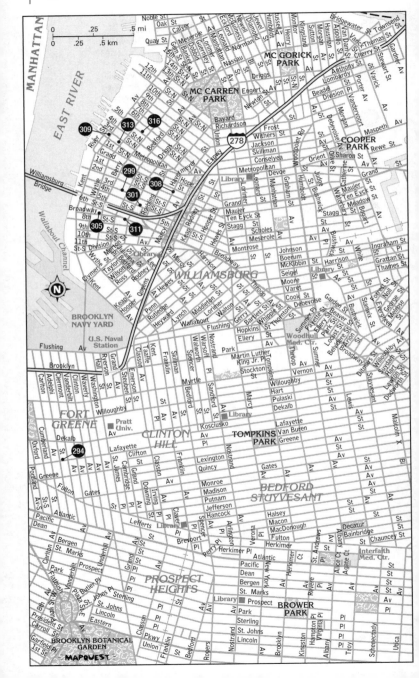

293 360
360 Van Brunt St
Brooklyn, NY 11231

295 Al Di La Trattoria
248 Fifth St
Brooklyn, NY 11215

296 Alma
187 Columbia St
Brooklyn, NY 11231

297 Blue Ribbon Brooklyn
280 Fifth Ave
Brooklyn, NY 11215

298 Blue Ribbon Sushi
278 Fifth Ave
Brooklyn, NY 11215

300 Chestnut
271 Smith St
Brooklyn, NY 11231

302 Convivium Osteria
68 5th Ave
Brooklyn, NY 11217

303 Cucina
256 Fifth Ave
Brooklyn, NY 11215

307 The Grocery
288 Smith St
Brooklyn, NY 11231

310 Patois
255 Smith St
Brooklyn, NY 11231

312 Pier 116
116 Smith St
Brooklyn, NY 11201

315 Saul
140 Smith St
Brooklyn, NY 11201

317 Smith Street Kitchen
174 Smith St
Brooklyn, NY 11201

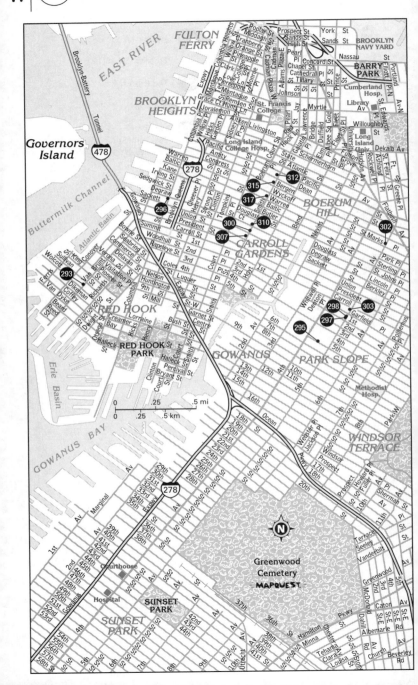

294   **A Table**
171 Lafayette Ave
Brooklyn, NY 11238

299   **Bonita**
338 Bedford Ave
Brooklyn, NY 11211

301   **Chickenbone Café**
177 S Fourth St
Brooklyn, NY 11211

305   **Diner**
85 Broadway
Williamsburg, NY 11211

308   **M Shanghai Bistro & Den**
138 Havenmeyer St
Brooklyn, NY 11211

309   **Miss Williamsburg Diner**
206 Kent Ave
Brooklyn, NY 11211

311   **Peter Luger Steak House**
178 Broadway
Brooklyn, NY 11211

313   **Relish**
225 Wythe Ave
Brooklyn, NY 11211

316   **Sea**
114 N Sixth St
Brooklyn, NY 11211

NEW YORK MAP LEGEND

METRO MAPS

CONTROLLED ACCESS HIGHWAYS

○ Free

® Toll; Toll Booth

Under Construction

1 ○——○ 12 Interchange & Exit Number

Rest Area; Service Area
Grey with facilities

® ® Ⓢ

OTHER HIGHWAYS

Primary Highway

Secondary Highway

Multilane Divided Highway
Primary and secondary highways only

Other Paved Road

HIGHWAY MARKERS

(12) Interstate Route

[12] U.S. Route

(12) State Route

A A12 County or Other Route

BUS 12 Business Route

○ 9 ○ Distance Markers

OTHER SYMBOLS

✈ Airport

Forest and/or Park

Trail

■ Point of Interest

ⓘ Visitor Information

Public/Private Golf
Professional tournament location

✚ Hospital

Ski Area

★ ★ National & State Capital

◉ County Seat

• Cities or Populated Places
Type size indicates relative importance

Urban Area

CITY MAPS

HIGHWAYS

Freeway & Tollway

Primary Highway

Other Paved Road

HIGHWAY MARKERS

(12) Interstate Route

[12] U.S. Route

(12) State Route

A A12 County or Other Route

BUS 12 Business Route

Parks

■ Point of Interest

Railroads

Point of Interest
Area fill

DOWNTOWN MAPS

HIGHWAYS

Freeway & Tollway

Divided Highway

Primary Highway

Other Paved Road

→ One way streets

‿ Tunnel

○ Subway stations

Parks

Point of Interest
Area fill

ALL MAPS

●000—000● Restaurant Locations

Introduction

Whether you're traveling to a city you've never visited or simply exploring a new area of town, one of the greatest joys of travel is eating. From gooey slices of pizza enjoyed standing up at the counter to plates of amazingly fresh sushi savored in an elegant and upscale restaurant, food brings instant gratification. Even if lousy weather threatens to ruin your trip, a great meal can save the day and brighten your mood instantly.

Food has been near and dear to our hearts at Mobil Travel Guide for the last 46 years. That's why we're so pleased to announce our newest series of books, focused exclusively on dining. We've highlighted the very best places to eat in New York, from fine-dining establishments to casual, family-friendly restaurants to hip and trendy hotspots. Pasta, steak, curry, dim sum—you name it, we've got it covered.

This book isn't just a boring A-to-Z list of restaurants, either. We tell you about the city's well-known chefs and specialties so that if your time is limited, you can sample the foods that really shine here. We include information about food-related attractions, from cooking schools to factory tours to shops that sell the latest kitchen gadgets. And we list some of the city's best groceries, markets, and bakeries so that you can take a little piece of New York home with you.

Our goal was to make this book as easy to use as possible. After an introduction to the city's dining scene, you'll find restaurant listings broken down by area of the city. Following the listings for the city itself are listings for outlying areas, again arranged geographically. Within each section, restaurants are listed alphabetically. If you're searching for a restaurant that is budget-friendly, that is suitable for a business meal, that invites romance, or that meets other special criteria, you'll find a variety of specialized indexes, as well as a general index, at the back of the book to help you find just the right spot.

The Mobil One- to Five-Star Ratings for Restaurants

The proprietary Mobil One- to Five-Star rating system, the oldest and most respected restaurant, hotel, and spa inspection and rating program in North America, puts us head and shoulders above other dining guides. We don't rely on the opinions of restaurant critics, whom restaurants often shower with special attention that a "normal" diner would never receive. And our star ratings are not based on popularity.

Definitions

The Mobil Star ratings for restaurants are defined as follows:

- ✪ ★ ★ ★ ★ ★ : A Mobil Five-Star restaurant offers one of few flawless dining experiences in the country. These establishments consistently provide their guests with exceptional food, superlative service, elegant décor, and exquisite presentations of each detail surrounding a meal.
- ✪ ★ ★ ★ ★ : A Mobil Four-Star restaurant provides professional service, distinctive presentations, and wonderful food.
- ✪ ★ ★ ★ : A Mobil Three-Star restaurant offers good food, warm and skillful service, and enjoyable décor.
- ✪ ★ ★ : A Mobil Two-Star restaurant serves fresh food in a clean setting with efficient service. Value is considered in this category, as is family friendliness.
- ✪ ★ : A Mobil One-Star restaurant provides a distinctive experience through culinary specialty, local flair, or individual atmosphere.

Allow us to emphasize that we do not charge establishments for inclusion in our guides. We have no relationship with any of the restaurants or businesses we list and rate; we act only as a consumer advocate. In essence, we do the investigative legwork so that you won't have to. We experience the restaurant as an average consumer would, receiving no special treatment and no discounts.

Approach

Since its founding in 1958, Mobil Travel Guide has served as an advocate for travelers seeking knowledge about hotels, restaurants, and places to visit. Based on an objective process, we make recommendations to our customers that we believe will enhance the quality and value of their travel experiences. Our process of rating each establishment includes:

- Unannounced facility inspections
- Incognito service evaluations for Mobil Four-Star and Mobil Five-Star properties
- Review of consumer feedback
- Senior management oversight

For each property, more than 450 attributes, including cleanliness, physical facilities, and employee attitude and courtesy, are measured and evaluated to produce a mathematically derived score, which is then blended with the other elements to form an overall score. These quantifiable scores allow comparative analysis among properties and form the basis that we use to assign our Mobil One- to Five-Star ratings.

This process focuses largely on guest expectations, guest experience, and consistency of service, not just physical facilities. It rewards those properties that continually strive for and achieve excellence each year.

Only facilities that meet Mobil Travel Guide's standards earn the privilege of being listed. Deteriorating facilities, run-of-the-mill restaurants or poorly managed establishments are not rated. A Mobil Travel Guide rating constitutes a quality recommendation from our staff; every listing is an accolade, a recognition of achievement. We strive to identify excellence within each star category, incorporating a commitment to diversity and variety throughout the Mobil One- to Five-Star Ratings.

All listed establishments have been inspected by experienced field representatives and/or reviewed by a senior incognito evaluator. Rating categories reflect both the features a property offers and its quality in relation to similar establishments across the country.

About the Restaurant Listings

All Mobil Star-rated restaurants listed in this book have a full kitchen and offer tables where you may sit to dine with a complete menu. In addition to a Mobil Star rating, each listing includes the restaurant's address, phone and fax numbers, and Web site (if it has one). We tell you the cuisine type, days of operation (if not open daily year-round), meals served, and price category. We also indicate if the restaurant does not accept credit cards and if valet parking is available. The price categories are defined as follows, per person, and assume that you order an appetizer or dessert, an entrée, and one drink:

- ✪ **$$$$** = $86 and up
- ✪ **$$$** = $36-$85
- ✪ **$$** = $16-$35
- ✪ **$** = $15 and under

At the ends of some listings, we include an icon that provides further information:

- ✪ 🚫 : The restaurant is not easily accessible to persons in wheel-chairs or with otherwise limited mobility.

 Although we recommend every restaurant we list in this book, a few stand out—they offer noteworthy local specialties or stand above the others in their category in quality, value, or experience. To draw your attention to these special spots, we've included the spotlight icon to the left of the listing, as you see here.

Keep in mind that the hospitality business is ever-changing. Restaurants—particularly small chains and standalone establishments—change management or even go out of business with surprising quickness. Although we make every effort to double-check information frequently, we nevertheless recommend that you call ahead to make sure the place you've selected is open and offers what you're looking for.

Tipping Guide

Tips are expressions of appreciation for good service. However, you are never obligated to tip if you receive poor service.

Before tipping in a restaurant, carefully review your check for any gratuity or service charge that is already included in your bill. If you're in doubt, ask your server.

Here are some general guidelines for tipping in restaurants:

- Coffee shop and counter service waitstaff usually receive 15 percent of the bill, before sales tax.
- In full-service restaurants, tip 18 percent or more of the bill, where deserving, before sales tax.
- In fine restaurants, where gratuities are shared among a larger staff, 18 to 20 percent is appropriate.
- In most cases, the maitre d' is tipped only if the service has been extraordinary, and only on the way out. At upscale restaurants in major metropolitan areas, $20 is the minimum.
- If there is a wine steward (sommelier), tip $20 for exemplary service, or more if the wine was decanted or the bottle was very expensive.
- Tip $1 to $2 per coat at the coat check.
- Tip valet parking staff $1 to $2.

Send Us Your Feedback

We hope that your travels are enjoyable and relaxing and that this book helps you get the most out of every meal you eat. If any aspect of your experience with this book motivates you to comment, please drop us a line. We depend a great deal on our readers' remarks, so you can be assured that we will read your comments and factor them into our research. General comments about our books are also welcomed. You can send an e-mail to info@mobiltravelguide.com or write to us at:

Mobil Travel Guide
1460 Renaissance Dr, Suite 401
Park Ridge, IL 60068

Mobil Four- and Five-Star Restaurants in This Book

★ ★ ★ ★ ★ RESTAURANTS

Alain Ducasse

Jean Georges

★ ★ ★ ★ RESTAURANTS

Aureole	Le Bernardin
Bouley	Le Cirque 2000
Daniel	March
Danube	Oceana
The Four Seasons Restaurant	Picholine
Gotham Bar & Grill	RM
Gramercy Tavern	Sugiyama
Kuruma Zushi	Veritas
La Grenouille	

New York

New York is the nation's most populous city, the capital of finance, business, communications, theater, and much more. It may not be the center of the universe, but it does occupy a central place in the world's imagination. Certainly, in one way or another, New York affects the lives of nearly every American. While other cities have everything that New York has—from symphonies to slums—no other city has quite the style or sheer abundance. Nowhere are things done in such a grandly American way as in New York City.

Giovanni da Verrazano was the first European to glimpse Manhattan Island (1524), but the area was not explored until 1609, when Henry Hudson sailed up the river that was later named for him, searching for a passage to India. Adriaen Block arrived here in 1613, and the first trading post was established by the Dutch West India Company two years later. Peter Minuit is said to have bought the island from Native Americans for $24 worth of beads and trinkets in 1626, when New Amsterdam was founded—the biggest real estate bargain in history.

In 1664, the Dutch surrendered to a British fleet and the town was renamed New York in honor of the Duke of York. One of the earliest tests of independence occurred here in 1734 when John Peter Zenger, publisher and editor of the *New York Weekly Journal,* was charged with seditious libel and jailed for making anti-government remarks. Following the Battle of Long Island in 1776, the British occupied the city through the Revolution, until 1783.

On the balcony of Federal Hall at Wall Street, April 30, 1789, George Washington was inaugurated as the first president of the United States, and for a time New York was the country's capital.

When the Erie Canal opened in 1825, New York City expanded vastly as a port. It has since consistently maintained its leadership. In 1898, Manhattan merged with Brooklyn, the Bronx, Queens, and Staten Island. In the next half-century several million immigrants entered the United States here, providing the city with the supply of labor needed for its growth into a major focal point. Each wave of immigrants has brought new customs, culture, and life, which makes New York City the varied metropolis it is today.

New York continues to capitalize on its image as the Big Apple, attracting more than 39 million visitors each year, and its major attractions continue to thrive in style. These, of course, are centered in Manhattan; however, vacationers should not overlook the wealth of sights and activities the other boroughs have to offer. Brooklyn has Coney Island, the New York Aquarium, the superb Brooklyn History Museum, Brooklyn Botanic Garden, Brooklyn Children's Museum, and the famous landmark Brooklyn Bridge. The Bronx is noted for its excellent Botanical Garden and Zoo and Yankee Stadium. Flushing Meadows-Corona Park, in Queens, was the site of two World's Fairs; nearby is Shea Stadium, home of the New York Mets. Uncrowded Staten Island has Richmond Town Restoration, a re-creation of 18th-century New York, rural farmland, beaches, salt marshes, and wildlife preserves.

The New York Dining Scene

New. York. City. Read those three little words, and you'll feel it. There it is: a stir of excitement. It's almost Pavlovian.

Indeed, of all the cities on this vast planet, Gotham is the place that makes people *feel*. It is a town that reminds us that we are alive. It is a metropolis that thrives on being ablaze with creativity, on being infused with individuality, and on pulsing with endless possibility. And when the sun sets behind the Hudson River at the end of the day, the city's varied inhabitants sleep reluctantly, for one reason, and one reason only—to be prepared to fully experience a new and exciting tomorrow. There's a lot to cover in a mere 24 hours. There's the theater, the museums, the galleries, the Met, Jazz at Lincoln Center, the Philharmonic, and more, but there's one thing that New Yorkers universally love to do (and then to argue about), and that is to eat out.

On any given day, on any given street, at any given hour you can find all sorts of folks—lawyers and construction workers, doctors and file clerks, master-of-the-universe types and high school teachers— digging into all kinds of eats. From the most haute ten-course tasting menu prepared by the hottest new chef with three French last names to a modest slice of tomato and mozzarella pizza baked in a coal oven by a family with a centuries-old recipe, this city is, at its core, one great place to fall in love with food.

Take this snapshot of a midweek lunch hour for starters. You'll find the sidewalks crowded with Middle Eastern and Greek street-cart vendors turning out tender marinated lamb sandwiches and chicken kabobs wrapped in thick, warm pita and drizzled with yogurt sauce to block-long lines of hungry construction and office workers. Over on 53rd and Park, you will find power brokers tucked inside pod-like banquettes at the sleek, super-mod Lever House, closing mega-million dollar deals over plates of heirloom tomato salad and organic roasted chicken with foie gras foam. Meanwhile, over at The Oyster Bar in Grand Central, the lunch counters are packed with lawyers, accountants, investment bankers, and various other well-suited types, all jammed in elbow-to-elbow but happy as clams (excuse the pun) to be there, slurping down oysters, digging into hearty bowls of Manhattan clam chowder, and wiping the mayo from their lips after that last bite of a lobster roll.

And that's just at lunch.

Dinner is another animal altogether, a spirited ritual that is as much about being seen as it is to see, and that is as much about eating as it is about eating at the right place at the right time. A night out in this town can go a number of ways. For a small tribe of friends out to meet and mingle, dinner can be a sort of mix-and-match crawl of drinks and eats that can begin with cocktails and nibbles at the bars of hotspots like Rande Gerber's Stone Rose Lounge in the Time Warner Center, Jean Georges and Gray Kunz's exotic wonderland Spice Market, Keith McNally's Schiller's Liquor Bar, or at Danny Meyer's bastion of barbecue and beer, Blue Smoke, and can evolve to a feast of antipasti and global small plates served at one of the city's thrilling new crops of wine bars like Punch & Judy, In Vino, Bar Jamon, Otto, and Joe and Jason Denton's wildly popular 'ino and 'inoteca. For others, dinner out can mean submitting to the seductive culinary powers of this town's chef deities like Thomas Keller at Per Se, Daniel Boulud at Daniel, Marcus Samuelsson at Aquavit, Scott

Conant at L'Impero, Eric Ripert at Le Bernardin, Gray Kunz at Café Gray, Jean-Georges Vongerichten at his namesake temple, and, for more adventurous gastronomes, the brilliant, avant-garde ways of chef/creative force Wylie Dufresne at WD-50 way down on the Lower East Side. Any way you choose to dine, you can't go wrong.

Speaking of the Lower East Side, if you thought it was all about pickles, knishes, and smoked fish, think again. Sure, you can still get the old-world goods, but New York City's oldest neighborhood has evolved from an ethnic enclave to one seriously happenin' 'hood. Thanks to pioneering restaurants like 71 Clinton Fresh Food, aKa Café, and Alias, the formerly downtrodden Lower East Side is now home to hipster destinations like Paladar, Suba, Schiller's, Peasant, and Apizz. And the change is not just restricted to the Lower East Side. It can be seen in the East Village as well, now a wonderland for dining with notable newcomers like The Tasting Room, Bao 111, Prune, and The Mermaid Inn, sharing real estate with old favorites like Veselka and Miracle Grill. And way up on the Upper West Side, we are finally seeing signs of life. Waking this stroller-filled latte-land from its culinary coma are restaurants like Ouest, 'Cesca, Aix, Nice Matin, and Compass. But what's perhaps even more interesting than Manhattan's dazzling neighborhood overhauls are the changes happening in the outer boroughs, notably the major crop of new spots sprouting up across the river in Queens and Brooklyn. The perpetual stepchildren of the city, Queens and Brooklyn (especially Brooklyn) are now trendsetting havens for folks fleeing sky-high rents and tiny apartments. Out in Queens, you'll find charming French bistros like Tournesol and Bistro 718 popping up between old Greek favorites like Christos Hasapo, while over in Brooklyn you'll find a garden of culinary flowers blossoming in places like Park Slope with Al Di La, Blue Ribbon, and Convivium Osteria; in Williamsburg with Diner, Relish, and Chickenbone Café; and in Cobble Hill with Chestnut, The Grocery, and Patois. Change never tasted so good.

Indeed, New York Ciy has it all. Whatever you crave, whether it's authentic Thai (Sripraphai), blistering Korean barbecue (Kum Gang San), out-of-this-world French (take your pick among Daniel, Atelier, Balthazar, and more), killer regional Mexican (Suenos, La Palapa, Rosa Mexicano, Rocking Horse Café), sublime Italian (Crispo, Babbo, Beppe, Lupa), seasonal New American (Blue Hill, Craft, Five Points, Union Square Café, Gotham Bar and Grill), sophisticated Japanese

(Sumile, Asiate, Nobu), a New England lobster roll (Mary's Fish Camp), a sky-high pastrami sandwich with a half-sour pickle (Katz's, Second Avenue Deli) or a messy pulled-pork sandwich and a cold beer (Virgil's, Blue Smoke, Pearson's), you can be sure this city's got it in numbers. Sure, Paris is lovely, San Francisco is a dream, and Chicago a contender, but there is no place like home, and New York City is every diner's hometown when it comes to the glorious world of eating.

We hope this guide helps make you feel right at home here, and that you fall in love over and over again with the grand and the small, the haute and the ordinary, and with all that makes this city such a thrilling place to eat. Cheers!

restaurants to watch

The following restaurants are too new to have earned a Mobil Star rating, but these hot new openings—many in the Time Warner Center—are generating lots of buzz.

Asiate
Mandarin Oriental Hotel
80 Columbus Cir (10019)
Phone 212/805-8881
www.mandarinoriental.com
Noriyuki Sugie's French-Asian restaurant in the second tower of the Time Warner Center serves lunch and dinner daily.

Café Gray
Time Warner Center
10 Columbus Dr (10019)
Phone 212/823-6338
www.cafegray.com
From Gray Kunz comes this European brasserie with Asian accents, designed by David Rockwell.

Charlie Trotter's
Time Warner Center
60 Columbus Dr (10019)
The Chicago svengali's as-yet-unnamed seafood restaurant will be less formal than its Windy City counterpart. There are plans for an oyster bar as well.

Jack's Luxury Oyster Bar
246 E 5th St (10003)
Phone 212/673-0338
Comprising the first two floors of Jack and Grace Lamb's own carriage house in the East Village, this tiny space turns out eclectic seafood fare.

Masa and Bar Masa
Time Warner Center
60 Columbus Dr (10019)
Phone 212/823-9800
Masa Takayama's intimate restaurant with a small sushi bar offers multicourse tasting menus at jaw-dropping prices.

Per Se
Time Warner Center
60 Columbus Dr (10019)
Phone 212/823-9335
A French-American restaurant from French Laundry legend Thomas Keller. Keller has also opened Bouchon Bakery, a bakery, pastry, and chocolate shop with a café open for breakfast, lunch, and early supper, one floor below.

V Steak House
Time Warner Center
60 Columbus Dr (10019)
A steakhouse from culinary Jean-Georges Vongerichten.

Upper West Side and Harlem

Primarily residential, the **Upper West Side** has traditionally been known as the liberal-leaning home of writers, intellectuals, musicians, dancers, doctors, lawyers, and other upper-middle-class professionals. A mix of ornate 19th-century landmarks, pre-World War II apartment buildings, and tenement houses, the Upper West Side stretches from 59th Street north to 110th Street and from Fifth Avenue west to the Hudson River. At its eastern border, between Fifth Avenue and Central Park West and 59th and 110th streets, Central Park sprawls out in a vast and beautifully landscaped expanse of green.

Anchoring the neighborhood to the south is one of its best-known addresses—the Lincoln Center for the Performing Arts (Broadway, between 62nd and 66th streets), which presents about 3,000 cultural events a year. Centering on a large, circular fountain, the 14-acre complex is home to such renowned institutions as the Metropolitan Opera House and Avery Fisher Hall. Many free outdoor concerts are presented on the plaza during the summer.

Directly across from Lincoln Center beckons a row of attractive restaurants and cafés, many with outdoor seating in the summer. The Museum of American Folk Art (Broadway, between 65th and 66th streets), one of the city's smaller and more unusual museums, is also here. Another dozen or so blocks farther north, the Museum of Natural History (Central Park West at 79th Street) is packed with everything from more than 100 dinosaur skeletons to artifacts from peoples around the world. Adjoining the museum on its north side is the state-of-the-art Rose Center for Earth and Space. Completed in 2000, the center is instantly recognizable for its unusual glass architecture revealing a globe within a triangle.

The Upper West Side didn't begin developing until the late 1800s, when a grand apartment building called the Dakota was built at what is now the corner of Central Park West and 72nd Street. At the time, the building was so far north of the rest of the city that New Yorkers said it was as remote as the state of Dakota—hence the name. Still standing today, the Dakota has been home to many celebrities, including Lauren Bacall, Gilda Radner, Boris Karloff, and John Lennon, who was fatally shot outside the building on December 8, 1980. In Central Park, directly across the street from the Dakota, is Strawberry Fields, a teardrop-shaped acre of land that Yoko Ono had landscaped in her husband's memory.

Central Park can be entered at major intersections all along Central Park West. Near the park's southern end, find Tavern on the Green (near Central Park West and 67th Street), a glittering extravaganza of a restaurant packed with mirrors and chandeliers. A bit farther north, find an odd-shaped body of water simply known as "The Lake" (between 72nd and 77th streets); rowboats can be rented at the Loeb Boathouse at the lake's eastern edge.

Stretching from 110th to 168th streets, between the Harlem and Hudson rivers, **Harlem** is in the midst of a renaissance. After years of being known primarily for its grinding poverty, drugs, and despair, the historic African-American neighborhood is sprucing itself up, attracting mainstream businesses such as Starbucks and Ben & Jerry's and becoming home once again to the middle class—both African American and Caucasian.

Harlem can be divided in two: west-central Harlem, which is primarily African American, and east Harlem, home to many Latinos and a smaller number of Italians. Between 110th and 125th streets west of Morningside Park is Morningside Heights, where Columbia University is located. Washington Heights, north of 155th Street, is home to Fort Tyron Park and the Cloisters, which houses the medieval collection of the Metropolitan Museum of Art.

First a farming community and then an affluent white suburb, Harlem began attracting African-American residents after the construction of the IRT subway in 1901, and soon became the nation's premier African-American neighborhood. The Harlem Renaissance boomed during the 1920s and 1930s, attracting writers and intellectuals such as Langston Hughes and W. E. B. DuBois, and the streets were packed with nightclubs, dance halls, and jazz clubs. Everything changed, however, with the Depression, when poverty took a strong hold that continues in many parts of the neighborhood today.

The heart of Harlem is 125th Street, where you'll find a new Magic Johnson Theater complex, several restaurants and sweet shops offering soul food and baked goods, and the famed Apollo Theater (253 W 125th St). Nearly every major jazz, blues, R&B, and soul artist to come along performed here, and the theater still presents its famed Amateur Night every Wednesday. Just down the street from the Apollo is the Studio Museum of Harlem (144 W 125th St), a first-class fine arts institution spread over several floors of a turn-of-the-century building. Another Harlem landmark is the Schomburg Center for Research in Black Culture (Lenox Avenue at 135th Street), founded by Arthur C. Schomburg, a Puerto Rican of African descent who was told as a child that his race had no history. Although primarily a library, the center also houses a large exhibit area where a wide array of changing exhibits is presented. Not far from Columbia University, which is centered on Broadway and 116th Street, the Cathedral of St. John the Divine (Amsterdam Avenue at 112th Street), is the world's largest Gothic cathedral, said to be big enough to fit both Notre Dame and Chartres inside. Another major attraction nearby is Grant's Tomb (122nd Street at Riverside Drive), an imposing mausoleum sitting high on a bluff overlooking the Hudson.

Restaurants on the Upper West Side and in Harlem

★ ★ @SQC ❶ (MAP C)
270 Columbus Ave (10023)
Phone 212/579-0100
www.sqcnyc.com
The Upper West Side traditionally has not been known as a culinary destination, but the one draw for years has been chef/owner Scott Campbell's wonderful creative American fare. Now at his own joint, he continues to offer locals and travelers his delicious brand of stylish seasonal fare like diver scallops wrapped in bacon, pork chops with cheddar grits, and lots of terrific daily specials. The restaurant has an easy, chic vibe that allows for lots of people-watching thanks to floor-to-ceiling sidewalk windows. A Valhrona hot chocolate and walnut tart for dessert should keep you smiling long after you leave. American menu. Breakfast, lunch, dinner, brunch. Bar. Casual attire.
$$$

★ BARNEY GREENGRASS ❷ (MAP C)
541 Amsterdam Ave (10024)
Phone 212/724-4707
www.barneygreengrass.com
If you don't mind lines that rival opening day of *The Lord of the Rings*, then you'll be fine at Barney Greengrass, an Upper West Side institution for brunch since 1908. The restaurant, still decked out like a vintage New York soda fountain, features a simple menu of eggs, waffles, pancakes, and assorted heavenly platters of smoked fish and bagels. From the menu to the waiters to the décor, Barney Greengrass hasn't really changed a whole lot in its century of doing business, and that is part of its distinct old-world charm. Deli menu. Breakfast, lunch, brunch. Closed Mon. Casual attire. No credit cards accepted. **$$**

food on foot

New York is a city of people on the go. Even tourists in the Big Apple are on the go, eager to take in as many sights, smells, and sounds as they can. Of course, many foods seem to be prepared with this intention in mind; they are cheap, fast, portable, and, most important, self-containing: not necessarily a meal, but more of a snack—sustenance to keep you going until the time comes to sit down and eat.

The hot dog is a street food found in many parts of the world, but as is the case elsewhere, New York has its own interpretation. Usually boiled, occasionally steamed, served in a mushy white bun with mustard and kraut or ketchup and onions (not raw but stewed in a sweet sauce), occasionally with relish on the side, the hot dog is everywhere. Although there are street carts a-million, practically one on every square block, a few places excel at the style that is known in this city.

- **Papaya King** (179 E 86th St, phone 212/369-0648, www. papayaking.com) is an institution where hordes of people line up out the door for the best dogs in the city. It's not to be confused with **Gray's Papaya** (402 Sixth Ave, phone 212/260-3532), another food soap opera for the history books, where excellent hot dogs are found at half the price. The similarity between the two, a reminder of the original relationship, is the watery papaya drink, consumed by many but enjoyed by few.

- The **Hallo Berlin Street Cart** (Fifth Ave at 54th St) serves a dog of more Germanic style with a variety of wursts, no less delicious than the standard Hebrew National variety found and coexisting side by side on an avenue of aggressive street sellers.

- **F & B** (269 W 23rd St, phone 646/486-4441) went creative on the hot dog, offering an array of flavors and preparations ranging from tofu dogs to deep-fried dogs, as if hot dogs weren't bad enough for you already.

- **Crif Dogs** (113 St. Marks Pl, phone 212/614-2728), the newest and most innovative in the bunch, brings standard and not-so-standard dogs to the East Village, offering a number of creative versions, some more appealing than others ("Good morning, I'll have a bacon-wrapped dog smothered with melted cheese and a fried egg"), in addition to the classics.

The frites phase took New York by storm, and now there are a number of places to find a cone of Belgian-style pommes frites served with a dizzying assortment of sauces, most appropriately imported mayonnaise-like frite sauce. **Pommes Frites** (123 Second Ave, phone 212/674-1234) was one of the first in on the craze and, like nearby **Le Frite Kot** (118 W 4th St, phone 212/979-2616), originally survived fueled by NYU students' insatiable appetite for greasy, single-ingredient foods. Now these tiny spots are perpetually packed with families, socialites, out-of-towners, and students alike feasting on crispy spuds dunked in sauces probably never imagined on the other side of the pond.

Falafel is a food that's probably as common in New York as it is in the Middle East where it originated. Cheap, compact, and easily customized to suit individual preferences, falafel meets all the requirements for a successful street food: fresh pita stuffed with chopped salad and fried falafel balls that vary in ingredients by country of origin, all topped with tahini sauce and, if requested, a fiery hot concoction sure to sear the roof of your mouth. Wrapped in a double shield of paper and foil, edges folded outward to catch any rogue toppings that might escape to a shirt or tie, falafel is sheer heaven. **Mamoun's** (119 MacDougal St, phone 212/674-8685) is one of the oldest and best, serving Egyptian-style falafel for $2 to students, actors, and longtime devotees. **Rainbow Falafel** (26 E 17th St, phone 212/691-8641) feeds countless sophisticates working in the Flatiron District, while **Moishe's** kosher cart (46th St just off Sixth Ave) does the same for the Midtown masses with only a minute to grab a bite at lunch. **Alfanoose** (150 Fulton St, phone 212/528-4669) went outside the box and constructed a tidy falafel for the banker, broker, and trader bunch by tightly rolling the fillings in a very thin, larger pita. **Bereket** (187 E Houston St, phone 212/475-7700) is a favorite destination for late-nighters and cabbies alike, as it stays open 24 hours and features the Turkish national pita snack, Doner Kebab, a tasty sandwich with a mixture of beef and lamb that has a marvelous flavor and the uncanny ability to absorb cheap booze.

Ice cream walks the streets year-round. Although there are plenty of Mr. Softie carts on blocks uptown and down, quite a few more innovative alternatives have gained popularity over the years. **Il Laboratorio del Gelato** (95 Orchard St, phone 212/343-9922, www.laboratoriodelgelato.com) was opened by the previous owner of Ciao Bella after he sold that company, got an MBA, survived as a trader, yet wasn't prepared to leave well enough alone. It certainly has the appearance of a laboratory, but there's nothing chemical about the gelato here. On St. Marks Place, there's a shop entirely devoted to milkshakes, **New York Milkshake Company** (37 St. Marks Pl, phone 212/505-5200), and they are well worth what seems a hefty price for flavor punches like pistachio and green tea. Even though **Fauchon** (1000 Madison Ave, phone 212/570-2211) has taken over what used to be St. Ambroseous, they continue to serve the same dreamy gelato, perfect for a shopping afternoon along Madison Avenue. It seems that the ice cream world in New York is filled with imports, and we are happy to have the Argentine brothers at **Cones** (272 Bleecker St, phone 212/414-1795). Made from scratch from luxurious ingredients, their ice cream and sorbet cones are not to be missed. A recent import from down under, **Australian Homemade** (115 St. Marks Pl, phone 212/288-5439) is chilling out happy customers with its mod storefront.

In Chinatown, there are many temptations of sidewalk cuisine, from the simplest coconut milk to the most complex Vietnamese sandwich, *banh mi*. The best place to sample these street foods is found under the Manhattan Bridge in a somewhat intimidating shopping mall. **Banh Mi Saigon** (108 Forsyth St, phone 212/941-1541) serves the traditional baguette sandwiches with pâté and a smattering of crunchy herbs and toppings. Avoiding the creative and confusing names, **Viet-nam Banh Mi So** (369 Broome St, phone 212/219-8341) offers a few different *banh mi* and can be easier to navigate for a novice. **Fried Dumpling** (99 Allen St, phone 212/941-9975) is a favorite of any frugal snacker, selling dumplings and steamed buns for the bargain price of $2—an easy encouragement to try both. Although it isn't quite a food, a popular Chinatown pickup is bubble tea. These tea drinks, offered with or without the large tapioca pearls, come in a dizzying range of flavors and variations, but one can't resist feeling hip after sipping away for a few moments. The number of outlets serving these beverages has proliferated, but the original was

Saint Alp's Teahouse (51 Mott St, phone 212/766-9889), a Taiwanese franchise arriving via Hong Kong that is rapidly expanding across the nation.

Amidst all the hot dogs, pretzels, mystery meat on a pita, falafel, fresh fruit, and bagel vendors selling their wares out of carts everywhere you look, a few tiny places in the heart of New York's busiest areas have focused on a unique offering and provide an alternative to the usual treats. Baked potato carts proliferate in congested areas during winter, luring cold lunch-seekers with their customized warmth. Although a baked potato is always satisfying, only one spot in the city focuses on sweet potatoes, a Japanese favorite. **Hero's** (30 E 13th St, phone 646/336-1685) sells steamed sweet potatoes topped or even wrapped any way you can imagine. Some are more appealing to the Western palate than others, but for sheer creativity, this tiny spot is worth a visit. Before the arrival of a sweet potato spot, a brave couple opened a tiny storefront selling two distinctly Japanese street snacks: oko-nomiyaki and takoyaki. Okonmiyaki are omelet-like pancakes, customized to taste with fillings and toppings. It's a treat to watch them being made. Takoyaki are usually fried balls of custard with savory eel inside, but **Otafuko** (236 E 9th St, phone 212/353-8503) offers the additional flavors of plain cus-tard and cheese-stuffed. Takoyaki are also topped with sauces and bonito flakes to taste. Eating both of these snacks while walking with chopsticks is challenging, but not impossible. Returning to more domestic flavors, **Daisy May's Chili Cart** (Sixth Ave at 50th St), a growing set of carts, feeds hungry folk from neighboring offices in the Financial District and Midtown. Texas chili may seem an odd thing to eat out of a moving cart, but one bite and you'll understand that the flavors intensify after many hours of simmering. The idea that the city now sup-ports a number of carts dedicated solely to *dosas*, a favorite South Asian street snack, shows the obsession and dedication to portable foods. **N.Y. Dosas** (W 4th St near Sullivan), a cart outpost of a storefront in Queens, serves delicious dosas, and the trend seems prepared to take off.

Pizza serves a number of different purposes in New York, and there are places to fill each need: delivery pies, sit-down pies, and, most common, the slice. Keep in mind that a place that makes a terrific slice may not produce a nearly adequate whole pie, so of course the destinations for each need are never the same. **Patsy's** (2287-91 First Ave, phone 212/534-9783) has one of the best slices in the city, and the location doesn't seem to put off those who favor the perfect balance of crust, sauce, and cheese. Not to be mixed up with the sit-down Patsy's Pizzeria's found in Manhattan, this Patsy's is all about food-on-the-go. **Joe's Pizza** (232 Bleecker St, phone 212/366-1182) has one of the most publicized slices in New York, although only this location can be trusted as the name proliferates. There is no comparison for one of these slices, oozing with melted cheese, consumed out on the sidewalk in the bustle of the Village. Although some residents and visitors are purists about the slice, a few places offer something outside the usual plain or pepperoni. **Pizza 33** (489 Third Ave, phone 212/545-9191) isn't decades old, but the lighter slices with carefully balanced flavors should be around for a long time to come. **Two Boots** (37 Ave A, phone 212/505-2276) was one of the first spots in the city to offer slices of a more creative variety, a blasphemy that had been succeeding in LA for years. The cornmeal crust and New Orleans-influenced toppings set these spots apart from the pack, and they're extremely popular with students and parents as the crowds often provide the desired background noise. **Pie by the Pound** (124 Fourth Ave, phone 212/475-4977) a newcomer and trendsetter, displays a number of long, rectangular, thin-crust pizzas with gourmet toppings, sold by the pound. Commonly found across Italy, this concept first appeared in the US here at Pie. Although the quality and variety of pizzas and toppings are awesome, the pounds in dollars add up quickly.

★ ★ ★ CAFÉ DES ARTISTES (MAP E)
1 W 67th St (10023)
Phone 212/877-3500
Fax 212/877-7754
www.cafenyc.com

Café des Artistes is a timeless New York City classic. Originally fashioned after the English Ordinary, a cozy bistro with a limited menu based on food available in the market, the Café was a regular meeting place where local artists in the neighborhood would come together to discuss their creative works. Today, the restaurant remains an old-guard favorite for its luxurious, sophisticated setting, impeccable service, and menu of up-to-the-minute, yet approachable, seasonal, French bistro fare. While elegant in its art-filled décor, the restaurant's menu does not try too hard, over-flourish, or over-think things. The kitchen stays true to its roots. French bistro menu. Dinner, brunch. Closed Dec 25. Bar. **$$$**

★ CARMINE'S ④ (MAP C)

2450 Broadway (10024)
Phone 212/362-2200
Fax 212/362-0742
www.carminesnyc.com

If you have an aversion to garlic, do yourself a favor and stay far
away from Carmine's, a loud, frenetic, oversized Italian spot in the
theater district. Garlic, a prominent ingredient here, reeks from
the walls. But if you crave hearty portions of zesty, family-style,
red-sauced Italian food at reasonable prices, this is your place.
Conversation is difficult as the noise level rivals a jet engine at close
range. The dining room, originally a hotel ballroom, is a re-creation of
a 1940s neighborhood Italian restaurant. Italian menu. Lunch, dinner.
Bar. Outdoor seating. **$$**

★★★ 'CESCA ⑤ (MAP C)

164 W 75th St (10023)
Phone 212/787-6300

Chef Tom Valenti is like Santa Claus for the Upper West Side—bringing
culinary treats for all the good neighbors strolling along Columbus
Avenue totting lattes and H&H Bagels. The follow-up to his slam hit
Ouest, 'Cesca is an earthy and lively restaurant specializing in rustic,
authentic, and often slow-cooked Italian fare like the oven-baked pasta
with meat ragu and a Fred Flintstone-sized braised pork shank. If at all
possible, go with an empty tummy so it can be filled all the way up.
And while a reservation is nice, the warm, chocolate-toned bar, decked
out in dark wood with amber lighting, is a perfect place to sit awhile,
drink some wine, and nosh (read: pig out). Italian menu. Dinner. Closed
Mon. Bar. Jacket required. Reservations recommended. **$$$**

★★ FIORELLO'S ROMAN CAFE ⑥ (MAP E)

1900 Broadway (10023)
Phone 212/595-5330
Fax 212/496-2471
www.cafefiorello.com

If you find yourself taking in a ballet or an opera at Lincoln Center
and you don't want to break the bank on dinner because you've just
spent your last dime on those tough-to-get tickets, Fiorello's is a
great choice for a reasonable, casual, and tasty meal. The convivial
restaurant has a large outdoor patio for summertime seating and
people-watching, while the indoor room is warm and welcoming,
making it equally charming in the winter months. The menu offers a

delicious selection of antipasti, pasta, meat, and fish prepared in the tradition of a Roman osteria, along with classic desserts like a creamy tiramisu. Italian menu. Lunch, dinner, late-night, brunch. Closed Dec 25. Bar. Casual attire. Reservations recommended. Outdoor seating. **$$$**

the great bagel

Any New Yorker (and hopefully all those who've made a visit to the Big Apple as well) knows that a bagel is not a bagel is not a bagel. Bagels are serious business, and residents always have a standby, a favorite, and a runner-up, each having significant individual characteristics. Some swear by toasting, while others argue that an excellent bagel needs no heat. Some go for the schmear (cream cheese), while others add a pile of smoked fish, whitefish salad, or pungent flavor spread to make it a meal to remember. There is no end to the argument of where to find the best bagel, but the following specialists usually get highest marks.

- **Ess-A-Bagel** (359 First Ave at 21st St, phone 212/260-2252; and 831 Third Ave, phone 212/980-1010; www.ess-a-bagel .com) has larger bagels with a fluffier interior.

- **H & H Bagels** (2239 Broadway at 80th St, phone 212/595-8003, www.handhbagel.com) have more of a crust; they even ship nationwide.

- **Tal** (333 E 86th St, phone 212/427-6811) is known not just for its terrific bagels but also for its friendly service and incredibly rich whitefish salad.

And then there's the bialy; perhaps not a sibling to the bagel but a second cousin. Lighter and smaller than a bagel with a noticeable onion flavor and no hole, the bialy is getting harder to find. Hopefully they'll make a comeback, saved by some rogue food trend, before they become extinct. Although they're often sold at the bagel shops mentioned above, true devotees go to **Kossar's Bialys** (367 Grand St, phone 212/473-4810, www.kossarsbialys.com) on the Lower East Side for the finest specimens.

★★ GABRIEL'S 7 (MAP E)

11 W 60th St (10023)
Phone 212/956-4600
Fax 212/956-2309
www.gabrielsbarandrest.com

Gabriel's is the creation of owner Gabriel Aiello, a charming host who knows how to make guests feel at home in this elegant Lincoln Center area spot for sumptuous Tuscan fare like tortelloni filled with lamb and tossed in a shiitake mushroom tomato sauce, artichoke Lasagna, and a daily house-made risotto. The restaurant is elegantly dressed with contemporary art cloaking the warm saffron-toned walls; wide, sleep-worthy green felt banquettes; well-spaced tables; soothing indirect lighting; and a 35-foot-long mahogany bar. While Gabriel's may look like a see-and-be-scene hotspot, the restaurant is warm and welcoming, without pretension, making an evening here a delight from start to finish. Italian menu. Lunch, dinner. Closed Sun; holidays. Bar. Casual attire. **$$$**

★ GABRIELA'S 8 (MAP C)

685 Amsterdam Ave (10025)
Phone 212/961-0574

From the people who brought you the large-scale Italian fare at Carmine's (see) comes Gabriela's, a breezy, colorful Mexican cantina that offers family-style portions of zesty south-of-the-border cuisine, without leaving you broke. The menu of spicy and fresh fare includes savory plates like shredded, spice-infused pork with rice and black beans, and fat burritos with vibrant sides of guacamole. Mexican menu. Lunch, dinner. Bar. Casual attire. **$**

★★★★★ JEAN GEORGES 9 (MAP E)

1 Central Park W (10023)
Phone 212/299-3900
Fax 212/299-3914
www.jean-georges.com

Perfection is a word that comes to mind when speaking of meals at Jean-Georges. Heaven is another word and divine yet another. Located in the Trump International Hotel and Tower across from Central Park, Jean-Georges is a shrine to haute cuisine. Drawing influences from around the world, the menu is conceived and impeccably executed by celebrity chef/owner (and author) Jean-Georges Vongerichten. Vongerichten is a man of meticulous discipline, and it shows on the plate. Nothing is present that shouldn't be there. Under Vongerichten's direction, ingredients shine, flavors spark, and the mouth trembles. Suffice it to say that you will be in heaven within minutes of the meal's commencement. The room is sophisticated and stunning, yet remains comfortable. You'll find that it's filled nightly with well-known names, high-powered financial moguls, actors, models, and local New Yorkers who are lucky enough to score reservations. Call well in advance. It is worth the time it may take you to get through. If you can't manage to secure a table, try your luck at Nougatine, the popular café in the outer bar area. It has a simpler menu but will give you a taste of what Vongerichten is capable of. The bar is also a lovely place to meet for an aperitif or a cocktail before dinner or a walk through the park. *Secret Inspector's Notes: On a lucky evening, Donald Trump may be dining at his favorite table with his guest du jour being catered to hand and foot by the proficient and attentive staff.* French menu. Dinner. Bar. Jacket required. Reservations recommended. Valet parking. Outdoor seating. **$$$$**

★ PATSY'S PIZZERIA **(MAP D)**
2287-91 First Ave (10035)
Phone 212/534-9783

Folks in New York take their pizza seriously, and with a pizza joint on what seems like every corner, the competition is fierce. But Patsy's remains a favorite among pie connoisseurs, consistently serving wonderful pizza with thin, crisp but chewy crusts, with an array of toppings for every appetite. Patsy's original location in Harlem is an easy, casual place, with gingham tablecloths, wood floors, and a welcoming, seasoned waitstaff. Pizza. Lunch, dinner. Casual attire. No credit cards accepted. **$**

★ ★ ★ ★ PICHOLINE **(MAP E)**
35 W 64th St (10023)
Phone 212/724-8585
Fax 212/875-8979

Picholine is a great choice for dinner if you happen to be attending an opera, ballet, or play at Lincoln Center. Don't feel like you need to be heading over to Lincoln Center in order to dine here, though; chef/owner Terrance Brennan's lovely, serene restaurant is easy to enjoy all by itself, which is probably why Picholine is often pleasantly packed with a savvy set of New Yorkers at both lunch and dinner, with no ticket stubs to be found. The menu changes with the seasons, and the chef uses organic and local ingredients as much as possible. Picholine is a safe bet for both adventurous diners and conservative eaters and for vegetarians and meat lovers alike. The menu runs the gamut from the exotic to the familiar, offering a wide selection of dishes from the land and the sea. Folks with a weakness for cheese are in the right place, as well. The cheese list (not to mention the great wine list) is one of the best in the city, and room must be saved to indulge in several types. The wine list, though seriously priced, offers a variety of selections to match all courses. *Secret Inspector's Notes: Picholine has by far the best cheese program in New York. True cheese lovers may want to just visit the bar for a full-bodied glass of wine and a mind-altering plate of cheese. Be forewarned, though; the dining room staff is unabashedly stuffy and snooty and must be ignored at times so as not to detract from the fantastic flavors offered by the talented kitchen.* Mediterranean menu. Closed holidays. Lunch, dinner. Bar. Jacket required. Reservations recommended. **$$$**

★★ ROSA MEXICANO 12 (MAP E)
61 Columbus Ave (10023)
Phone 212/977-7700
www.rosamexicano.com
One of the first restaurants to introduce New Yorkers to authentic Mexican cuisine, Rosa Mexicano was founded by chef Josefina Howard in the early '80s and today remains an essential stop for anyone who craves strong, chilly, perfectly mixed margaritas (frozen or on the rocks), and bright, fresh, vibrant bowls of guacamole mixed tableside to your desired level of heat (mild to scorching). The menu is a beautiful tribute to the regional home-cooking of Mexico—steamy pork tamales, chicken in a rich savory blanket of mole, terra-cotta cazuelas brimming with shrimp, tomatoes, garlic, and chiles, and a long-time entrée signature—budin Azteca, a wonderful tortilla casserole with layers of shredded chicken and cheese. Expect a crowd with as much spice and attitude as the food. Mexican menu. Lunch, dinner, late-night. Bar. Casual attire. **$$$**

zabar's

Zabar's is one of those places that makes New York the yummy place that it is. This second-generation gourmet food market, considered sacred by those who enjoy fine eating, has graced Manhattan's Upper West Side since 1934. Occupying close to one city block and employing 250 people, Zabar's sells sinful breads and pastries, meats, cheeses, smoked fish, condiments, and cookware. The shop's babka (Russian coffee cake) makes life worth living. Since Zabar's is one of the rare establishments in New York that's open every day of the year, you can treat your taste buds anytime you like. Forget diets and just enjoy. *2245 Broadway at 80th St (10024). Phone 212/787-2000. www.zabars.com.*

★★ SARABETH'S WEST (MAP C)

423 Amsterdam Ave (10024)
Phone 212/496-6280
Fax 212/787-9655
www.sarabeths.com

Sarabeth's is known for some of the most delicate and delicious pastries, scones, and muffins in the city, so brunch here is a must for anyone who craves buttery cakes with coffee in the morning. Aside from the pastry arena, Sarabeth's offers a wonderful brunch of wild berry pancakes, brioche French toast, and plates of fluffy eggs, as well as a seasonal American menu for dinner nightly. Don't forget to pick up some baked goods for the next morning on your way out. American menu. Breakfast, lunch, dinner, brunch. Closed Dec 25. Bar. Casual attire. Outdoor seating. **$$**

★★ SHUN LEE CAFÉ (MAP E)

43 W 65th St (10023)
Phone 212/595-8895
Fax 212/799-3598

You won't find typical white-carton options at this urban Chinese outpost with an eclectic menu. The drama is evident in the décor and on the plates—from the white ceramic monkeys hanging off the bar to the specialty sweetbreads with black mushrooms. Chinese menu. Lunch, dinner. Closed Thanksgiving. Bar. Casual attire. Reservations recommended. **$$$**

★★ TAVERN ON THE GREEN (MAP E)

Central Park at W 67th St (10023)
Phone 212/873-3200
Fax 212/580-4265
www.tavernonthegreen.com

Ornate, over the top, and brash, Tavern on the Green is the Cher of the New York restaurant scene. Like the one-name singer, it's still popular after all these years, it's had a lot of work done, and it's tacky but loved anyway. If you're in the mood for a serviceable meal and extra-high prices, go for it; otherwise, you may want to steer clear of this tourist trap. The food is straightforward and fine, and the view of Central Park is romantic, but the restaurant has morphed into more of a theme park than a serious dining destination. American menu. Lunch, dinner, brunch. Bar. Valet parking. **$$$**

★ ★ ★ TERRACE IN THE SKY (MAP C)
400 W 119th St (10027)
Phone 212/666-9490
Fax 212/666-9490
www.terraceinthesky.com
Set high in the sky on the top floor of a prewar Upper West Side building, Terrace in the Sky offers breathtaking panoramic views of the city and a rich selection of eclectic fare to match. The haute menu of seared sweetbreads, foie gras torchon, smoked salmon, lobster, and caviar make dining here seem very posh. If you have love on your mind, this is *the* place to go. Terrace in the Sky is ideal for romance with its elegant linen-topped tables, soft candlelit ambience, and views that are truly beyond compare. French, Mediterranean menu. Lunch, dinner. Closed Mon. Bar. Casual attire. Reservations recommended. Outdoor seating. **$$$**

Upper East Side

Long associated with New York society, much of the Upper East Side—stretching from 59th Street north to 106th Street and Fifth Avenue east to the East River—is filled with elegant mansions and brownstones, private clubs, and museums. Many of the city's most famous museums—including the Metropolitan Museum of Art—are located here, along with several posh hotels and Gracie Mansion, sometime residence of New York City's mayor.

But the neighborhood is about more than just wealth. Remnants of what was once a thriving German community can be found along the 86th Street-Second Avenue nexus, while a Puerto Rican and Latin community begins in the upper 80s, east of Lexington Avenue. At the corner of 96th Street and Third Avenue is a surprising sight—the Islamic Cultural Center, a modern, gold-domed mosque flanked by a skinny minaret.

Many of the Upper East Side's cultural institutions are located on Fifth Avenue, facing Central Park, along what is known as "Museum Mile." The Frick Collection, housing the private art collection of the former 19th-century industrialist Henry Clay Frick, marks the mile's southernmost end, at 70th Street. El Museo del Barrio, dedicated to the art and culture of Latin America, marks the northernmost end, at 104th Street. In between reign the grand Metropolitan Museum of Art (at 82nd Street), with huge flags flapping out front, and the circular, Frank Lloyd Wright-designed Guggenheim Museum (at 88th Street)—to name just two.

The Plaza Hotel beckons from the southern end of the Upper East Side (Fifth Avenue, between 58th and 59th streets). This magnificent French Renaissance-style edifice was built in 1907 and is now owned by Donald Trump. Directly across Fifth Avenue from the hotel, FAO Schwarz is an imaginative toy store that's as much fun for adults as it is for kids. Central Park is directly across 59th Street. Horse-drawn hansoms and their drivers congregate along the streets here, waiting hopefully for tourists interested in taking a clip-clopping tour. The small but state-of-the-art Central Park Zoo can be found in the park near Fifth Avenue and 65th Street.

Shoppers will want to take a gander at the many upscale boutiques lining Madison Avenue between 57th and 90th streets, or take a stroll over to Bloomingdale's (Lexington Avenue at 59th Street). Fifty-Seventh Street holds numerous world-famous galleries, including PaceWildenstein (32 E 57th St) and Andre Emmerich (41 E 57th St), as well as such popular tourist stops as the Warner Brothers Studio Store (57th Street at Fifth Avenue) and Niketown (6 E 57th St). The infamous St. Patrick's Day Parade, attracting hordes of rowdy revelers, travels down Fifth Avenue from 86th Street to 44th Street every March 17.

Restaurants on the Upper East Side

★ ★ ★ ★ AUREOLE ⑰ (MAP E)
34 E 61st St (10021)
Phone 212/319-1660
www.aureolerestaurant.com
Hidden away inside a lovely brownstone, Aureole is inviting and warm and feels like a special place to dine. The waitstaff's gracious hospitality ensures that you continue to feel that way throughout your meal. The luxurious space is bathed in cream tones and warm lighting, and is furnished with overstuffed wine-colored banquettes. (An enclosed courtyard garden opens for warm-weather dining.) Diners at Aureole are generally here to celebrate something, as it is one of New York's most impressive eateries. The crowd is mostly middle-aged and from the upper echelon of New York society, although Aureole is not a stuffy place. It is friendly and cozy and well suited for just about any occasion, from couples looking for romance to colleagues looking to have a delightful business dinner together. Owner and celebrity chef Charlie Palmer offers his guests the delicious opportunity to dine on a wonderfully prepared menu of what he calls Progressive American fare. But it doesn't really matter what label you give it, because it's all great. There are always two tasting menus—one vegetarian and another inspired from the market—in addition to a parade of terrific à la carte selections. The extensive and celebrated wine program includes bold wines from California, Spain, and Italy. *Secret Inspector's Notes: Aureole has impressed diners for more than ten years and, amazingly enough, continues to improve over time, always getting a little bit better and brighter.* American menu. Lunch, dinner. Closed Sun; holidays. Bar. Jacket required. Reservations recommended. **$$$$**
🅳

★★ BEYOGLU ⓲ (MAP D)

1431 Third Ave (10028)
Phone 212/650-0850

There is much to love about this family-run Turkish restaurant. From the service, which is warm and friendly, to the dining room, a spacious, stylish, low-lit space, to the easygoing crowd of neighborhood folks, Beyoglu beckons you back as soon as you enter. The real star here is the food, which includes delicious warm pita bread drizzled with olive oil to start and moves on to a terrific variety of mezze and a heavenly spiced selection of fragrant rice and assorted kabobs that will leave you in want of a ticket to Istanbul ASAP. Mediterranean, Turkish menu. Lunch, dinner. Bar. Casual attire. Outdoor seating. **$$**

fantastic food markets

Three things reign supreme in the world of New York's residents: delivery, takeout, and the gourmet market. Each neighborhood has its Gucci of gourmet food stores, each with a unique personality, clientele, specialty, and reputation.

Any market related to the Zabar empire comes with its own family drama, and Fairway was recently dragged into the food market soap stories as well. There is no love lost between **Zabar's** (2245 Broadway, phone 212/787-2000, www.zabars. com), one of the oldest and most democratic markets in the city, and Eli Zabar (**Eli's**, 1411 Third Ave at 80th St, phone 212/787-8100; and **The Vinegar Factory,** 405 E 91st St, phone 212/987-0885; www.elismanhattan.com), who consistently achieves gourmet food of skyscraper proportions and prices. The story of the family split is worthy of a screenplay, but both sides have done quite well for themselves.

Those who reside on the Upper East and West sides are fortunate enough to have quite a few markets to choose from:

• **Agata & Valentina** (First Ave at 79th St, phone 212/452-0690) is a palace of Italian fare.

• **Citarella** (Broadway at 75th St, phone 212/874-0383; and Third Ave at 75th St, phone 212/874-0383; www.citarella .com) offers seafood delights.

- **Fairway** (both uptown and downtown: 2127 Broadway at 74th St, phone 212/595-1888; and 2328 Twelfth Ave, phone 212/234-3883; www.fairwaymarket.com) has a produce selection fit for a king, at prices for the pawns.

- **Grace's Marketplace** (1237 Third Ave at 71st St, phone 212/737-0600, www.gracesmarketplace.com) has an old-school feel and a knowledgeable staff.

Downtown residents are more limited but by no means deprived, with **Dean & DeLuca** (560 Broadway, phone 212/226-6800, www.deandeluca.com) taking the prize for most expensive and **Gourmet Garage** (Broome and Mercer sts, phone 212/941-5850, gourmetgarage.com) having the most affordable flower selection of the bunch. **Chelsea Market** (75 Ninth Ave between 15th and 16th sts, www.chelseamarket.com) contains a number of smaller specialists, ranging from Fat Witch Bakery to Ronnybrook Farms Dairy. Luckily, in this neighborhood residents never complain about running from one small shop to another along Bleecker Street with the produce abundance that is the glorious **Union Square Greenmarket.**

★ ★ BOATHOUSE CAFE (MAP C)
72nd St in Central Park (10028)
Phone 212/517-2233
Fax 212/517-8821
www.thecentralparkboathouse.com

Central Park is one of the most wonderful places to spend a day in Manhattan. It really doesn't matter what the season. The same can be said of the Boathouse Cafe, an open, airy, and romantic New York icon/restaurant with views of the rowboaters making their way across the unfortunately green Central Park pond. Sure, summer is the ideal time to settle in for cocktails on the patio under the cherry blossoms, but this restaurant is equally idyllic in the winter, when snow blankets the park in a soft hush. The menu at the Boathouse is New American, with steak, fish, pasta, and salads sure to please any and all culinary desires. Brunch in warmer months is a winner here, but the lines are long, so call ahead for a table. American menu. Lunch, dinner, Sun brunch. Bar. Children's menu. Casual attire. Reservations recommended. Outdoor seating. **$$$**

★ ★ ★ CAFÉ BOULUD (MAP D)

20 E 76th St (10021)
Phone 212/772-2600
Fax 212/772-7755
www.danielnyc.com

Daniel Boulud is one very committed chef. So committed, in fact, that he is the chef-king of a little empire of French restaurants in New York City. Café Boulud is his less formal version of his haute temple of French gastronomy, Daniel (see). But less formal is a relative term. Café Boulud is a majestic space, perfect for quiet conversation and intimate dining. The service is helpful and unobtrusive. The chef is a whiz at pleasing the palate and offers a choice of four à la carte menus: La Tradition (French Classics and Country Cooking), La Saison (The Rhythm of the Seasons), Le Potager (Vegetarian Selections from the Farmers' Market), and Le Voyage (a menu inspired from a changing international destination—Mexico, Morocco, etc.). The wine program is ambitious, and the staff is unintimidating and eager to assist with pairings, making the total dining experience like a little slice of French heaven. French menu. Lunch, dinner. Bar. Jacket required. Reservations recommended. Outdoor seating. **$$$$**

★ ★ CAFÉ NOSIDAM (MAP E)

768 Madison Ave (10021)
Phone 212/717-5633
Fax 212/717-4436

A jewel of a restaurant, Café Nosidam is known for its intimate setting, gracious service, and delectable Italian cuisine. The pastas are the restaurant's best-loved dishes, but the seafood and meat entrées also score high marks. For fans of Caesar salad, this one is a simple, shining star. This is the sort of place that welcomes you with open arms. Don't be surprised if your waiter is more like a friend by the time you leave. Italian, American menu. Lunch, dinner, Sun brunch. Bar. Casual attire. Reservations recommended. Outdoor seating. **$$$**

★ CAFÉ SABARSKY (22) (MAP D)

1048 Fifth Ave (10028)
Phone 212/288-0665

Located in the Neue Galerie, facing the magnificent Central Park on Fifth Avenue, Café Sabarsky offers a taste of Austria in a spectacular New York City setting. With sky-high ceilings, marble pillars, crystal chandeliers, and elegant brocade banquettes, Café Sabarsky feels like a royal chateau in the Austrian Alps. The divine menu, prepared by wonder-chef Kurt Gutenbrunner of Wallse, includes delicious and authentic Viennese pastries and savory Austrian dishes. The wine list is extensive and includes wonderful Austrian red and white varietals. Austrian menu. Lunch, dinner. Bar. Casual attire. **$$**

★ ★ CENTOLIRE 23 (MAP D)
1167 Madison Ave (10028)
Phone 212/734-7711
Fashionable Upper East Siders use Pino Luongo's Centolire as their elegant dining room and watering hole. The space, soothing and all aglow in ultra-flattering light, has a serene vibe with an air of money and power subtly floating in the background. This is not to say that Centolire is pretentious, it's not. The service is gracious and the Italian menu of simple, well articulated flavors is wonderful. However, if you are used to a downtown crowd, you may feel out of place among all the glitzy guests. Italian menu. Lunch, dinner. Bar. Casual attire. **$$$**

★ ★ COCO PAZZO 24 (MAP D)
23 E 74th St (10021)
Phone 212/794-0205
Fax 212/794-0208
www.cocopazzo.com
For more than a decade, Pino Luongo has been serving the wonderful cuisine of his native Tuscany in this sunny, airy space. Your senses will be seduced upon entry by tables crowded with Italian cheeses and roasted vegetable displays. After you're seated, dense homemade breads arrive, along with vibrant green olive oil. Try to save some room for dinner, though. The kitchen masters classics like tomato bruschetta, spaghetti with meatballs, and osso bucco, and also excels in modern dishes like a seasonal salad made from goat cheese, brussels sprouts, pumpkin, and endive. Italian menu. Lunch, dinner. Closed holidays. Bar. Jacket required. Reservations recommended. **$$$**

★ ★ ★ ★ DANIEL 25 (MAP E)
60 E 65th St (10021)
Phone 212/288-0033
Fax 212/933-5250
www.danielnyc.com
Daniel Boulud is one of those chefs who could make scrambled eggs taste like manna from heaven. He has a magic touch that warms you from the inside out. For this reason, Daniel is a dining experience. It is not dinner. The experience starts when you enter the palatial front room, continues as you sip an old-fashioned cocktail in the romantic,

low-lit lounge, and is taken to new heights when you take a seat at your table, your home for the hours you will spend as the fortunate culinary guest of Boulud. French food at other restaurants is good. With Boulud facing the stove, it is sublime. Potato-crusted sea bass is a signature. The crisp, golden coat, fashioned from whisper-thin slices of potatoes, protects the fish while it cooks and seals in its juices so that it melts on the tongue. It is wonderful. Wine service is another perk. Friendly and helpful, the staff wants you to learn and wants to help you choose the right wine for your meal and your wallet. You will have a new favorite wine before leaving. After dessert, you will think that you're free to go, but not so fast. There are petit fours, of course, and then the pièce de resistance: madeleines. Daniel is famous for these delicate, fluffy, lemony little cakes served warm, just seconds out of the oven. When you are finally free to go, you may not want to. *Secret Inspector's Notes: The atmosphere at Daniel is unlike any other. Lively, pulsating, and elegant all at once, it is an experience well worth the cost. Whether for drinks or dinner, Daniel is always a hotspot, filled with celebrities, captains of industry, and plenty of other international elite. Go for the flowers, the festivity, the fanciness, and the fun.* French menu. Dinner. Closed Sun. Bar. Jacket required. Reservations recommended. **$$$$**

★ ★ ★ **GEISHA** **26** (MAP E)
33 E 61st St (10021)
Phone 212/813-1113
Set in a modern, posh townhouse in the east 60s, Geisha is seafood whiz kid Eric Ripert's inspired translation of Japanese cuisine. While he is still manning the stoves at Le Bernardin (see), here at Geisha, his love affair with Asian-tinged seafood is in full bloom. The food at Geisha delivers Zen enlightenment in plates of coconut-marinated fluke with coconut ponzu, lime vinaigrette, and orange essence; bowls of tiger shrimp dumplings with toasted pumpkin in a green curry broth; and dishes of

kitchen arts & letters

Great cooks and novices alike can spend hours in this store, which features more than 10,000 cookbooks from all over the world. You can find the hottest new books by the most popular chefs, as well as those that have been out of print for years. Whether you want to prepare complicated desserts or perfect the art of the grilled cheese sandwich, this store will have the right cookbook for you. *1435 Lexington Ave, between 93rd and 94th sts (10128). Phone 212/876-5550.*

dayboat cod with warm pepper and snow pea salad in soy ginger butter, not to mention gorgeous platters of sushi, sashimi and signature rolls prepared by a pair of seriously skilled sushi chefs. Japanese tea and an extensive sake list will keep you well hydrated and spiritually centered. Japanese menu. Lunch, dinner. Bar. Casual attire. **$$$**

★ ★ ★ HARRY CIPRIANI **27** (MAP E)
781 Fifth Ave (10022)
Phone 212/753-5566
Fax 212/308-5653
www.cipriani.com
If you are searching for a place to see and be seen by some of New York's most moneyed crowds, Harry's is your spot. Located across the street from Central Park, this posh restaurant has not been renovated in a while and could use a facelift, but perhaps because many of its patrons have already had work done, the owners don't feel as obligated to make over the room. The menu is Italian, the prices are high, the service is gracious, and the entire experience very old-world charming. Be prepared to hear the word "daaahhling" with alarming regularity. Italian menu. Breakfast, lunch, dinner. Bar. Jacket required. Reservations recommended. **$$$$**

★ JACKSON HOLE **28** (MAP D)
1611 Second Ave (10028)
Phone 212/737-8788
If you crave a thick, juicy burger and don't mind a loud crowd and a fast-paced, sometimes frenetic setting, then Jackson Hole is the place for you. This is a top spot to feast on burgers offered in various sizes and weights with an almost infinite variety of toppings. All are served with piles of steak fries and thick slices of red onion and ripe tomatoes. Jackson Hole restaurants are fun joints where cold beer and great beef burgers are the draw. American menu. Breakfast, lunch, dinner. Closed Thanksgiving, Dec 25. Bar. Outdoor seating. **$**

★ ★ ★ JO JO **29** (MAP F)
160 E 64th St (10021)
Phone 212/223-5656
Fax 212/755-9038
Located in a charming old townhouse, Jo Jo was one of the first restaurants from acclaimed star-chef and restaurateur Jean-Georges Vongerichten. It was recently renovated and given a turn-of-the-century feel, with deep jewel tones, velvet and silk fabrics, and 17th-century terra-cotta tiles. While the dining room has been made

over, the menu has stayed much the same, with dishes that highlight Vongerichten's French-Asian style, such as goat cheese and potato terrine with chive oil, roast chicken with chickpea fries, and tuna spring rolls with soybean coulis. Jo Jo is a wonderful spot for elegant, restful, special-occasion dining. American menu. Lunch, dinner. Closed holidays. Bar. Casual attire. **$$$$**

★ ★ ★ KAI 30 (MAP E)

822 Madison Ave (10021)
Phone 212/988-7277

Specializing in kaiseki, artistic meals made up of precious, miniature courses, Kai is a slim, shoebox-size restaurant with clay walls and chocolate-brown plank floors that you will find tucked into a sliver of a space above a Madison Avenue Japanese tea shop. The procession of food is breathtaking, each dish an artistic portrait composed of delicate vegetables, flavorful tea-smoked meats, and glistening seafood. After your harmonic meal, settle in with some tea, steeped and poured with skill from stunning, Asian-deigned iron kettles. To replicate the experience at home, stop by at the tea shop downstairs and purchase one to go. Japanese menu. Lunch, dinner. Closed Sun; holidays. Casual attire. **$$$**

★ ★ KINGS' CARRIAGE HOUSE 31 (MAP D)

251 E 82nd St (10028)
Phone 212/734-5490
www.kingscarriagehouse.com

Located on a tree-lined block, Kings' Carriage House is an exquisite and intimate restaurant with all the comforts of an antique-filled Irish manor house. Owned by former food stylist Elizabeth King and her husband, Paul Farell, a native of Dublin, this is indeed one of Manhattan's most enchanted and personal restaurants. Special treats include Sunday afternoon tea and the Sunday roast dinner, but the everyday menu with dishes like shrimp bisque and Irish smoked salmon is winning as well. Irish, English menu. Lunch, dinner. Closed Dec 25. Bar. Reservations recommended. **$$$**

★ ★ ★ LE REFUGE 32 (MAP D)

166 E 82nd St (10021)
Phone 212/861-4505
Fax 212/736-0384
nyc.lerefugeinn.com

Located within walking distance of the Metropolitan Museum of Art and the lush greenery of Central Park, Le Refuge is a classically charming French restaurant that offers a small slice of Paris in New York, without the smoking, of course. Aside from the lack of cigarette smoke, the difference between the two is negligible. The upper crust of society gathers at Le Refuge for its Parisian elegance and its impressive wine list that pairs up perfectly with the selection of simple, bistro-style fare, like farm-raised duck with fresh fruit and filet mignon with peppercorn sauce. French menu. Lunch, dinner, brunch. Closed holidays. Casual attire. Outdoor seating. **$$$**

★ ★ ★ LENOX ROOM ③③ (MAP D)

1278 Third Ave (10021)
Phone 212/772-0404
Fax 212/772-3229
www.lenoxroom.com

Restaurateur Tony Fortuna has managed to bring a bit of slick, downtown style to this quiet, residential (some might say culinarily comatose) neighborhood. Thanks to Fortuna, the vibrant life inside Lenox Room more than makes up for the lack of a pulse beating at nearby eateries. At Lenox, you will find a sexy bar and lounge with cool cocktails and inventive tiers of cocktail cuisine, and a swanky, intimate dining room offering a smart New American menu. Lenox is a sure thing for a business lunch, a ladies-only cocktail outing, or a spirited dinner with friends. Not only will the food win you over, but Fortuna's gracious hospitality will have you scheduling your next visit before you leave. American menu. Lunch, dinner, Sun brunch. Closed holidays. Bar. **$$$$**

★ ★ LUSARDI'S ③④ (MAP D)

1494 Second Ave (10021)
Phone 212/249-2020
Fax 212/585-2941
www.lusardis.com

This well-established neighborhood staple is a favorite among Upper East Siders craving reliable Italian fare in a modest, warm setting. The menu sticks to the things Italian restaurants do best—lavish plates of antipasti, fresh composed salads, hearty bowls of pasta, olive oil-grilled fish, and tender slow-cooked meats braised in red wine. This is a lovely restaurant with a gracious staff and a wonderful wine list to complement the cuisine. Italian menu. Lunch, dinner. Closed holidays. Bar. Casual attire. Reservations recommended. **$$$**

★ ★ ★ MAYA   35 (MAP F)
1191 First Ave (10021)
Phone 212/585-1818
Fax 212/734-6579

A native of Mexico City, Maya's chef/owner Richard Sandoval knows authentic Mexican cuisine. His popular Upper East Side outpost is perpetually packed with smart, sexy neighborhood locals who understand that Mexico does more than just refried beans and cheesy enchiladas. At Maya, you'll find a soothing hacienda-style room—wood-paneled walls accented with native art, and terra-cotta tiled floors—a comfortable, stylish place to relax for dinner. And speaking of dinner, you'll be treated to a thrilling menu of authentic regional Mexican dishes like Cordero en Mole Verde—lamb shank braised in mole verde with pan-roasted potatoes, chayote squash, and baby carrots, and the house Mariscada—a mammoth bowl bobbing with sea scallops, shrimp, mussels, and clams, served with black rice and a coriander seed-red pepper emulsion. The food goes down almost as easily as the terrific selection of one hundred tequilas and mezcals. Take two aspirin before bed. Mexican menu. Dinner, Sun brunch. Closed Jan 1, Dec 25. Bar. Casual attire. Reservations recommended. **$$$**

★ ★ OUR PLACE   36 (MAP D)
1444 Third Ave (10028)
Phone 212/288-4888
Fax 212/744-3620

Our Place could be mistaken for just another neighborhood Chinese joint, but once you try their sophisticated cuisine, you'll agree it's a notch or two above. The dining room and staff are so pleasant and professional it's worth dining in, but if you must stay at home it's by far the highest-quality Chinese delivery on the Upper East Side. On weekends, don't miss their dim sum brunch for a fun change from the usual brunch destinations. Chinese menu. Lunch, dinner, brunch. Closed Thanksgiving. Bar. **$$$**

★ ★ ★ PARK AVENUE CAFE   37 (MAP F)
100 E 63rd St (10021)
Phone 212/644-1900
Fax 212/688-0373
www.parkavenuecafe.com

Sophisticated and savvy New Yorkers head to Park Avenue Cafe for luxurious lunch meetings, intimate dinners, and large party outings. The warm, blond-wooded room is bright and airy and feels easy and comfortable. The menu of inspired seasonal dishes uses clean, simple flavors that please the palate. Desserts whipped up by famed pastry chef Richard Leach make you feel like a kid again; finger-licking may be necessary. American menu. Lunch, dinner, Sun brunch. Closed Jan 1, Dec 25. Bar. Casual attire. **$$$$**

🔲

★ ★ ★ PAYARD PATISSERIE AND BISTRO (MAP D)

1032 Lexington Ave (10021)
Phone 212/717-5252
Fax 212/717-0986
www.payard.com

Willpower must be left outside of Payard. Aside from the great selection of sandwiches, salads, and Parisian bistro staples served in this lovely, butter-yellow French pastry shop, the desserts are as tempting as they come. But this should come as no surprise considering that the baker in question is François Payard, a master of sweets and treats. While lunch and dinner are good choices, Payard's afternoon tea is a wonderful way to get acquainted with his talents. French menu. Lunch, dinner. Closed Sun; holidays. **$$$**

🔲

★ ★ PEARSON'S TEXAS BARBECUE 39 (MAP D)

170 E 81st St (10028)
Phone 212/288-2700
www.pearsonsbbq.com

Now more conveniently located on the Upper East Side, Pearson's claims to serve the most authentic barbecue this side of the Mississippi. Once you step inside, it sure feels like a roadside BBQ stand, with gingham-checked tablecloths, memorabilia galore, and smoky smells wafting through the dining room. The menu of ribs, pulled pork, beans, slaw, onion rings, and sausages offers something for everyone, and the casual staff makes this an easy choice for families and groups. Expect to have to wait for a table, as Pearson's does not take reservations and has developed a loyal following over the years. Barbecue menu. Lunch, dinner. Children's menu. Casual attire. Outdoor seating. **$$**

★ ★ PIG HEAVEN 40 (MAP D)

1540 Second Ave (10028)
Phone 212/744-4887
Fax 212/744-2853

The name may be intimidating but they're not guilty of false advertising one bit. The spare ribs, roast pork, and suckling pig are some of the best found outside Chinatown. The roast duck is fantastic as well and after a delightful renovation a few years ago, Pig Heaven is just as much for dining out as for dining in. Nancy Lee, the well-known hostess, will make sure you enjoy the best food Pig Heaven has to offer. Chinese menu. Lunch, dinner, brunch. Bar. Reservations recommended. **$$**

★ ★ ★ THE POST HOUSE 41 (MAP E)
28 E 63rd St (10021)
Phone 212/935-2888
Fax 212/371-9265
www.theposthouse.com

New York has many steakhouses, and The Post House is one of the power lunch club's favorites. The comfortable dining room, with a long bar, has an easy feel thanks to polished parquet floors, wooden wainscoting, and leather armchair seating. The menu sports a super selection of salads, signature appetizers like cornmeal-fried oysters, and a shimmering raw bar in addition to entrées like grilled chicken, rack of lamb, and meat-eater delights like prime rib, filet mignon, and the signature "Stolen Cajun Rib Steak." An extensive wine list emphasizes California wines and some rare gems from Burgundy and Bordeaux. Steak menu. Lunch, dinner. Closed Jan 1, Thanksgiving, Dec 25. Bar. Casual attire. **$$$**

★ ★ ★ ★ RM 42 (MAP E)
33 E 60th St (10022)
Phone 212/319-3800
Fax 212/319-4955

After ten years at the helm at Oceana, chef Rick Moonen decided to set off on a ship of his own. At RM, his sparkling new namesake eatery, seafood remains the star attraction. Moonen has a gift with the ocean's bounty, and with the new space, he has found new inspiration and a source of revitalization. The New American menu at RM sets off sparks, focusing on the freshest catches and perfectly blending seasonal ingredients with vibrant global flavors. The sophisticated dining room is dressed in soothing neutral tones, with lots of blond wood and warm, golden lighting, lending the restaurant a Zen vibe. Despite the high-income power crowds that fill the restaurant for business lunches and civilized, exquisite dinners, the dining room remains a serene retreat from Manhattan stress. Seafood menu. Lunch, dinner. Closed Sun. Reservations recommended. **$$$$**

★★ SERAFINA FABULOUS PIZZA (MAP D)
1022 Madison Ave (10021)
Phone 212/734-2676
At this mini-chain of velvet-roped pizza joints, you can start the evening off with a simple meal of tasty Italian fare like wood-fired pizzas, salads, antipasti, pasta, seafood, and meat and then stay and hang out in the bar to sip cool cocktails and listen to the DJs spinning tunes. Serafina is casual but hip, with a generally young and gorgeous European crowd that comes in more for the see-and-be-scene vibe than the terrific pizzas. Pizza. Lunch, dinner, late-night. **$$**

★ SERENDIPITY 3 (44) (MAP F)
225 E 60th St (10022)
Phone 212/838-3531
Fax 212/688-4896
www.serendipity3.com
Most restaurants rest on their savory menus. Not at Serendipity 3, a loud, kid-in-a-candy-store sort of a place that is fashioned after a vintage soda parlor. Decorated with Tiffany lamps and stained-glass windows, with a fun boutique up front, this is one restaurant where desserts rule the roost. Sure, you can grab sandwiches, burgers, salads, and the like, but really, this is one place to have dessert for dinner. Monster-sized sundaes, gooey chocolate layer cake, mountain-size cheesecake, and the signature frozen hot chocolate—a birdbath-sized chocolate seducer—are great dinner dishes. Who needs protein? American menu. Lunch, dinner. Closed Dec 25. **$$**

★★★ SUSHI OF GARI (45) (MAP D)
402 E 78th St (10021)
Phone 212/517-5340
Sushi of Gari is one of those spots frequented by New Yorkers in the know. Nobu's divine, sure, but Sushi of Gari stays true to Japanese fare rather than infusing Latin ingredients. The problem is that, like Nobu, Sushi of Gari is always packed to capacity with sushi-seeking trendsetters, and at times, it's hard to hear yourself order, let alone have a conversation. But try to keep your ears tuned to other tables as they order, since many regulars come in and order amazing dishes that are not on the menu. Either eavesdrop or feel free to ask your neighbors for their recommendations—New Yorkers love to talk about food. If you're sticking to the basics, the raw fish—like the kanpachi (Japanese yellowtail) and the toro (fatty tuna)—is silky and luscious. Japanese menu. Dinner. Casual attire. **$$$$**

★ ★ ★ WILLOW 46 (MAP D)

1022 Lexington Ave (10021)
Phone 212/717-0703
Fax 212/717-0725

It's easy to miss this tiny corner restaurant tucked away at street level, but make a point of being vigilant. This is a neighborhood gem. Serving a French-American bistro menu, Willow is an easy charmer, with amber lighting, cozy banquettes, and seasonal floral arrangements. If you are planning a romantic dinner, or if you are looking for a place to catch up in peace with an old friend, you can't go wrong here. French bistro menu. Lunch, dinner, Sun brunch. Closed Dec 25. Casual attire. Reservations recommended. Outdoor seating. **$$$**
🄳

Midtown

Stretching from 34th Street to 59th Street, the Harlem River to the East River, Midtown is the heart of Manhattan. Most of the city's skyscrapers are here, along with most of its offices, major hotels, famous shops, the Empire State Building, Times Square, the Broadway theaters, the Museum of Modern Art, Rockefeller Center, Grand Central Station, and the New York Public Library.

Fifth Avenue is the center of Midtown, dividing the city into east and west. Although nothing more than a line on a map as late as 1811, the thoroughfare had become New York's most fashionable address by the Civil War. It began to turn commercial in the early 1900s and is now lined with mostly shops and office buildings.

Towering over the southern end of Midtown is the Empire State Building (350 Fifth Ave at 34th St), one of the world's most famous skyscrapers. Built in the early 1930s, the building took just 14 months to erect and remains an Art Deco masterpiece.

Forty-Second Street is lined with one major attraction after another. On the corner of Third Avenue soars the magnificent Chrysler Building, another Art Deco masterpiece; Grand Central Station, whose magnificent concourse was recently restored to the tune of $200 million, is at Lexington Avenue. At Fifth Avenue beckons the New York Public Library, behind which spreads Bryant Park, where many free events are held during the summer months.

West of Seventh Avenue along 42nd Street begins Times Square, which stretches north to 48th Street along the Seventh Avenue-Broadway nexus. The best time to come here is at night, when the huge state-of-the-art neon lights that line the square begin to shine. Much cleaned up in recent years, Times Square is also a good place to catch street performers and, of course, Broadway theater. Many of the city's most famous theaters are located on the side streets around Times Square.

North and a little east of Times Square, Rockefeller Center reigns as an Art Deco complex stretching between 48th and 51st streets, Sixth and Fifth avenues. Built by John D. Rockefeller during the height of the Depression, Rockefeller Center is home to the landmark Radio City Music Hall, the NBC Studios, and a famed skating rink filled with outdoor enthusiasts during the winter months.

Along Fifth Avenue just south and north of Rockefeller Center, find some of the city's most famous shops—Saks Fifth Avenue, Tiffany's, Steuben Glass, and Cartier, along with Trump Tower at 56th Street. Between 50th and 51st streets soars the Gothic Saint Patrick's Cathedral, the largest Roman Catholic cathedral in the United States; the Museum of Modern Art, a must-stop for any art lover, is on 53rd Street just west of Fifth.

Restaurants in Midtown West and Chelsea

★★★ 21 CLUB   (MAP E)
21 W 52nd St (10019)
Phone 212/582-7200; toll-free 800/721-2582
Fax 212/974-7562
www.21club.com
This one-time speakeasy is now one of New York City's most celebrated spots for lunch, dinner, and lots of drinks—at least for the well-heeled Wall Street, media, and superstar regulars who frequent its best tables. Chef Erik Blauberg turns out stellar, seasonal American-French fare, with standards that shine and inventive twists that delight. The restaurant has a distinguished air to it, with a clubby, brass-railed bar (often the sight of dealmakers clinking martini glasses), luxurious linen-lined tables, golden lighting, antique oil paintings, and old photos hung on wood-paneled walls. The deep wine list explores the world at large and works well to complement the cuisine. American menu. Lunch (Mon-Fri in the Bar Room), dinner. Closed Sun; holidays. Bar. Jacket required in Upstairs at 21. **$$$**

★★★★★ ALAIN DUCASSE 48 (MAP E)
155 W 58th St (10019)
Phone 212/265-7300
www.alain-ducasse.com
When word came that the famed French wizard of gastronomy, Alain Ducasse, was opening a restaurant in New York, the city's food world began salivating. And while the excess, such as the choice of half a dozen pens to sign the bill, drew some criticism at its opening, people started to embrace the restaurant once they experienced Ducasse firsthand. Ducasse has superhuman culinary powers; food doesn't taste this way anywhere else, and it sure doesn't arrive at a table this way anywhere else. Elegant to the point of being regal, Ducasse is a restaurant designed to please every one of the senses: sight, sound, smell, taste, and touch. The room frequently fills with attractive diners. Hours later, when dinner is over and you attempt to get up

and walk to the door, you receive a gift for breakfast the next morning: a gift-wrapped buttery, fruit-laced brioche that will make you swoon. If you manage not to dig into it in the cab on the way back to your hotel, you have a will of steel. But divine excess does not come without its price. Dinner at Ducasse will set you back several pretty pennies, but really, isn't paying your mortgage a dull way to spend your money? *Secret Inspector's Notes: Food is only one of the amazing aspects of a dinner at Alain Ducasse. The service, décor, presentations, and wine service are only a few of the other details that Ducasse handles in an unparalleled way.* French menu. Dinner. Closed Sun; also mid-July–early Aug. Jacket required. Reservations recommended. **$$$$**

new yorker food

There are a few foods that New Yorkers can't live without. Discussions and arguments regarding the superiority and foundation of each of these foods are common. Of course, these foods are found outside New York, but the sheer variety and passion regarding each one is a cultural phenomenon unparalleled elsewhere. Many of these foods are packed with nutritional guilt, a sharp contrast to the slender, health-conscious folks you usually find hungrily waiting to enjoy these forbidden pleasures.

Cheap and portable, the hot dog is everywhere. But the Special is truly a New Yorker food. Found at many Jewish delis around the city, Specials are larger, meatier, and more satisfying, with a richer flavor and more texture. **Katz's** grills theirs, while **Pastrami Queen** serves them steamed. Specials are eaten sans bun, removed from the casing with ample deli mustard.

Pastrami is like a religion for those who partake. The rules are rigid, and to go outside the rye-bread-and-mustard-on-the-side paradigm is to risk excommunication. Occasionally, it's permitted to marry with another meat, such as corned beef or tongue, for a double-decker, but in general it's best to play by the rules. **Second Avenue Deli** (156 Second Ave, phone 212/677-0606, www.2ndavedeli.com) is assuredly one of the two most devout sources of pastrami, providing crispy fries, feathery matzo balls, and dense blintzes to an infrequently kosher crowd. The other spiritual leadership resides at **Katz's**

(205 E Houston St, phone 212/254-2246, www.katzdeli.com), where the countermen (why bother with table service?) are generous enough to feed you a taste of the pastrami as they thickly slice it for your sandwich. The ancient payment system is a perpetual reminder that if it ain't broke, don't fix it. **Carnegie Deli** (854 Seventh Ave, phone 212/757-2245, www.carnegiedeli.com) is a frequent stop on the tourist trail and serves excellent pastrami via an unnecessarily surly staff. The size of the sandwiches, multiplied by price, makes them worthwhile to share or take home half for later. Though not quite members of the supreme triumvirate, **Sarge's** (548 Third Ave, phone 212/679-0442) and **Pastrami Queen** (1269 Lexington Ave, phone 212/828-0007) offer worthy alternatives if the geography is more manageable.

Pizza is as New York a pastime as baseball. Whether delivered to the door, eaten in a restaurant, or snacked on as a slice, pizza is the everyman food. Preferences are strong and the variations subtle, but the thin-crust pie is the New York standard—no slow-baking deep-dish in this town. When it comes to sit-down, eat-in pizza, everyone has a preferred joint, and an accompanying salad is requisite not for vegetable provision but the balancing acidity of vinegar. **Lombardi's** (32 Spring St, phone 212/941-7994, www.lombardipizza.com), the oldest pizzeria in both New York and the nation, has excellent pizza in a somewhat cramped and crowded space. **John's** (278 Bleecker St, phone 212/243-1680), one of the remaining coal-burning-oven pizza spots, is warm and casual with dark wood booths and a friendly staff. **Grimaldi's** (19 Old Fulton St, phone 718/858-4300, www.grimaldis.com), a former relative of the Patsy's in Harlem, is well worth the subway trip, while **Patsy's Pizzeria** (distantly related to Harlem Patsy's of slice fame, 61 W 74th St, phone 212/579-3000) is the most appealing of the bunch décor-wise and a favorites of families. When it comes to pizza, a name is a powerful thing. **Totonno's** (1524 Neptune Ave, Coney Island, phone 718/372-8606, www.totonnos.com), like Patsy's, has the original location, where terrific pies are found, and unrelated locations throughout the city, where the pizza is much more average and mainstream. Many may question who would make the trek to Coney Island just for pizza, but once you make the pilgrimage and consume the coal-burning-oven charred crust, it seems a minor complication. Often favored by those who prefer the spots free from family feuds, **DiFara Pizza** (1424 Ave J, phone 718/258-1367) makes one delicious pie. Little details like freshly ground Parmigiano for topping set this place apart from others. **Arturo's** (106 W Houston St, phone 212/677-3820) may not have the best pizza in the running, but the lively atmosphere, festive crowd, and loud entertainment make it more of a destination.

What's most amazing about New York is how many ethnic foods become a common part of the city's vocabulary. Suddenly everyone has an opinion on the best pad Thai, dim sum, moules frites, Ethiopian dive, cheese selection, sushi chef, tamale, and on and on. Foods that are generally common to a specific ethnic group become part of the mainstream, and it's impossible to imagine what life was like before. Certainly a knish is not a common find in Kansas City, but **Yonah Shimmell's Knishes** (137 E Houston St, phone 212/477-2858, www.knishery.com) is a destination for many, and the knowledge that they ship all over the country is a comfort for those who don't live nearby. The pickle, an essential accompaniment, is found almost anywhere across the city, but **Gus's Pickles** (87 Orchard St) is the best place to stock up and to find the freshest pickled tomatoes and pickles of any adaptation imaginable. Smoked and pickled fish are items that many novices turn their noses up at until they enjoy the finest pickled herring from **Russ & Daughters** (179 E Houston St, phone 212/475-4880), rich smoked sable from **Sable's** (1489 Second Ave, phone 212/249-6177), or sturgeon from **Barney Greengrass** (541 Amsterdam Ave, phone 212/724-4707, www.barneygreengrass.com), self-declared "sturgeon king." Suddenly life seems empty without. And who ever thought babka would become famous through a *Seinfeld* episode capturing the ease with which this seemingly simple food can create insanity? If it's a black-and-white cookie, beware the imposters; you'd better head to **Glaser's Bake Shop** (1670 First Ave, phone 212/289-2562), where you can get them in mini-versions too.

★★★ AMUSE (MAP E)

108 W 18th St (10011)
Phone 212/929-9755

Amuse is a unique restaurant, which is quite an accomplishment in the scheme of New York City dining. The kitchen offers a clever menu of different-sized plates—$5, $15, or $20 each, depending on portion size—for tasting, sharing, passing, and, above all, enjoying. The menu spans the globe and features lots of full-flavored snacks, appetizers,

and entrée-type plates from comfort food favorites to inventive
haute creations. This design-your-own-dinner formula fits seamlessly
with the slick cocktail-crazed crowds that come in for the scene
as much as the terrific and, as the restaurant's name promises, fun
food. American menu. Lunch, dinner. Closed Sun. Bar. Casual attire.
Reservations recommended. **$$$**

★ ★ ★ AQUAVIT (MAP E)

13 W 54th St (10019)
Phone 212/307-7311
Fax 212/265-8584
www.aquavit.org
Chef/partner (and culinary heartthrob) Marcus Samuelsson intro-
duced New York to his splashy brand of modern Scandinavian cuisine
a decade ago at Aquavit, an elegant two-story restaurant housed in a
historic Midtown townhouse, just a stone's throw from the Museum
of Modern Art and the shops of Fifth Avenue. After ten years and a
facelift, the restaurant still has a sleek, sophisticated vibe, and the
cuisine is even more spectacular. While ingredients like herring, lamb,
salmon, caviar, and dill show up with regularity on this Scandinavian-
inspired menu, the food here is more uniquely Samuelsson than
anything else. What this means is that every dazzling plate achieves
a startlingly delicious harmony as the result of the chef's careful and
creative combination of textures, flavors, temperatures, ingredients,
and the cooking styles of France, Asia, and Sweden. A shot of smooth,
citrus-tinged aquavit complements dinner nicely, as does a selection
from the impressive wine list. Scandanavian menu. Lunch, dinner.
Closed holidays. Bar. Casual attire. **$$$$**

★ ★ ★ ATELIER 51 (MAP E)

50 Central Park S (10019)
Phone 212/521-6125
www.ritzcarlton.com
Located across from Central Park in the posh Ritz-Carlton hotel,
Atelier is a stunning, civilized restaurant that feels like luxury from
the moment you are seated in one of its cushy banquettes. To match
the surroundings, the kitchen offers beautiful dishes for adventurous
and high-minded foodies—this is super-modern French cuisine of the
haute variety. The food is often cloaked in foams, gelees, and mousses
with lots of contrasting textures and flavors dancing on the plate
for a wild and delicious meal. French menu. Breakfast, lunch, dinner,
brunch. Bar. Jacket required. Reservations recommended. **$$$$**

★ ★ BARBETTA (MAP E)
321 W 46th St (10036)
Phone 212/246-9171
Fax 212/246-1279
www.barbettarestaurant.com

Barbetta is the grand old dame of the theater district. This classic Italian restaurant opened its doors in 1906 and is still owned by the same loving family, the Maioglios. Located in a pair of historic early-19th-century townhouses, this restaurant is a classic charmer that's all about super-elegant, old-world dining. The menu doesn't aim anywhere other than where its heart is—Italy—but don't expect just pasta. The kitchen offers a great selection of seafood, poultry, and beef prepared with seasonal ingredients and lively flavors. The tree-lined outdoor garden is an enchanted spot to unwind over dinner or drinks. Italian menu. Lunch, dinner. Closed Sun. Outdoor seating. **$$$**

★ ★ BECCO (MAP E)
355 W 46th St (10036)
Phone 212/397-7597
Fax 212/977-6738
www.becconyc.com

Becco, a charming Italian restaurant in the theater district, is a delightful place to relax over a delicious Italian supper before or after the theater, or at lunch for a business meeting. Becco offers great food, gracious service, and a lovely, airy atmosphere. The pre-theater special for which it has become famous offers authentic homemade pastas in an all-you-can-eat format. You choose three pastas, and they keep dishing them out until you say "Uncle!" or until you can't rise from the table, whichever comes first. Italian menu. Lunch, dinner. Closed Dec 25. Casual attire. Reservations recommended. **$$$**

★ ★ ★ BEN BENSON'S STEAKHOUSE (MAP E)
123 W 52nd St (10019)
Phone 212/581-8888
Fax 212/581-1170
www.benbensons.com

At this popular testosterone-infused steakhouse, you'll find yourself elbow to elbow with celebrities, politicians, sports stars, and the city's financial elite. As you might expect from a power steak spot, the menu is as big as the egos in the room and includes solid standards like salads, poultry, and seafood that are simply and impeccably prepared. But the magnetic pull here is the restaurant's signature selection of USDA Prime dry-aged beef, served in the form of about a dozen cuts and portion sizes. The huge steaks are matched in size

by lobsters the size of small pets. Don't miss the house's signature crispy hashed browns. When the sun is shining, grab a seat outside in the sidewalk dining room, appointed in the same style as the indoor space with deep armchairs, formal white linens, and green-and-white wainscoted planters—an ideal alfresco setting. Steak menu. Lunch, dinner. Closed holidays. Bar. Casual attire. Outdoor seating. **$$$**
🅳

★ ★ ★ THE BILTMORE ROOM   (MAP E)
290 Eighth Ave (10001)
Phone 212/807-0111
www.thebiltmoreroom.com

Located on a nondescript block of Chelsea, The Biltmore Room appears like a mirage in the desert, its magnificent façade marked by guilded gates and marble columns that make the entranceway feel like an old palace. Once inside, the design continues to please the eye, with marble floors; a long, sexy bar; high ceilings; and loveseat-styled banquettes set around the dining room like an elegant old-world parlor. The bar, where the impressive cocktails are made from the freshest ingredients, draws the beautiful people crowd, a mix of sophisticated foodies and hipsters in scant dress. As if the design and the drinks weren't enough, the food, by chef/partner Gary Robbins, is already creating legions of fans. The menu features a savvy fusion style of American and Asian flavors with dishes accented with chiles, mango, lime, sweet spices, fresh mint, basil, and other savory herbs. The Biltmore Room is the rare spot that lacks pretension despite its fabulous food and design, which makes it a perfect spot for drinks, a special occasion, or a night out with friends. American, pan-Asian menu. Dinner. Closed Sun. Bar. Business casual attire. Reservations recommended. **$$$$**

★ ★ ★ BLUE FIN   (56) (MAP E)
1567 Broadway (10036)
Phone 212/918-1400
www.whotels.com

Located in the heart of Times Square in the swanky W Times Square Hotel, Blue Fin is restaurateur Steve Hanson's (Blue Water Grill, Dos Caminos—see both) most elaborate seafood palace. On two levels, with a breathtaking aquatic-themed design, Blue Fin features high-end fish dishes and a stunning array of sushi, sashimi, and maki. The bar on the ground floor is always packed to the gills with suits sipping tall, cool cocktails, while the upstairs bar is more mellow but may still be a struggle for intimate conversation at peak times. Blue Fin offers terrific food in a stylish and slick setting that makes it a great spot for pre-theater, a dinner with a large group, or a business lunch. American, seafood, sushi menu. Breakfast, lunch, dinner, late-night. Bar. Children's menu. Casual attire. Outdoor seating. **$$$**

★ ★ ★ BRASSERIE 8½ (MAP E)
9 W 57th St (10019)
Phone 212/829-0812
www.restaurantassociates.com/brasserie8andahalf
Located in the sleek, Gordon Bunshaft-designed "9" building in the heart of West 57th Street, Brasserie 8 1/2 is the perfect spot for all sort of plans. It's a great pick for a power lunch or for shimmering cocktails after work. The long, backlit bar is a mecca for stylish men and women in search of one another. It's also a wise choice for pre-theater dinner and a terrific selection for those who want to relax in a slick, modern setting and enjoy a leisurely meal of updated brasserie classics tweaked to modern attention. The kitchen incorporates accents from Asia and the Mediterranean into these classic dishes, varying each dish just enough from its original base. Be warned that the spacious banquettes are so soft and comfortable that you may never want to get up. American menu. Lunch, dinner. Bar. Jacket required. Reservations recommended. **$$$**

★ ★ BRYANT PARK GRILL (MAP E)
25 W 40th St (10018)
Phone 212/840-6500
Fax 212/840-8122
www.arkrestaurants.com
Located behind the New York Public Library in the leafy tree-lined Bryant Park, the Bryant Park Grill is an airy, vaulted, and stylish spot to relax over dinner or hammer out a complex business transaction over lunch. The simple American menu features salads, steaks, fish, sandwiches, and pasta on a straightforward, seasonal menu. The bar is a zoo in the summertime, so if mingling with happy hour crowds is your thing, make Bryant Park Grill your destination. American menu. Lunch, dinner. Bar. Children's menu. Casual attire. Outdoor seating. **$$$**
🄳

★ ★ CAFETERIA 59 (MAP E)
119 Seventh Ave (10011)
Phone 212/414-1717
This Chelsea restaurant is a hotspot late at night—and at all times in between—for its easy-to-love American menu in a minimalist white-washed setting. Cafeteria is a sleek, ramped-up diner with good food,

fun cocktails, and lots of fabulous attitude that makes it a second home to lots of size 2 babes, metrosexuals, and buff Chelsea boys. American menu. Breakfast, lunch, dinner, late-night. Bar. Children's menu. Casual attire. Outdoor seating. **$$**

★ CARNEGIE DELI 60 (MAP E)
854 Seventh Ave (10019)
Phone 212/757-2245
Fax 212/757-9889
www.carnegiedeli.com

Sandwiches are the specialty of Carnegie Deli, and by sandwich we mean at least a pound of freshly sliced meat, cheese, cole slaw, and assorted condiments stuffed between two slices of rye bread. Take note—this is not a place for dainty eaters. The Carnegie Deli is a loud, hectic, and chaotic whirlwind of a place with a bustling lunch crowd that is equally crazy in the evenings, when the old-fashioned booths fill up with eager sandwich lovers. Deli menu. Breakfast, lunch, dinner, late-night. **$$**

★ ★ CHELSEA BISTRO AND BAR 61 (MAP E)
358 W 23rd St (10011)
Phone 212/727-2026
Fax 212/727-2180

Chelsea Bistro and Bar is a lovely neighborhood bistro that goes beyond the call of the average local spot. Warm service, a charming atmosphere, wonderful food, and romantic lighting make this an ideal choice for almost any type of evening plans. A bite at the bar makes you feel like a regular even if you are from miles away. French bistro menu. Dinner. Bar. **$$**

chelsea

Primarily middle-class residential and still somewhat indus-trial, Chelsea—stretching between 14th and 30th streets, from Sixth Avenue to the Hudson River—is not the most tourist-oriented of areas. However, the neighborhood does offer an exciting, avant-garde arts scene, as well as many lovely quiet blocks lined with attractive row houses and rustling trees. A new gay community has moved in recently, bringing with it trendy cafés, shops, and bars, while an enormous, state-of-the-art sports complex, the Chelsea Piers, beckons from the river's edge (between 18th and 22nd streets).

Most of Chelsea was once owned by Captain Thomas Clarke, whose grandson, Clement Charles Clarke, laid out the residential district in the early 1800s. Clement Charles was also a scholar and a poet who wrote the famous poem beginning with the line, "'Twas the night before Christmas..." Another of Clement Charles's legacies is the General Theological Seminary, a peaceful enclave of ivy-covered buildings bounded by the block between Ninth and Tenth avenues and 20th and 21st streets.

Also on the western edge of Chelsea are many of the city's foremost art galleries, which began moving here in the early 1990s as rents in SoHo—their former home—began skyrocketing. An especially large number can be found on West 21st and 22nd streets between Tenth and Eleventh avenues; among them are the Paula Cooper Gallery (534 W 21st St), the Maximum Protech Gallery (511 W 22nd St), and the Dia Center for the Arts (548 W 22nd St). One of the pioneers of the area, the Dia Center is really more a museum than an art gallery and usually hosts a variety of eye-popping exhibits, along with an open-air sculpture garden on the roof.

Most of Chelsea's thriving shops, restaurants, and bars—some of which are predominantly gay, some not—stand along Sixth and Eighth avenues between 14th and 23rd streets. Some of the neighborhood's prettiest blocks, lined with elegant row houses, are West 20th, 21st, and 22nd streets between Eighth and Tenth avenues. Also, be sure to take a gander at the Chelsea Hotel (222 W 23rd St, near Eighth Ave), a maroon-colored landmark that has all-black gables, chimneys, and balconies. Built in 1884, the Chelsea has housed dozens of artists, writers, and musicians over the years, including Arthur Miller, Jackson Pollock, Bob Dylan, and Sid Vicious.

Just north of Chelsea lies the underground Pennsylvania Station (Seventh Ave at 32nd St), topped with circular Madison Square Garden, and the General Post Office (Eighth Ave, between 31st and 33rd sts)—a gorgeous building designed by McKim, Mead & White in 1913. The Garment District, centering on Seventh Avenue in the 30s, also begins here.

★★ CHURRASCARIA PLATAFORMA   62 (MAP E)

316 W 49th St (10019)
Phone 212/245-0505
Fax 212/974-8250
www.churrascariaplataforma.com

Succulent Brazilian barbecue is served in delicious abundance at Churrascaria Plataforma, a loud, high-energy eatery in the theater district. This authentic Riodizio offers grilled and skewered beef, pork, chicken, sausage, lamb, and fish in all-you-can-eat portions (you give your server the green light by flipping the small disc at your place setting, indicating "Go!"), accompanied by intoxicating caiparinas—tangy, lime-soaked cocktails made from cachaca, a potent alcohol similar to rum. Brazilian menu. Lunch, dinner. Closed Dec 25. Bar. Casual attire. Reservations recommended. **$$$**

★★★ CITÉ   64 (MAP E)

120 W 51st St (10020)
Phone 212/956-7100
Fax 212/956-7157
www.citerestaurant.com

Located in the heart of Midtown, Cité is an elegant, civilized spot for wining and dining. The restaurant is known for its wonderful prix fixe meals paired with four complimentary wines, making this power spot a meat and wine lover's paradise. The signature tender prime filet mignon (piled high with golden French fries) is a dish made for the restaurant's bold reds from France, Spain, and around the world. Seafaring diners, fret not: you too can rejoice in lobster, salmon, and meaty crab cakes, with lots of crisp whites to complement them. American, French menu. Lunch, dinner. Closed holidays. Bar. Casual attire. **$$$**

★ CITY BAKERY   63 (MAP E)

3 W 18th St (10003)
Phone 212/366-1414

Maury Rubin, the owner and creator of City Bakery, would probably have a warrant taken out on him if he ever closed City Bakery. Literally, New Yorkers would revolt and hunt him down. This hall of out-of-this-world baked goods is perpetually jammed with trendy locals craving his rich and creamy hot chocolate with house-made marshmallows, and his signature try-and-stop-at-one pretzel crois-sants. Aside from his selection of baked goods, he offers a dreamy buffet stocked with sandwiches, salads, antipasti, and soups made from the freshest seasonal ingredients. Just try and leave without loosening your belt buckle. American menu. Breakfast, lunch, dinner. Casual attire. **$**

★ ★ ★ DB BISTRO MODERNE 65 (MAP E)
55 W 44th St (10036)
Phone 212/391-2400
Fax 212/391-1188
www.danielnyc.com/dbbistro

This cool, sexy, ultra-stylish bistro in Midtown is Daniel Boulud's most casual restaurant. But he succeeds in making it a hotspot for foodies and moguls of all sorts without making it ordinary. For Boulud, making a regular restaurant is simply not possible. It's like asking Frank Sinatra to hum a simple tune. In many dishes, Boulud has a magic touch, transforming simple into spectacular with ease. His signature DB Burger is an excellent example of his creative interpretations. He builds the fattest, juiciest round of beef and stuffs it with short ribs and sinful amounts of foie gras and truffles. He serves it on a homemade Parmesan brioche bun, with house-stewed tomato confit (instead of ketchup) and a great big vat of fries. Don't think that this will be too much food for you to eat alone—you'll regret offering to share after the first bite. French menu. Lunch, dinner, late-night. Closed holidays. Casual attire. Reservations recommended. **$$$**

★ ★ ELMO 66 (MAP E)
156 Seventh Ave (10011)
Phone 212/337-8000

Located in the heart of Chelsea, Elmo is a convivial American eatery with a bustling bar serving comfort food that has been tweaked a bit for a fashionable New York City crowd. There are dishes as retro as Alphabet Soup with fluffy, dill-accented chicken dumplings; a hearty mac and cheese; and easy-to-love Hungry Man-type meals featuring meat and potatoes. There's even a Duncan Hines devil's food cake for dessert. Mom would be proud. American menu. Lunch, dinner. Bar. Casual attire. Outdoor seating. **$$**

★ ★ ★ ESTIATORIO MILOS 67 (MAP E)
125 W 55th St (10019)
Phone 212/245-7400
Fax 212/245-4828
www.milos.com

Milos, as it's called for short (try saying "Estiatorio" over and over again and you'll understand why), is a luxurious, cavernous, white-washed eatery decorated with umbrella-topped tables and seafood market-style fish displays. Showcasing simple, rustic Greek cooking, this elegant, airy restaurant takes you from the hustle of Midtown to the shores of the Mediterranean in the whirl of a revolving door. Seafood is priced by the pound and is prepared either perfectly grilled over charcoal or in the Greek style called *spetsiota*—filleted and baked with tomatoes, onions, herbs, and olive oil. Greek menu. Lunch, dinner. Closed Jan 1, Dec 25. Bar. Casual attire. **$$$$**

★ ★ ★ FIREBIRD (MAP E)
365 W 46th St (10036)
Phone 212/586-0244
Fax 212/957-2983
www.firebirdrestaurant.com

Firebird is an ode to the glamour and gluttony of St. Petersburg, sometime around its heyday in 1912. Set in a lavish, double town-house, this restaurant and cabaret is furnished like a majestic Russian palace, with ornate antique furniture, intricate china and etched glass, old-world oil paintings, and 19th-century photographs. The extravagance extends to the food, with Russian classics like blinis with sour cream and caviar, zakuska (the Russian equivalent of tapas), borscht made with pork and dill, and sturgeon baked in puff pastry. Vodka flows like water in a fast-running stream, and the wine list is deep as well. Russian menu. Dinner. Closed Mon; holidays. Bar. Outdoor seating. **$$$$**

🅟

★ ★ ★ GALLAGHER'S (MAP E)
228 W 52nd St (10019)
Phone 212/245-5336
Fax 212/245-5426
www.gallaghersnysteakhouse.com

The theater district has some great longtime restaurant hotspots to choose from, and Gallagher's is one of its brightest stars. This steakhouse is a New York City landmark and former speakeasy, and remains decorated as it was the day it opened in November 1927, with plain-planked floors, red-checked tablecloths, and dark wood-paneled walls covered in old photos. Specializing in dry-aged beef, the kitchen stays true to simple American fare rather than straying off course for global flourishes that have no place in such a comfort-able, back-to-basics establishment. The tried-and-true formula is winning; after all these years, Gallagher's is a perennial favorite on Theater Row. American, steak menu. Dinner. Bar. Casual attire. **$$$**

🅟

★★ GASCOGNE (MAP E)

158 Eighth Ave (10011)
Phone 212/675-6564
Fax 212/627-3018
www.gascognenyc.com

At this charming neighborhood restaurant, the robust regional cuisine of Gascogne fills the air. Paying tribute to the southwest of France, the kitchen offers heavenly plates of fill-in-the-blank confit, Armagnac-soaked prunes and foie gras terrine, cassoulet, and monkfish casserole, and a lovely list of wines to match. This is a spot for romance, as the dining room is intimate and candlelit, and the garden out back makes you feel like you are miles from the city. French menu. Lunch, dinner. Closed holidays. Bar. Casual attire. Outdoor seating. **$$**

★ HARLEY-DAVIDSON CAFÉ 70 (MAP E)

1370 Ave of the Americas (10019)
Phone 212/245-6000
Fax 212/245-5417
www.harley-davidsoncafe.com

This bustling two-level eatery in Midtown is a true slice of Americana: favorites like burgers, home-style meatloaf, and chicken pot pie are whipped up in the kitchen; a massive American flag covers the ceiling; and bright, shiny Harley-Davidson motorcycles—along with motorcycle jackets and other Harley memorabilia—are displayed throughout. While visiting, don't miss your chance to climb on one of the Hogs for a photo op! American menu. Lunch, dinner. Children's menu. Outdoor seating. **$$**

★★★ JUDSON GRILL (MAP E)

152 W 52nd St (10019)
Phone 212/582-5252
Fax 212/265-9616

Judson Grill, located in the heart of Midtown, has a lively bar crowd, but the large, high-ceilinged dining room, filled with widely spaced tables and deep, plush banquettes and decorated with tall, seasonal branch and floral arrangements, remains a serene and civilized place to dine. Chef Bill Telepan honors the seasons and regional farmers' produce with pride, weaving these pristine ingredients together on the plate with creative New American style. While the menu changes often to reflect the best of the markets, you'll always find a great selection of fish, poultry, beef, and vegetarian options, as well as a terrific domestic farmstead cheese plate. A wonderful wine list pulls it all together. American menu. Lunch, dinner. Closed Sun; holidays. Bar. Casual attire. **$$$**

★ LA BONNE SOUPE 72 (MAP E)

48 W 55th St (10019)
Phone 212/586-7650
Fax 212/765-6409
www.labonnesoupe.com

La Bonne Soupe is one of those restaurants that fits like an old shoe, in the best sense of the word. Comfortable and easy, the room feels like a Parisian bistro with checked tablecloths, long banquettes, and lovely French waitresses. The menu keeps the illusion of Paris alive with dishes like fluffy quiche, an excellent bouillabaisse, and of course, a delicious French onion soup capped with a thick and gooey blanket of melting Gruyère cheese. For a pre-theater meal, keep this gem in mind. French menu. Lunch, dinner, Sun brunch. Closed holidays. Bar. Children's menu. Casual attire. Outdoor seating. **$**

angelika film center.

18 W Houston St (10012). Phone 212/995-2000. www.angelika filmcenter.com. Get a taste of genuine SoHo living at this cultural institution that has attracted lovers of artsy movies for years. But the Angelika is even more than that. It is a special place—a world away from today's overcrowded, noisy multiplexes teeming with soccer moms and screaming kids. You'll find a generally urbane crowd at the independent films shown at the theater. And the **Angelika Café** in the lobby area is a great little place to grab a latté and a scone before the flick or a soda and a sandwich after the movie. On Sunday mornings, you'll find locals relaxing in the café, enjoying their coffee and *The New York Times.* Hang out here for a while and you'll feel more like a real New Yorker than a tourist.

ninth avenue international food festival

This late-May event epitomizes all the gastronomical diversity that is New York City. Taking place during the third weekend in May in the ethnically mixed Hell's Kitchen neighborhood, the two-day festival is a 20-block extravaganza of food booths and entertainment. From burritos to jerk chicken to curried chicken, you can find any kind of food imaginable in this ultimate of block parties. More than 1 million visitors have showed up in the past to this annual festival that's been going strong for 28 years, so prepare for crowds. Wear comfortable shoes and loose-fitting clothes so that you can pig out in total comfort. *Ninth Ave, between 37th and 57th sts (10018). Take the A/C/E subway to 34th St and 8th Ave. Phone 212/581-7029. www.9th-ave.com.*

★ ★ ★ ★ LE BERNARDIN (MAP E)
155 W 51st St (10019)
Phone 212/554-1515
Fax 212/554-1100
www.le-bernardin.com

If you crave the fruits of the sea, if you dream of lush, shimmering plates of pristine, perfectly prepared seafood, if you are a fan of soft, sinking seats, if your idea of paradise is a long, luxurious meal, you will be very happy at Le Bernardin. The restaurant, born in Paris in 1972, has been impressing foodies and novices alike since it moved across the ocean to Manhattan in 1986. After you experience the food and service, it's easy to see why. Le Bernardin is elegant everything—elegant service, elegant food, elegant crowd. It's all very civilized and sophisticated, and it's not the type of place to go for a quick bite. This is real dining at its finest. The sauces are light, aromatic, and perfectly balanced. The ingredients are seasonal and stunning. The presentations are museum-worthy in their perfection. All these elements combined with flawless service make dinner at Le Bernardin an experience that will stay with you for days, even months. The food is thoughtful and innovative, yet simple and approachable. It is the sort of menu that makes you want to try new things. But those craving beef need not enter. Seafood is the star at this distinguished, elegant New York restaurant, and the menu reflects the kitchen's passion for this food. Mind-altering fish first courses are divided between "Simply Raw" and "Lightly Cooked." Equally stellar entrées are completely from the sea, with a reluctant addition of meat at the end, in a section entitled "Upon Request." This is not the strength of

the talented kitchen. Enjoy all courses of that which once swam when
you're at Le Bernardin, and you won't regret it. *Secret Inspector's Notes:
The décor at Le Bernardin is as spectacular as the food. Be sure to take
a peek into the kitchen on your way to the rest room to see a talented
machine in action. Over the years, this grown-up destination continues
to be ideal for serious dining moments.* French, seafood menu. Lunch,
dinner. Closed Sun; holidays. Bar. Jacket required. **$$$$**

★★LOLA ⬤135 (MAP E)
30 W 22nd St (10010)
Phone 212/675-6700
Fax 212/675-6760
www.lolany.com
If enjoying the sounds of gospel music and the smells of fresh
biscuits and fluffy omelettes seems like a nice way to spend a Sunday
afternoon at brunch, then Lola is the place for you. This lively, chic
downtown restaurant has been serving sophisticated soul food in
easy, low-country style for years. While brunch remains a destination for hearty dishes like Carolina breakfast shrimp with creamy
cheddar grits, dinner offers exciting takes on Southern soul food as
well. Southern/Soul menu. Dinner, late-night, brunch. Closed Mon;
holidays. Bar. Casual attire. Outdoor seating. **$$**

★★MESA GRILL ⬤201 (MAP E)
102 Fifth Ave (10011)
Phone 212/807-7400
Fax 212/989-0034
www.mesagrill.com
In the ten years since the Southwestern haven known as Mesa Grill
opened its tall blond-wood doors and chef/owner Bobby Flay reached

union square greenmarket

This bustling year-round farmers' market, held on Monday,
Wednesday, Friday, and Saturday, is located at Union Square
between 14th and 17th streets and Broadway and Park
Avenue. It's a chance to experience a bit of the country in
the Big Apple, as farmers and other vendors sell fresh fruits,
vegetables, cheeses, homemade pies, herbs, cut flowers, and
potted plants. Plan to arrive early for the best selection. *14th
St and Broadway (10001). The 4, 5, 6, N, and R subways stop at
Union Square. Phone 212/477-3220. www.cenyc.org.*

stardom on cable TV's Food Network, he has, impressively, managed to keep his creative eye on this, his first restaurant. The vaulted, lively room remains a popular spot for margarita-soaked happy hours, as well as a top choice for superb Southwestern-inspired American fare. The vibrant menu changes with the seasons, but famous plates include the cotija-crusted quesadilla stuffed with goat cheese, basil, and red chiles, topped with a charred corn salsa; and the 16-spiced chicken with mango garlic sauce and cilantro-pesto mashed potatoes. Flay's food is not shy, so keep a cold margarita handy to soothe the heat. Southwestern menu. Lunch, dinner. Closed Dec 25. Bar. Casual attire. **$$$**

★ MICKEY MANTLE'S (MAP E)
42 Central Park S (10019)
Phone 212/688-7777
Fax 212/751-5797
www.mickeymantles.com
Located on Central Park South, Mickey Mantle's is an easy and smart choice when you want to catch a game and have a good meal minus the roar of a crowded sports bar. This elegant dining room is a good option if you're wandering around Central Park and get hungry for straightforward, tasty American fare. Burgers, steaks, seafood, and pastas are on the menu, and in season, the Yankees are always on TV here. As you'd expect, you'll also find a nice collection of baseball memorabilia and sports-themed art on the walls. American menu. Lunch, dinner. Bar. Children's menu. Outdoor seating. **$$**

★ ★ ★ MIX NEW YORK (MAP E)
68 W 58th St (10019)
Phone 212/583-0300
www.mixny.com
After startling New Yorkers with sky-high prices at his flagship restaurant, Alain Ducasse (see), Mix in New York is Ducasse's latest attempt at wooing the city's finicky dining public, and by all indications, it's working. A sleek, high-styled, modern space, Mix offers French and American comfort food created from stunning ingredients and presented with whimsical style. Macaroni and cheese takes on a glamorous cast, plated on fine china and topped with artisanal cheese, while more elegant takes on duck confit, tuna niçoise, and roast chicken grand mere make your head swirl with delight. All meals start with homemade peanut butter and jelly for your table's bread, and end with Madelines straight from the oven served with Nutella—the perfect way to end a meal. American, French menu. Lunch, dinner. Bar. Business casual attire. Reservations recommended. **$$$**

★ ★ ★ MOLYVOS (MAP E)

871 Seventh Ave (10019)
Phone 212/582-7500
www.molyvos.com

Located just steps from Carnegie Hall and City Center, Molyvos is a
great choice for before or after a dance or concert, with a wonderful
menu of modern Greek specialties like assorted mezze served with
warm, puffy pita; grilled whole fish; stunning takes on lamb; and an
impressive international wine list. The restaurant feels like it fell from
the shores of the Mediterranean, with blue and white tiles and sturdy
wooden tables. The lively bar and front room is ideal if you're in the
mood for a light bite and a glass of wine before a show, while the
more refined dining room offers leisurely diners a place to unwind
without rushing. Greek menu. Lunch, dinner. Bar. Casual attire.
Reservations recommended. **$$$**

★ ★ OSTERIA AL DOGE (MAP E)

142 W 44th St (10036)
Phone 212/944-3643
Fax 212/944-5754
www.osteria-doge.com

Osteria al Doge is a warm restaurant that feels like a seaside town
near Venice. The room is decorated warmly with blue, green, and
yellow and has a balcony overlooking the main dining area. The
kitchen is not breaking culinary ground, but it doesn't really need to.
This restaurant is a solid standby for Venetian-inspired seafood dishes
like whole branzino with cherry tomatoes, olives, and potatoes; a
bouillabaisse-style seafood stew; and house-made trenette pasta with
crabmeat. Those craving more substantial meals can dig into veal,
poultry, and beef. A good choice for pre-theater dining. Italian menu.
Dinner. Closed Jan 1, Dec 25. Bar. **$$**

★ ★ OSTERIO DEL CIRCO (MAP E)

120 W 55th St (10019)
Phone 212/265-3636
Fax 212/265-9283
www.osteriodelcirco.com

Owned by Sirio Maccioni of Le Cirque 2000 (see), Osterio del Circo carries on his signature brand of homespun hospitality in a more casual,
yet no less spirited, atmosphere. The rustic menu of Italian fare includes
delicious homemade pastas made from Maccioni Mama Egi's lick-your-
plate-clean recipes, as well as thin Tuscan-style pizzas, classic antipasti,
and signature main courses like salt-baked Mediterranean seabass and

brick-pressed chicken. Because it's located near Carnegie Hall and City Center, it's a great place to stop by before or after the theater. Italian menu. Lunch, dinner. Closed holidays. Bar. Casual attire. **$$$**

★ ★ ★ PERIYALI   **81** (MAP E)

35 W 20th St (10011)
Phone 212/463-7890
Fax 212/924-9403
www.periyali.com

Offering authentic Greek fare in a soothing Mediterranean-accented setting, Periyali is a wonderful place to experience the delicious seaside cuisine of Athens and beyond. Classics on the menu include octopus marinated in red wine, sautéed sweetbreads with white beans, grilled whole fish, and mezze like taramosalata (caviar mousse), melitzanosalata (grilled-eggplant mousse), and spanakopita (spinach and cheese pie). Periyali has been around for a while, but the restaurant's popularity has not waned. You'll find it full of regulars most days at lunch, although at night the pace is calmer, making it a great choice for a leisurely dinner. Greek menu. Lunch, dinner. Closed Sun. Casual attire. **$$$**

★ ★ ★ PETROSSIAN   **82** (MAP E)

182 W 58th St (10019)
Phone 212/245-2214
Fax 212/245-2812

Caviar, caviar, and caviar are the first three reasons to head to Petrossian, an elegant restaurant in Midtown featuring, you guessed it, caviar, served on perfect blinis and crème fraiche. In addition to the great salty roe, you'll find an ultra-luxurious brand of Franco-Russian cuisine that includes classics like borscht, assorted Russian zazuska (tapas) like smoked salmon (served with cold shots of vodka—ask for Zyr, one of the best from Russia), and other glamorous plates, including foie gras prepared several different ways and, of course, beef Stroganoff. But don't miss the caviar. Russian menu. Dinner, brunch. Bar. Casual attire. **$$$$**

★ ★ THE RED CAT   **211** (MAP E)

227 Tenth Ave (10011)
Phone 212/242-1122
www.theredcat.com

Jimmy Bradley, chef/owner of The Red Cat, is one of those restaurateurs who knows exactly what New Yorkers are looking for in

a dining experience: a cool, hip scene? Check. An innovative and exciting menu? Check. A solid international wine list with lots by the glass and a tempting selection of sexy house cocktails? Check, check. Indeed, Bradley delivers it all at his West Chelsea haunt for inspired Mediterranean-accented fare set in a New England-chic space trimmed with white-and-red wainscoting, hurricane lamps, and deep, long banquettes. This is one place you will want to return to, even if it's just to figure out how to replicate his formula in your own town. American menu. Dinner. Closed Jan 1, Dec 24-25. Bar. Casual attire. **$$$**
🗓

★ ★ REDEYE GRILL 83 (MAP E)
890 Seventh Ave (10019)
Phone 212/541-9000
Fax 212/245-6840
www.redeyegrillgroup.com
You can't miss the bright red entrance to Redeye Grill, which sits just 50 feet from Carnegie Hall. Its name comes from the dreaded over-night flight linking the West and East coasts, and that link is exactly what inspires its seafood-heavy menu and its design. The soaring dining room features Mission-style furnishings and is anchored by a shrimp, sushi, and smoked fish bar, flanked by giant bronze shrimp sculptures. Nightly jazz on the balcony keeps diners' toes tapping. American, seafood menu. Lunch, dinner, brunch, late-night. Bar. Casual attire. Outdoor seating. **$$$**
🗓

★ ★ REMI 84 (MAP E)
145 W 53rd St (10019)
Phone 212/581-4242
Fax 212/581-7182
The cuisine of Venice is the focus of the menu at Remi, an airy, lofty restaurant decorated with ornate Venetian blown-glass lights and murals of the Italian city's romantic canals. Remi has long been a favorite for local businesspeople to dish over lunch, but also makes a terrific choice for drinks, dinner, or a visit before or after a theater show. The kitchen's specialty is brilliant handmade pastas, but the menu also features contemporary Mediterranean takes on fish, beef, poultry, and game. A ciccetti menu of Venetian tapas is also avail-able at the bar for nibbling while working through the restaurant's impressive Italian wine list. Italian menu. Lunch, dinner. Closed holi-days. Casual attire. Reservations recommended. Outdoor seating. **$$**

★ ★ RENÉ PUJOL (MAP E)
321 W 51st St (10019)
Phone 212/246-3023
Fax 212/245-5206
www.renepujol.com
René Pujol is a theater district charmer, offering Gallic cuisine updated with a modern sensibility. The restaurant is warm and convivial, with butter-colored walls, a brick hearth, and snug, cozy tables. The menu offers refined takes on French dishes that are hearty and savory, like the lamb shanks with white beans, a house specialty. French menu. Lunch, dinner. Closed Mon; holidays. Jacket required. **$$$**
Ⓓ

★ ★ ROCK CENTER CAFÉ ⁸⁶ (MAP E)
20 W 50th St (10020)
Phone 212/332-7620
Fax 212/332-7677
www.restaurantassociates.com
Located in Rockefeller Center, this American restaurant is an ideal place to relax under blue summer skies with cool cocktails, or to grab a seat and watch the ice skaters slip, slide, and crash all winter long under the twinkling Christmas tree. The Rock Center Café is one of those places that never fails to satisfy with a broad menu of terrific salads, sandwiches, burgers, and generously sized seasonal American entrées. American menu. Breakfast, lunch, dinner, brunch. Outdoor seating. **$$**

★ ★ ★ SAN DOMENICO ⁸⁷ (MAP E)
240 Central Park S (10019)
Phone 212/265-5959
Fax 212/397-0844
www.sandomenicony.com
Tony May's San Domenico is like an Armani suit—classic, elegant, and perfect for every occasion. Located on Central Park South with views of the horse-drawn carriages lined up along the edge of Central Park just outside, San Domenico is one of city's most well regarded restaurants for sophisticated, contemporary Italian cuisine. Pasta, fish, and meat dishes manage to feel rustic yet updated, as the chef teams new-world ingredients and twists with authentic old-world recipes and style. An impressive wine list from the motherland of Italy enriches every bite. Italian menu. Dinner. Closed Jan 1, Thanksgiving, Dec 25. Bar. Casual attire. **$$$$**
Ⓓ

★★ SARDI'S (MAP E)

234 W 44th St (10036)
Phone 212/221-8440
Fax 212/302-0865
www.sardis.com

This icon in the theater district, established in 1921, is one of those old-time favorites that seems to stay the same year after year. For some places, though, no change is a good thing. Sardi's still serves as a cafeteria of sorts for many theater celebrities, and still offers hearty Italian signatures like stuffed cannelloni (veal, beef, or sausage), serviceable antipasti (this is not the restaurant's strong suit), and solid simple dishes like rotisserie roasted chicken and grilled filet mignon. Yes, the brilliant baked Alaska is still on the menu, and it's still a monster—a tasty one at that. Italian menu. Lunch, dinner, late-night. Closed Mon. Bar. Casual attire. **$$$**

★★ THE SEA GRILL (MAP E)

19 W 49th St (10020)
Phone 212/332-7610
Fax 212/332-7677
www.restaurantassociates.com/theseagrill

The Sea Grill is home to some of the most delicious seafood in the city. This lavish, ocean-blue restaurant dressed up in aquamarine and off-white tones sports a slick bar and prime wintertime views of ice skaters twirling (and crashing) on the rink under the twinkling Christmas tree at Rockefeller Plaza. Summertime brings alfresco dining and lots of icy cool cocktails to pair up with veteran chef Ed Brown's fantastic contemporary seafood menu. Crab cakes are his signature, and they deserve to be ordered at least once. Other dishes—salmon, cod, halibut, skate, you name it—are just as special, as Brown infuses his cooking with techniques and flavors from Asia and the world at large. Seafood menu. Lunch, dinner. Closed Sun; holidays. Bar. Casual attire. Outdoor seating. **$$$**

★★ SHAAN (90) (MAP E)

57 W 48th St (10020)
Phone 212/977-8400
Fax 212/977-3069

Shaan offers traditional northern Indian cuisine of the distinctly delicious variety. The restaurant is located just a stone's throw from Rockefeller Center, so it makes a great pit stop during holiday shopping and skating. Shaan offers dishes from the clay tandoor oven, as well as savory vegetarian, lamb, chicken, and fish dishes served with steaming bowls of fragrant rice. A heavenly selection of

breads, like naan, poori, and roti, makes mopping up the wonderfully aromatic sauces easy work. On Friday and Saturday nights, the
restaurant usually hosts classical Indian musicians for a transporting
evening. Indian menu. Dinner. Closed holidays. Bar. Casual attire.
$$$

★ **SIAM GRILL**　**91**　(MAP E)
586 E Ninth Ave (10036)
Phone 212/307-1363
At this warm and cozy Thai grill in the theater district, you'll find that
it's easy to kick back and relax for dinner. The service is pleasant and
prompt, and the menu is filled with tasty traditional Thai dishes like
pad Thai and Bammee curry, as well as house specialties like crispy
duck in red curry and steamed fish in ginger and bean threads. The
prices seem a bit high for the fare, but considering Siam Grill's location,
they aren't out of line. Thai menu. Lunch, dinner. Closed holidays. **$$**
🄳

★ **STAGE DELI**　**92**　(MAP E)
834 Seventh Ave (10019)
Phone 212/245-7850
Fax 212/245-7957
www.stagedeli.com
Stage Deli is one of New York's most favored between-the-bread
restaurants, offering lovely sandwiches crafted from rye bread,
pastrami, tongue, brisket, mustard, mayo, and half-sour pickles, as

chelsea piers sports and entertainment complex

For the best in recreational activities all in one location, keep
heading west until you hit Chelsea Piers. The 1.7-million-square-
foot complex features an ice skating rink, a bowling alley, climbing
walls, a driving range, basketball, in-line skating, and more. There
also are pubs and restaurants to grab a meal after doing all these
activities. Stop in for a cold one at the **Chelsea Brewing Co.**, the
state's largest microbrewery. Make a point to visit the complex at
sundown, to view the beautiful sunset off the river. Both kids and
adults can spend a nice few hours at this mega sports center. *24th
St and West Side Hwy (10011). Piers 59-62 on the Hudson River from
17th to 23rd sts. The entrance is at 23rd St. Take the C/E subway to
23rd St. Phone 212/336-6666. www.chelseapiers.com.*

well as comforting standards like chicken noodle soup. This is a hectic and bustling deli, with a ton of energy that exemplifies life in the Big Apple. Kosher deli menu. Breakfast, lunch, dinner, late-night. Children's menu. Casual attire. **$$**

★ ★ SUEÑOS   218 (MAP E)
311 W 17th St (10011)
Phone 212/243-1333
Walk by Sueños and you will most likely spy a crowd of people gathered on the sidewalk, looking through a large rectangular window, drooling. The porthole gives sidewalk voyeurs a bird's eye view of the kitchen, where Mexican-cuisine diva (chef/owner) Sue Torres executes orders of her addictive modern regional Mexican cuisine. There are fat, steamy empanadas filled with fava beans and drunken goat cheese, heavenly pork tamales steamed in banana leaves and plated in a fiery lather of ancho beurre blanc, and tortilla-crusted Chilean sea bass with a chile rajas tamale. The restaurant is lively and hip, decorated in bright colors and filled with the sweet smell of fresh corn tortillas, which are made by hand in the main dining room. The margaritas are a must. Mexican menu. Dinner. Closed Sun-Mon. Bar. Casual attire. Reservations recommended. **$$$**

★ ★ ★ ★ SUGIYAMA   93 (MAP E)
251 W 55th St (10019)
Phone 212/956-0670
Fax 212/956-0671
If you're searching for an oasis of calm in the center of Midtown Manhattan, head to Sugiyama and your blood pressure will drop upon entry. The dining room is warm and tranquil and has a Zen air to it. The spare, warm room fills up quickly at lunch with strikingly well-appointed businesspeople on expense accounts. But even filled to capacity, it maintains a soothing energy. Sugiyama's specialties are prix fixe kaiseki-style meals. Those who are not well suited to culinary adventures should search for calm somewhere else. It's not worth the visit to order only sushi. Kaiseki are multicourse meals that were originally part of elaborate, traditional Japanese tea ceremonies, but at Sugiyama they have evolved into a procession of precious little plates, holding petite portions that are as tasty as they are appealing to the eye. Lead by head chef and owner Nao Sugiyama, the chefs here have a talent for presentation—every dish is a work of art. Meals are tailored to suit your appetite and preferences and start with sakizuke (an amuse bouche) followed by a seasonal special (zensai), soup, sashimi, sushi, salad, and beef or seafood cooked over a hot stone (ishiyaki), among other sumptuous Japanese delicacies. Soups

are Nao's specialty, and warm broths have never been so dynamic and exciting. Dining at Sugiyama is an unexpected adventure. The chef's enthusiasm and energy are contagious, and you can't help departing with a giant grin knowing that you've just had an experience like no other. *Secret Inspector's Notes: Enjoying kaiseki at Sugiyama is undoubtedly one of the most fun and educational dining experiences to be had.* Japanese menu. Lunch, dinner. Closed Sun-Mon. **$$$$**

★★★ TOWN (MAP E)
15 W 56th St (10019)
Phone 212/582-4445
www.chambershotel.com
Located in the swanky Chambers Hotel, Town is an oasis of hipness, featuring a white-hot, low-lit lounge and bar with some of the most inventive and well-made cocktails in the city. Move downstairs to the sexy, oversized-banquetted, David Rockwell-designed dining room, and you'll find it filled edge to edge with high-powered media and fashion folks digging into chef/owner Geoffrey Zakarian's brilliant high-styled, modern American fare. American menu. Lunch, dinner. Bar. Casual attire. Reservations recommended. **$$$**

★★★ TRATTORIA DELL'ARTE (MAP E)
900 Seventh Ave (10019)
Phone 212/245-9800
Fax 212/265-3296
www.trattoriadellarte.com
Trattoria dell'Arte is the perfect choice if Carnegie Hall or a performance at City Center is on your list. Owned by Shelly Fireman, this lively and popular restaurant offers easy, approachable Italian cuisine in a comfortable, neighborly setting. The scene here is festive, so expect it to be loud with diners who are clearly enjoying the generous plates of homemade pastas, selections from the spectacular antipasti bar, seafood, and meats, all prepared in simple Mediterranean style. Italian menu. Lunch, dinner, brunch. Closed Thanksgiving, Dec 25. Bar. Casual attire. **$$$**

★★ TUSCAN SQUARE (MAP E)
16 W 51st St (10020)
Phone 212/977-7777
Fax 212/977-3144
www.tuscansquare.com
Restaurateur Pino Luongo is a native Italian whose airy, comfortable Tuscan Square restaurant brings his idyllic homeland to life, warding

off all cases of homesickness here in the big, boisterous city. Located in Rockefeller Center, Tuscan Square is a great place to relax and unwind at lunch or dinner. It offers a taste of the Italian countryside with a sunny, frescoed dining room and impressive antipasti and homemade pastas, as well as more robust regional specialties that match up well with the deep selection of Chianti, Barbaresco, Barolo, Montepulciano, Orvieto, and Pinot Grigio. Italian menu. Lunch, dinner. Closed Sun; holidays. Casual attire. **$$$**

★★ VICTOR'S 97 (MAP E)
236 W 52nd St (10019)
Phone 212/586-7714
Long before the mojito became as popular as the cosmopolitan, these minty rum drinks from Cuba were the cocktail of choice at Victor's, a popular theater district restaurant that feels like an elegant throwback to Havana, decorated with tall palm trees and filled with the rhythmic sounds of Cuban jazz. Aside from the terrific cocktails, Victor's is a festive place to feast on top-notch contemporary Cuban cuisine, like roasted marinated pork with rice and beans, picadillo, fried plantains, and tostones. Cuban menu. Lunch, dinner. Bar. Casual attire. **$$**

★ VIRGIL'S REAL BARBECUE   (MAP E)
152 W 44th St (10036)
Phone 212/921-9494
Fax 212/921-9631
www.virgilsbbq.com
While everyone has an opinion about barbecue, most will agree that Virgil's is a super choice. Manners are thrown to the wind at Virgil's, a sprawling hog pit where ribs, juicy chicken, tomato-based pulled pork, Memphis pit beans, and spicy collard greens are gobbled up in record time. The noise can be deafening, but there really isn't time to talk once the food arrives. The warm, fluffy buttermilk biscuits usually quiet everyone down rather quickly. Barbecue menu. Lunch, dinner, late-night. Closed Dec 25. Bar. Children's menu. Casual attire. **$$**

Restaurants in Midtown East, Murray Hill, and Gramercy Park

★ ★ ★ AL BUSTAN (99) (MAP F)
827 Third Ave (10022)
Phone 212/759-5933

If you've ever wondered what Lebanese cuisine is like, head to Al Bustan and discover a world of aromatic and exquisite food. Many have already made the discovery, which means that Al Bustan is very popular, especially at lunch, as its Midtown location makes it a nice choice for dealmakers. But when the sun sets, Al Bustan becomes an elegant respite for dinner, offering guests a luxurious upscale Lebanese dining experience that includes some of the best bread in the city, served with a magnificent array of mezze, not to mention a full menu of authentic Lebanese dishes. Middle Eastern menu. Lunch, dinner. Casual attire. Reservations recommended. **$$$**

★ ★ AMMA (100) (MAP F)
246 E 51st St (10022)
Phone 212/644-8330

At Amma, an elegant, petite Midtown spot serving excellent Indian fare, you'll find tables jammed with eager curry lovers kvelling over dishes of Goan shrimp, piles of toothsome bhel puri, and plates of frizzled okra with tomatoes and onions. This is not your ordinary curry house though. Amma is stylish and serene, and the service is efficient and fine. The chef, formerly of Tamarind (see), knows his way around the tandor oven, and you should by all means order several tandoori dishes like stuffed chicken breasts, crisp and spiced shrimp, or the succulent yogurt-infused lamb chops. Save room for dessert; the rasmalai dumplings are a showstopper. Indian menu. Lunch, dinner. Children's menu. Casual attire. **$$**
🄳

★ ★ ARTISINAL (101) (MAP E)
2 Park Ave (10016)
Phone 212/725-8585

Say cheese! Artisinal is chef/owner Terrance Brennan's ode to the stuff, and it is a glorious tribute at that. (Brennan is also chef/owner of Picholine—see also.) In addition to one of the best cheese selections this side of the Atlantic, you'll find lovely brasserie standards like moules frites, gougères (warm, cheese-filled brioche puffs that melt in your mouth and are impossible to stop eating), frisée au lardons, and of course, cheese fondue—the house specialty. If you are more inclined to eat a meal at the bar, Artisinal's is a terrific spot to hunker down and sample some of the best cheeses from the United States and around the world, not to mention wines, all 120 of which are available by the glass. Located in the east 30s, this is also just about the best place to eat before or after a Madison Square Garden event. French menu. Lunch, dinner. Bar. Casual attire. **$$**

★★ AVRA (102) (MAP F)
141 E 48th St (10017)
Phone 212/759-8550

At this terrific, airy, and elegant estiatorio, you can eat like they do on the Greek islands, feasting on fresh fish (priced by the pound) simply grilled with lemon, herbs, and olive oil; salads of fresh briny feta and tomato; and loaves of fluffy, warm pita to dip into assorted garlicky mezze like hummus and tzatziki. Save room for dessert, as the sticky-sweet honey-soaked baklava is not to be missed. Greek menu. Lunch, dinner. Bar. Casual attire. Reservations recommended. Outdoor seating. **$$$**

★ BAR JAMON (103) (MAP F)
125 E 17th St (10003)
Phone 212/253-2773

Mario Batali is turning Spanish on us. After mastering the art of simple Italian fare at Babbo, Lupa, Otto (see all three), and Esca, he is taking on the Iberian Peninsula with Bar Jamon. Yes folks, a ham and wine bar set adjacent to Casa Mono (see), where he serves up a menu of Catalan small plates in a convivial setting straight out of Barcelona. A miniature spot with dark wood accents and a marble bar, this crowded watering hole features all sorts of Spanish jamon (pronounced haah-mon), cheeses (manchego, queso de tetilla, valdeon, calabres), and olives. More exciting plates include smoked trout salad with olives and cava-soaked grapes and classics like torti-lla d'Espana—all perfectly suited to Spanish wine and sherry. Spanish, tapas menu. Lunch, dinner, late-night. Casual attire. **$$**

★★ BEPPE (104) (MAP E)
45 E 22nd St (10010)
Phone 212/982-8422

Walk into Chelsea's Beppe, and you may feel yourself leaving the city of New York and entering the lovely land of Italy. At this warm, weathered eatery filled with all the charm of an Italian farmhouse kitchen, you can sample some of chef/owner Cesare Cassella's earthy and divine pasta; a terrific selection of Tuscan-style wood-fired seafood, meat, and game; and a wine list that focuses on gems from Tuscany and Italy's lesser-known regions. Italian menu. Lunch, dinner. Closed Sun. Bar. Casual attire. **$$$**

★★ BLUE SMOKE (MAP F)
116 E 27th St (10016)
Phone 212/447-7733

With elegant restaurants like Union Square Cafe and Gramercy Tavern (see both) in his repertoire, Danny Meyer might come as a surprise as the man behind Blue Smoke, a sleek, casual barbecue joint packed nightly with a loud and boisterous crowd. But Meyer hails from St. Louis, and barbecue has been his longtime passion. This love of 'cue shines through in saucy, meaty ribs; pulled pork sandwiches; and fried catfish, paired with super sides like smoky bacon-laced pit beans, messy slaw, and, for dessert, a perfect banana cream pie. Barbecue menu. Lunch, dinner, late-night. Bar. Children's menu. Casual attire. **$$**

★★ BLUE WATER GRILL (MAP E)
31 Union Sq W (10003)
Phone 212/675-9500

Overlooking Union Square Park, Blue Water Grill is a buzzing shrine to seafood, with a raw bar and an extensive menu of fresh fish prepared with global accents and a terrific array of sushi, sashimi, and creative maki rolls. The dining room is massive and magnificent, with marble columns and floors, and sky-high ceilings. The crowds are always here because the food is tasty, inventive, and fun, which means the vibe is spirited and lively. Be warned that conversation may be difficult to conduct above the roar at peak times. Seafood menu. Lunch, dinner. Bar. Casual attire. Outdoor seating. **$$**

★★ BOLO 229 (MAP E)
23 E 22nd St (10010)
Phone 212/228-2200
Fax 212/228-2239
www.bolorestaurant.com

Chef, restaurateur, Food Network star, and author Bobby Flay is one busy celebrity chef. Lucky for us, fame hasn't gone to his head. The food at Bolo, the Spanish restaurant he opened a decade ago, keeps getting better. Since taking trips to Barcelona, Flay has reinvented the menu at Bolo, adding a delicious menu of tapas (and a nice list of sherries) to his lively, contemporary Spanish menu. While the food continues to excite, the room at Bolo could use a facelift and feels worn at the seams. Nevertheless, the bar is still alive with regulars, and the restaurant has a warm energy that makes it a wonderful place to dine. Spanish, tapas menu. Lunch, dinner. Closed Dec 25. Bar. Casual attire. **$$$**

★★ BRASSERIE 107 (MAP E)

100 E 53rd St (10022)
Phone 212/751-4840
Fax 212/751-8777
www.restaurantassociates.com

As you enter Brasserie, you may feel all eyes on you, which is probably because they are. The dining room is set down a level, and when you enter, you must walk down a futuristic glass staircase, a dramatic walkway that calls all eyes up. In case the folks at the backlit bar and seated along the long, luxurious banquettes are too busy feasting on the tasty brasserie fare (like duck cassoulet, frisée aux lardons, onion soup, escargots, or goujonettes of sole) to look up and catch your entrance, 15 video screens broadcast images of incoming diners; you'll be captured on film for repeat viewing later. It's best just to get over your stage fright and relax, because it's so easy to enjoy a meal here. French, American menu. Breakfast, lunch, dinner, Sun brunch. Bar. Casual attire. **$$$**

★★★ BULL AND BEAR STEAKHOUSE 108 (MAP E)

49th St and Lexington Ave (10022)
Phone 212/872-4900
Fax 212/486-5107
www.waldorfastoria.com

Located in the stately Waldorf Astoria Hotel, the Bull and Bear Steakhouse is a testosterone-heavy, meat-eater's haven. The street-level dining room is elegant in a clubby, macho sort of way, and the steaks, all cut from certified aged Black Angus, are fat, juicy, and the way to go, even though the menu does offer a wide variety of other choices, including chicken, lamb, pot pie, and assorted seafood. Classic steakhouse sides like creamed spinach, garlic mashed potatoes, and buttermilk fried onion rings are sinful and match up well with the rich beef on the plate. A terrific selection of red wine will complete your meaty meal nicely. American menu. Lunch, dinner. Bar. **$$$**

★★ CANDELA RESTAURANT ⑩⑨ (MAP F)

116 E 16th St (10003)
Phone 212/254-1600
Fax 212/614-8626
www.candelarestaurant.com

Located near Union Square Park, Candela is an ideal choice for a romantic dinner, a large gathering of friends, or a light bite and a drink at the long, inviting, low-lit bar. Candela, as the name suggests, is filled with ivory-pillared candles of varying sizes, giving the large dining room dressed in dark wood a sexy, amber glow. The space gets its medieval vibe from heavy hanging tapestries, beamed ceilings, and dark oak-planked floors. The menu is sort of like the Gap, offering something for everyone at reasonable prices. Expect a nice selection of Mediterranean, Italian, and Asian dishes like garlicky hummus, lobster and corn ravioli, and sushi dishes like a tempura-battered spicy tuna roll or black cod with a rich miso glaze. Eclectic/International menu. Lunch, dinner, Sun brunch. Bar. Casual attire. Reservations recommended. **$$**

★★ CASA MONO ②③① (MAP F)

52 Irving Pl (10003)
Phone 212/253-2773

With Casa Mono (which means "monkey house"), a snug little restaurant on the corner of 17th and Irving Place, Mario Batali has stepped off of familiar Italian earth and onto the culinary and fashion hotbed known as Barcelona. Grab a seat in this cozy restaurant and watch as the chefs in the open kitchen deliver a menu that excites and invigorates in its simplicity. Popular picks include the sepia a la plancha (grilled squid), quail with quince, and oxtail-stuffed piquillo peppers. This is the sort of place that makes you smile until your face hurts. Claim your sliver of real estate and be patient. You'll soon be rewarded. Spanish menu. Lunch, dinner. Casual attire. **$$$**

★ CHAT'N'CHEW ⑪⑪ (MAP E)

10 E 16th St (10003)
Phone 212/243-1616

Walk by Chat'n'Chew on a Saturday afternoon and you'll walk straight into a line of twentysomethings, married couples with strollers, and red-eyed partiers waiting to get inside to feast on one of the best and most reasonably priced brunch menus in the city. Filled with vintage décor and thrift store restaurant finds, this crowded Union Square diner is about quantity (portions are giant) and comfort food. There's roast turkey with gravy, mac 'n' cheese, and hearty breakfast fare like eggs, hash browns, French toast, and pancakes. It's not fancy, it's inexpensive, and it's all good. American menu. Lunch, dinner, brunch. Casual attire. Outdoor seating. **$**

🔳

★ ★ ★ CRAFT   ⑫ (MAP E)
43 E 19th St (10003)
Phone 212/780-0880

Chef/owner Tom Colicchio's Craft (Colicchio is also a partner and the executive chef at Gramercy Tavern—see also) is a restaurant for two types of people: inventive, adventurous sorts who like to build things and gourmets who appreciate perfectly executed portions of meat, fish, fowl, and vegetables. Why these two sorts of folks? Because at Craft, lovers of Legos delight in creating dinner from the listlike menu of meat, fish, vegetables, mushrooms, and condiments. You choose what two delicious morsels should come together on your plate. (Those who prefer to defer to the chef may opt for a preplanned menu.) Dinner at Craft is a unique, interactive, exciting, and delicious adventure that should be experienced at least once, with like-minded builders. American menu. Closed holidays. Lunch, dinner. Bar. Casual attire. **$$$$**

🔳

★ ★ CRAFTBAR   ⑬ (MAP E)
47 E 19th St (10003)
Phone 212/780-0880

After the runaway success of Craft (see), chef/owner Tom Colicchio's magnificent temple to the season's best ingredients, it was only a matter of time before he opened a smaller, more intimate and casual offshoot. Located right next door to its fancier sibling, craftbar is part wine bar, part Italian trattoria, and part American eatery, serving small plates like the signature fried, stuffed sage leaves and crisp fried oysters with preserved lemon, alongside beautiful salads, soups, crusty panini, game, fish, and the most extraordinary veal ricotta meatballs in the country, if not the world. The wine list is extensive, and a meal at the bar is a great way to go if you can't score a table. American, Italian menu. Lunch, dinner. Bar. Casual attire. Reservations recommended. **$$**

★ ★ DAWAN (MAP F)
210 E 58th St (10022)
Phone 212/355-7555
Fax 212/355-1735

Located on the eastern edge of Midtown, just a stone's throw from Bloomingdale's, Dawat is one of the city's first (and best) high-end Indian restaurants. Serving elegant haute cuisine in a posh, hushed townhouse setting, Dawat is one of the most popular destinations for seekers of upscale, authentic Indian cuisine, including curries, rice dishes, poori, naan, and chutneys. Indian menu. Lunch, dinner. Casual attire. Reservations recommended. **$$**

★ ★ DELEGATES DINING ROOM (MAP F)
UN General Assembly Bldg (10017)
Phone 212/963-7625
Fax 212/963-2025

The United Nations may not be the first place you think of in terms of dining options, but the Delegates Dining Room offers a rotating buffet of international cuisine, often prepared by chefs who are visiting America from their native lands. Expect exotic menus from far-off places like Thailand, Korea, and India, as well as more traditional spots like Italy, Greece, and France. The restaurant is an elegant place to dine, and with its floor-to-ceiling windows, it provides some of the city's most captivating, panoramic views of the East River. International menu. Lunch. Closed Sat-Sun; holidays. Jacket required. Reservations recommended. Photo identification is required. **$$**

★ ★ DIWAN   116 (MAP F)
148 E 48th St (10017)
Phone 212/593-5425

Indian cuisine may not seem glamorous, but it is at Diwan—one of the city's most acclaimed Indian restaurants, serving amazing, upscale dishes in a swanky, newly remodeled setting smack dab in the center of Midtown. The lunchtime hour finds Diwan packed with businesspeople leaning in over tables to seal deals, while dinner is more relaxed and intimate, with an extensive menu of Bombay-inspired dishes that will satisfy your strongest craving for great Indian cuisine. Indian menu. Lunch, dinner. Casual attire. **$$**

★★ DOS CAMINOS (MAP F)
373 Park Ave S (10016)
Phone 212/294-1000

Steve Hanson has built a New York City restaurant empire with Blue Water Grill (see), Ruby Foo's, and Fiamma (see). With Dos Caminos, he has introduced the regional cuisines of Mexico to his winning formula of hip scene, cool bar, and crowd-pleasing eats. Dos Caminos is loud and always crowded, so don't plan on intimate dining, but certainly plan on tasty food. The menu reflects the diverse regions of Mexico, including guacamole made tableside to your desired level of spiciness; warm homemade tacos filled with chile-rubbed shrimp, steak, or pulled pork; and snapper steamed in banana leaves. To wash it all down, margaritas are potent and tasty. Mexican menu. Lunch, dinner. Bar. Casual attire. **$$$**

★★★ ELEVEN MADISON PARK (MAP E)
11 Madison Ave (10010)
Phone 212/889-0905
Fax 212/889-0918
www.elevenmadisonpark.com

Located across from the leafy, historic Madison Square Park, Danny Meyer's grand New American restaurant is a wonderful, soothing spot to take respite from the frenetic pace of a day in New York City. The magnificent dining room boasts old-world charm with vaulted ceilings, clubby banquettes, giant floor-to-ceiling windows, and warm, golden lighting. The crowd is equally stunning: a savvy blend of sexy, suited Wall Street types and chic, fashion-forward New Yorkers. The contemporary seasonal menu features updated American classics as well as a smart selection of dishes that borrow accents from Spain, France, and Asia. Meyer, who also owns Gramercy Tavern and Union Square Cafe (see both), continues to offer his gracious brand of

lexington avenue

It may be only a three-block area just south of Murray Hill, but this neighborhood is brimming with the sights and sounds of India. Stores sell Indian and Pakistani spices, pastries, videos, cookware, saris, and fabrics. Restaurants cater to both Muslim and Hindu tastes, suiting both beefeaters and vegetarians. The low prices are a treat as well. To get there, take the 6 Lexington Avenue subway to 28th Street.

warmth and hospitality at Eleven Madison Park. You will feel at home in an instant. American menu. Lunch, dinner. Closed Jan 1, Labor Day, Dec 24-25. Bar. Casual attire. **$$$**

★ ★ ★ FELIDIA ⑱ (MAP F)

243 E 58th St (10022)
Phone 212/758-1479
Fax 212/935-7687
www.lidiasitaly.com

Celebrated chef and TV personality Lidia Bastianich is the unofficial matriarch of Italian-American cuisine. Her restaurant, Felidia (she and son Joe are partners in Becco (see), Babbo (see), and Esca as well), is warm and elegant and draws an elite New York crowd, although it remains free of pretense. The lovely dining room is bathed in golden, amber light and decorated with rich wood-paneled walls, hardwood floors, magnificent flowers, and seasonal vegetable and fruit displays. The menu focuses on a wide array of Italian dishes that you would discover if you journeyed throughout the country's varied culinary regions. Diners are expected to eat as they do in Italy, so you'll start with a plate of antipasti or a bowl of zuppe (soup), move on to a fragrant bowl of fresh pasta and then to a grilled whole fish, and finally have a bit of dolci for dessert. The Italian wine list is extra-special, so be sure to pair your meal with a few glasses. Italian menu. Menu changes daily. Closed Sun; holidays. Lunch, dinner. Bar. Jacket required. **$$$**

Ⓓ

★ ★ ★ FIFTY SEVEN FIFTY SEVEN ⑲ (MAP E)

57 E 57th St (10022)
Phone 212/758-5757
Fax 212/758-5711
www.fshr.com

A power spot to meet for (at least two) martinis, Fifty Seven Fifty Seven, at the über-civilized Four Seasons Hotel on the magnificent shopping mile of 57th Street, is indeed a hotspot for the city's movers and shakers. This is not to say that mere mortals can't sit down for dinner. Despite the moneyed crowd at the bar, the 22-foot coffered-ceiling dining room remains an oasis of calm, with glossy maple floors and bronzed chandeliers. The gifted crew in the kitchen dresses up classic American fare to suit a demanding urban sensibility. The restaurant also boasts an award-winning international wine list in addition to a fantastic selection of martinis and other perfectly shaken and stirred classic cocktails. American menu. Dinner, Sun brunch. Bar. Piano bar. Business casual attire. Valet parking. **$$$$**

★ ★ ★ FLEUR DE SEL (MAP E)
5 E 20th St (10003)
Phone 212/460-9100

Located on a sleepy block of East 20th Street, Fleur de Sel sneaks up on you like a ray of sunshine through the clouds. This lovely buttercup-colored cottage-like restaurant is one of the most enchanted hideaways in the city, serving sophisticated French-American fare in a serene dining room decorated with sheer curtains, soothing creamy walls, and precious bouquets of fresh flowers. It is, quite simply, a lovely setting to enjoy a dinner of stunningly presented, delicate, and deliciously prepared food. French menu. Dinner. Closed Sun. Bar. Casual attire. Reservations recommended. **$$$**

🄓

★ ★ ★ ★ THE FOUR SEASONS RESTAURANT (MAP E)
99 E 52nd St (10022)
Phone 212/754-9494
Fax 212/754-1077

The Four Seasons is truly a New York classic. Since 1959, it has been the de facto dining room of media powerhouses, financial movers and shakers, publishing hotshots, legal dealmakers, and the generally fabulous crowd that follows them. Lunch can be an exercise in connect-the-famous-faces, as is the bar, a must for a pre-dinner cocktail or a quick bite. As for what you'll eat when you take a break from gawking at the stars, the food at the Four Seasons is simple but well prepared and takes its cues from around the world. You'll find classically French entrées as well as more contemporary American fare accented with flavors borrowed from Asia, Morocco, and Latin America. Guests at the Four Seasons are often some of the highest rollers, and the room has an energetic buzz that epitomizes the life and breath of the city that never sleeps. It is a scene. Dining here is fun, especially at lunch, if only to be a fly on the wall as deals are made and fortunes are won and lost. *Secret Inspector's Notes: The pool in The Four Seasons has been the scene of many a scandalous moment when celebrity guests or ladies who lunch kick off their shoes and enjoy Champagne and misbehavior while splashing around. The food and service may disappoint, but the atmosphere and décor never will.* American menu. Breakfast, lunch, dinner. Closed holidays. Bar. Jacket required. Reservations recommended. **$$$$**

★ ★ ★ ★ GRAMERCY TAVERN (MAP E)

42 E 20th St (10003)
Phone 212/477-0777
Fax 212/477-1160
www.gramercytavern.com

Dining at Gramercy Tavern is for people who don't have trouble being very well taken care of. Owner Danny Meyer's perpetually bustling New York eatery oozes warmth and charm without a smidgen of pretension. Chef/co-owner Tom Colicchio delivers on the food in much the same way. While his menu is inventive, it is not overfussed. Pristine, seasonal, locally sourced ingredients shine, and every bite allows the flavors to converse quietly yet speak individually as well. Though formal and elegant in tone, Gramercy Tavern is a fun place to dine. Colicchio's food is so good that you can't help but have a great time, and the waitstaff's enthusiasm for the chef's talent shows, adding to the appeal. In the glorious main room, you can choose from a pair of seasonal tasting menus or a wide array of equally tempting à la carte selections. And if you don't have a reservation, don't fret. Meyer is a fan of democracy and accepts walk-ins in the front Tavern Room. Stroll in, put your name on the list, and you'll have the chance to sample Colicchio's spectacular food (the menu is different than in the main dining room but just as wonderful) and rub elbows with the city's sexy locals. There's a terrific house cocktail list as well, so make a nice toast while you're there. *Secret Inspector's Notes: Gramercy Tavern continues to achieve excellence in both service and food. No restaurant in New York has a staff that conveys such incredible warmth and food that expresses flavor so eloquently.* American menu. Lunch, dinner. Bar. Casual attire. **$$$$**

★ ★ ★ I TRULLI 123 (MAP F)

122 E 27th St (10016)
Phone 212/481-7372

i Trulli envelops you with warmth, whether in the winter with its hearth-style, wood-burning fireplace, or in the summer when the lovely outdoor courtyard garden opens up for dining under the stars. This is a true neighborhood place, with charming service that features the rustic Italian cuisine of the Apulia region. Favorites include ricotta-stuffed cannelloni, orchiette with veal ragu, and fantastically fat calzones made by hand and baked to a golden brown in the wood-burning oven. Italian menu. Lunch, dinner. Bar. Casual attire. Reservations recommended. Outdoor seating. **$$$**

★ ★ KITCHEN 22 (MAP E)

36 E 22nd St (10010)
Phone 212/228-4399

At this low-lit neighborhood bistro in the Flatiron neighborhood, you'll be treated to a three-course prix fixe menu of seasonal American fare for an unbelievably affordable price of $25 for dinner. This Charlie Palmer restaurant provides a winning formula for hip locals who crowd in for drinks and delicious meals in a dark, sexy setting. The crowded bar up front is a popular spot for regulars to gather and sip martinis in style. American menu. Dinner. Closed Sun. Bar. Casual attire. **$$**

★ ★ ★ ★ KURUMA ZUSHI 125 (MAP E)

7 E 47th St, 2nd floor (10017)
Phone 212/317-2802
Fax 212/317-2803

Kuruma Zushi is New York's most secreted sushi spot. Located on the second floor of a less-than-impressive Midtown building, with only a tiny sign to alert you to its presence, it is tough to find but well worth the search. Fresh, supple, mouthwatering fish is served with freshly grated wasabi and bright, fiery shavings of ginger. This sushi temple has quite a following, among them Ruth Reichl, the former *New York Times* restaurant critic and current editor of *Gourmet* magazine, who is vocal about her love of the restaurant's spectacular fish. You will be dreaming about this fish for weeks after your meal has ended. While many consider this the pinnacle of sushi, it does come with quite an insane price tag. Dinner per person can easily hit the $100 mark, which may be why the restaurant, an earth-colored, minimalist room, is most popular with business people on expense accounts and true devotees. Japanese menu. Lunch, dinner. Closed Sun. **$$$$**

★ ★ L'EXPRESS 126 (MAP E)

249 Park Ave (10003)
Phone 212/254-5858

Open 24 hours a day for omelettes, frisée au lardons, steak frites, and other traditional bistro fare, L'Express is a perfect choice for an off-hour snack, a late-night meal, or a quiet breakfast of eggs, coffee, and a newspaper. At prime lunch and dinner hours, this replica of a French brasserie can get a bit frenetic, but if you don't mind the hustle and bustle, you'll have yourself a nice Parisian-style meal. French bistro menu. Breakfast, lunch, dinner, late-night. Bar. Casual attire. **$$**

★ ★ ★ L'IMPERO (MAP F)
45 Tudor City Pl (10017)
Phone 212/599-5045

L'Impero arrived on the New York City dining scene in 2002, and with it, the landscape of elegant Italian cuisine was permanently changed. Chef/partner Scott Conant takes you to new heights with his interpretation of the Italian cucina. There are simple plates of pasta, like a gorgeous bowl of perfect handmade spaghetti garnished with fresh tomato and basil that will renew your love of a dish tossed aside long ago. His signature capretto (that would be goat) is moist-roasted until fork-tender and saturated with rich, delicious flavors. His takes on crudo (raw, brightly accented sashimi-style dishes of fish) are luminous. The service is flawless, the wine list is an Italian encyclopedia, and the décor is serene and civilized, warmed with chocolate and blue tones. L'Impero is a must-visit for a special occasion or for a well-deserved renewal of a love affair with Italian food. Italian menu. Lunch, dinner. Closed Sun. Bar. Casual attire. Outdoor seating. **$$$**

★ ★ ★ ★ LA GRENOUILLE (128) (MAP E)
3 E 52nd St (10022)
Phone 212/752-1495
Fax 212/593-4964
www.la-grenouille.com

Yes, frogs' legs are on the menu at La Grenouille, whose name literally means "The Frog." This stunning Midtown restaurant is the epitome of a classic. If you're craving some sort of fusion hotspot with a loud crowd and a lengthy cocktail list that contains the word Cosmopolitan, you won't be happy here. La Grenouille is elegant and conservative in style and substance. The room is quiet, lovely, and modest; the kitchen serves authentic, sophisticated French cuisine at its finest; and the staff offers service that is refined and seemingly effortless. Now back to those frogs' legs, which appropriately are the restaurant's signature. They are served sautéed, Provençal style, and are a must for adventurous diners who have never indulged in them. This is certainly the place to have your first experience with them, although it may spoil you for life. The wine list is mostly French, although some American wines have managed to make the cut as well. Indulging in a cheese course is a nice way to finish your meal, as it is in France. The restaurant is popular at lunch and is frequently crowded with well-preserved businesspeople on lunch hour, being in the heart of Midtown. It is also a wonderful spot to take a civilized siesta from hours of shopping along Fifth Avenue and recharge your batteries for the afternoon ahead. *Secret Inspector's Notes: The flowers at La Grenouille are a part of the overall atmosphere that pleasantly mimics the French in elegance. They are one of the most charming additions to this transporting dining spot.* French menu. Lunch, dinner. Closed Sun-Mon; also Aug. Bar. Reservations recommended. **$$$$**

★ ★ **LA MANGEOIRE** **(MAP F)**
1008 Second Ave (10022)
Phone 212/759-7086
Fax 212/759-6387
www.lamangeoire.com
La Mangeoire is a perfect place for a business lunch or a quiet, intimate dinner. The warm dining room is charming and cozy, and the menu offers enough of a selection of contemporary French fare—escargots, Provençal fish soup, and the caramelized onion tart are signatures—to please even the most high-maintenance diners. The staff is gracious, and hospitality flows effortlessly. French menu. Lunch, dinner, Sun brunch. Closed holidays. Casual attire. Reservations recommended. **$$$**

★ ★ ★ ★ **LE CIRQUE 2000** **(MAP E)**
455 Madison Ave (10022)
Phone 212/303-7788
Fax 212/303-7712
www.lecirque.com
Located in the stunning New York Palace Hotel, Le Cirque has set the standard for New York City dining for 20 years. The restaurant, designed by Adam Tihany, combines old-world charm with modern design. Bright swirls of neon lights and bold, primary-colored banquettes evoke a playful, 21st-century circus theme, while mahogany walls, vintage carpets, and crown moldings maintain the elegance of the original palace-like space. The kitchen does a wonderful job of balancing old and new as well, creating meals (both prix fixe and à la carte) that challenge yet feel safe, and manage to satisfy every taste and appetite. The à la carte menu is divided into several sections: Appetizers, Pasta, Main Courses, Classics, and From the Grill. Desserts are wonderful, showy, artistic creations and should not be turned down. They are worth any added inches on the hips. An extensive wine list and a menu of caviar accent the meal and bring the dining experience into another realm of luxury. Le Cirque is perpetually crowded and with an eclectic mix of socialites, tourists, fashion-forward New Yorkers, influential visitors, and other elite. It is constantly buzzing, yet the energy is not overwhelming. Quite the

opposite. The place makes you feel alive and giddy, like a kid in a toy store anticipating many gifts. French menu. Lunch, dinner. Bar. Jacket required. Reservations recommended. Outdoor seating. **$$$$**

★★ LE COLONIAL 132 (MAP F)

149 E 57th St (10022)
Phone 212/752-0808
Fax 212/752-7534

Serving sophisticated French-Vietnamese fare, Le Colonial is a Midtown favorite for lunch and dinner. The room feels like colonial Saigon come to life, with tall bamboo, spinning ceiling fans, lazy palms, and soft lighting. The menu offers the vibrant chile-tinged signature dishes of the region and includes such treats as glossy spring rolls filled with shrimp, pork, and mushrooms; tender ginger-marinated duck with a tamarind dipping sauce; and grilled loin of pork paired with a lively mango and jicama salad. Vietnamese, French menu. Lunch, dinner. Closed July 4, Thanksgiving, Dec 25. Bar. Casual attire. **$$$**

★★★ LE PERIGORD 133 (MAP F)

405 E 52nd St (10022)
Phone 212/755-6244
Fax 212/486-3906
www.leperigord.com

Le Perigord is one of New York's old-time favorites for sophisticated French dining. The menu of classic dishes, including the restaurant's signature game selection (in season), is geared for diners who define luxury in terms of impeccable, attentive service; elegant furnishings; inspired haute cuisine of the nouvelle French variety; and the quiet of a dining room filled with people enjoying a civilized meal. The food here is delicate and serene, in perfect harmony with the peaceful and majestic dining room. French menu. Lunch, dinner. Closed July. Bar. Jacket required. **$$$**

★★ LES HALLES 134 (MAP F)

411 Park Ave S (10016)
Phone 212/679-4111

Chef Anthony Bourdain (author of behind-the-scenes memoir *Kitchen Confidential*) brought Les Halles into the culinary limelight a few years back. Despite all the hype, this brasserie remains a genuine star for amazing cuts of steak and terrific takes on pork, chicken, moules, and, of course, lots of frites. The front serves as a French-

terence conran shop

This British-based retailer has finally come to the Big Apple, with a shop built right into a pavilion at the Queensboro Bridge. With international flair and a sense of style, the store sells fine—and sometimes unusual—home furnishings, kitchenware, and jewelry familiar to those who read *Wallpaper* and *British Elle Décor*. If you don't blow your budget on these irresistible, ultra-modern accessories, stop for a bite next door at Gustavino's, a French-American restaurant that is just as chic as the store. *415 E 59th St (10022). Phone 212/755-9079. www. conran.com.*

style butcher shop, while the crowded bistro-style dining room feels like it just fell out of some super-fabulous arrondisement in Paris. French menu. Lunch, dinner, brunch. Bar. Casual attire. **$$**

★ ★ ★ MALONEY & PORCELLI (MAP E)
37 E 50th St (10022)
Phone 212/750-2233
Fax 212/750-2252
www.maloneyandporcelli.com
Named for the restaurant owners' attorneys, Maloney & Porcelli is an easy, smart choice for an urban business lunch or a simple dinner out with a group of friends who favor simple, well-executed cuisine served in a classic, clubby environment without fuss or pretense. The New American menu offers straight-ahead choices like a raw bar, thin-crust pizza, and filet mignon from consulting chef David Burke. The wine list contains some real gems as well, making Maloney & Porcelli a favorite for Midtown dining. American menu. Lunch, dinner. Closed Jan 1, Dec 25. Bar. **$$$**

★ ★ ★ ★ MARCH 137 (MAP F)
405 E 58th St (10022)
Phone 212/754-6272
Fax 212/838-5108
www.marchrestaurant.com
Many people have issues with indulgence. Chef/owner Wayne Nish is not one of them. He believes that his guests should be indulged from the moment they enter his jewel-like, turn-of-the-century-townhouse restaurant to the moment they sadly must part. And a meal at March is just that—pure, blissful indulgence—from start to finish.

For this reason (and because it's one of the most romantic spots in New York City), it is truly a special-occasion place, and reservations should be secured well in advance. Nish's menu, of what he calls "New York City Cuisine," is fabulous. Dishes focus on fresh, seasonal products sparked to attention with luxurious ingredients from around the world. Choose from three-, four-, five-, or six-course tasting menus; each is available with or without wine pairings. Go for the wine. Co-owner Joseph Scalice is a gifted wine director, and you're in for a treat. Alfresco dining on the townhouse's rooftop terrace and mezzanine is magical in warm months. *Secret Inspector's Notes: The service is incredibly accommodating at March, and the kitchen is receptive to guest modifications of tasting menus. The food is inconsistent, though; while some courses are like a taste of heaven, others seem to miss the mark.* American menu. Lunch, dinner. Closed holidays. Jacket required. Reservations recommended. Outdoor seating. **$$$$**

★ ★ ★ MORTON'S OF CHICAGO   (MAP E)
551 Fifth Ave (10017)
Phone 585/972-3315; toll-free 800/972-3315
Fax 585/972-0018
www.mortons.com
This steakhouse chain, which originated in Chicago in 1978, appeals to serious meat lovers. With a selection of belt-busting carnivorous delights (like the house specialty, a 24-ounce porterhouse), as well as fresh fish, lobster, and chicken entrées, Morton's rarely disappoints. If you just aren't sure what you're in the mood for, the tableside menu presentation may help you decide. Here, main course selections are placed on a cart that's rolled to your table, where servers describe each item in detail. Steak menu. Lunch, dinner. Closed holidays. Bar. Jacket required. Reservations recommended. **$$$**

★ ★ ★ MR. K'S   139 (MAP F)
570 Lexington Ave (10022)
Phone 212/583-1668
Fax 212/583-1618
www.mrksnyc.com
In general, most movers and shakers in the world of finance, media, and power know of Mr. K's—it is their daily cafeteria for grease-less, elegant Chinese food. Forget what you may have ever thought about Chinese food, because Mr. K's breaks all the rules, bringing New Yorkers wonderful, upscale, exotic dishes from the various regions of China and serving them in an ultra-elegant, posh setting filled with fresh flowers, plush cushioned banquettes, and most notably, waiters

who know the meaning of service. The restaurant, which is a clone of the DC original, is a wonderful choice for a big party to celebrate a special occasion, even if it's just being able to share a dazzling meal at Mr. K's together. Chinese menu. Lunch, dinner. Casual attire. Reservations recommended. **$$$**

★ ★ ★ NADAMAN HAKUBAI (MAP E)
66 Park Ave (10016)
Phone 212/885-7111
www.kitano.com
Located in the posh Kitano Hotel, Nadaman Hakubai offers authentic Japanese fare in a tranquil, Zenlike space. The menu features a myriad of traditionally prepared seafood dishes like ika shiokara (chopped salted squid), karuge-su (vinegar-marinated jelly fish), and karei (fried, grilled, or simmered flounder). For a special treat, call ahead and reserve a private room for the multicourse chef's choice menu ($120 to $150), or, to savor a simpler meal, choose from the restaurant's swimming selection of sushi, sashimi, and maki rolls, as well as udon and soba noodle dishes. Japanese menu. Lunch, dinner. Casual attire. **$$$$**

★ ★ ★ ★ OCEANA (MAP E)
55 E 54th St (10022)
Phone 212/759-5941
Fax 212/759-6076
www.oceanarestaurant.com
Oceana has been one of New York's most lauded seafood spots for more than a decade. Although ten years could have derailed the restaurant, it has stayed a steady course and its mission is as clear as ever: stunning, just-shy-of-swimming seafood tinged with subtle, precise flavors from around the globe. You'll find practically every glorious fish in the sea on the menu, from halibut to tuna, dorade to turbot. Scallops, lobster, and glistening oysters are also on the menu. But there's a nod to the issue of overfishing here as well. Oceana is known for serving only sustainable seafood that is not in danger of becoming extinct. The service is warm and efficient, and the cream-colored, nautical-themed room (portholes dot the walls) is peaceful and comfortable, making Oceana a perennial favorite for power lunchers and pre-theater diners. The wine list is impressive, with a good number of seafood-friendly options at a variety of price points. A signature selection of American caviar from sturgeon, paddlefish, and rainbow trout makes a strong argument for forgoing osetra, beluga, and sevruga. American menu. Lunch, dinner. Closed Sun; holidays. Jacket required. Reservations recommended. **$$$$**

★★★ OLIVES 248 (MAP F)
201 Park Ave S (10003)
Phone 212/353-8345
www.whotels.com
Celebrity chef-restaurateur Todd English's New York debut is a branch
of his mega-successful Boston-based bistro. Located in the swanky
W Union Square Hotel, the inviting and bustling restaurant has an
open kitchen, with buttery walls, an open hearth fireplace, and deep,
oval banquettes for luxurious relaxation all night long. The menu
stars English's standard (but delicious) Mediterranean formula: boldly
flavored, luxurious dishes that are impeccably prepared and artfully
presented on the plate. His signature tart filled with olives, goat
cheese, and sweet caramelized onions is a winner, but the menu
offers a dish for every taste, including lamb, fish, homemade pastas,
and pizzas from the wood oven. Mediterranean menu. Breakfast,
lunch, dinner. Bar. Casual attire. Outdoor seating. **$$$**

★★ OYSTER BAR 142 (MAP E)
Grand Central Terminal, Lower Level (10017)
Phone 212/490-6650
Fax 212/949-5210
www.oysterbarny.com
Chaos has never been more fun than at the Oyster Bar. Packed to
the gills at lunch and dinner daily, this Grand Central Station icon
is one of the best places to gorge on all sorts of seafood. The room
makes you feel as though you have gone back in time, with vaulted
subway-tiled ceilings and waiters who have been working here since
Nixon was in the White House. As for the grub, there are more than
two dozen varieties of oysters to choose from, as well as all sorts of
chowders, fish sandwiches, fish entrées, and, well, you get the idea. If
it swims or even sits in water, it's on the menu. If you're on the run,
don't worry: grab a seat at the bar or at one of the old-fashioned
lunch counters for a quick lunch. Seafood menu. Lunch, dinner.
Closed Sun; holidays. Bar. Casual attire. **$$**

★★★ PATROON 143 (MAP F)
160 E 46th St (10017)
Phone 212/883-7373
Fax 212/883-1118
Owner Ken Aretsky's popular, clubby, low-lit Patroon is more than a
boys' club for juicy steaks. You'll also find women feasting at Patroon,
as his American restaurant has that edge that other steakhouses
don't—a terrific kitchen with talent for more than just beef (although
the beef is fabulous). Of the USDA Prime selections, Steak Diana

(named for Aretsky's wife) is a house specialty and is prepared tableside with brown butter, shallots, and wine for an arresting visual presentation. The kitchen also gussies things up with hearty dishes like pork shanks, short ribs, and lighter fare like oysters, shrimp, lump crab, and a slew of stunning seafood. A wide rooftop deck makes summertime fun with great grilled fare and chilly cocktails. American menu. Dinner. Closed Sun; holidays. Bar. Casual attire. Outdoor seating. **$$$**

★★ PIPA 144 (MAP E)
38 E 19th St (10003)
Phone 212/677-2233
Pipa, a lively and sultry restaurant and tapas bar in the Flatiron District, serves up some of the most delicious modern Spanish food in the city in a sexy, candlelit, antique-filled setting worthy of a designer's dream. The eclectic flea market décor should come as no surprise, as the restaurant occupies the ground floor of ABC Carpet & Home, one of the city's swankiest furniture and accessories stores, making it the perfect shopping pit stop. Spanish menu. Lunch, dinner. Bar. Casual attire. Reservations recommended. Outdoor seating. **$$$**

★ REPUBLIC 254 (MAP E)
37 Union Sq W (10003)
Phone 212/627-7172
Fax 212/627-7010
www.thinknoodles.com
Located on Union Square West, Republic is perpetually packed with trendy locals who seek out the restaurant's signature Asian noodle dishes. Be ready to sit on communal picnic tables and shout above the din, but the decibels and the less-than-comfy seating vanish when the steaming bowls arrive, brimming with Thai, Japanese, and other East Asian recipes for all sorts of delicious noodles. Asian menu. Lunch, dinner. Closed Memorial Day, Dec 25. Bar. Casual attire. Outdoor seating. **$**

★★★ RIINGO 145 (MAP F)
205 E 45th St (10017)
Phone 212/867-4200
riingo.com
Marcus Samuelsson, the heartthrob, boy-wonder chef behind the very popular contemporary Scandinavian spot Aquavit (see), is the man behind Riingo, a white-hot Asian restaurant in Midtown's Alex Hotel.

Japanese for apple, Riingo is a sleek and sexy bi-level space featuring dark ebony woodwork and bamboo floors, and luxurious banquettes that swallow you up in warmth. It's tough not to feel fabulous here, seated in magnificent surroundings while nibbling on Samuelsson's inventive brand of Japanese-American fare. This stylish restaurant comes equipped with the requisite swanky lounge, an extensive house-infused sake list, full sushi bar, and look-at-me crowds. Riingo is the perfect apple for the Big Apple. Pan-Asian menu. Lunch, dinner. Business casual attire. Valet parking. **$$$**

★★★ SAKAGURA (MAP F)
211 E 43rd St (10017)
Phone 212/953-7253

At this subterranean hideaway in Midtown, you'll find one of the most extensive sake collections in the city, as well as a talented knife-wielding team of sushi chefs turning out some of the most delicious sashimi you've ever tasted. (There is no sushi here, as it is forbidden to serve rice with sake.) Sakagura may be a bit tough to find—you enter through the lobby of an office building and follow a small gold sign that points you toward this buried basement space. But once you have found it, you will be hesitant to leave. The space is very Zen/minimalist and is leanly decorated with bamboo plants and paper lanterns. Between the soothing atmosphere and the potent sake, you'll sleep like a baby after your evening here. Japanese menu. Lunch, dinner. Bar. Casual attire. Reservations recommended. **$$**

★★★ SAN PIETRO (MAP E)
18 E 54th St (10022)
Phone 212/753-9015
Fax 212/371-2337
www.sanpietro.net

San Pietro is one of the restaurants where you walk in a customer and leave a part of the family. Located on a busy Midtown street, San Pietro is owned and run by the three Bruno brothers, who grew up on a family farm along the Amalfi Coast in the southern Italian region of Campagna. At San Pietro, the brothers pay homage to their homeland by serving traditional dishes—antipasti, pasta, poultry, fish, veal, and beef—accented with seasonal ingredients and lots of Italian charm. The wine list contains a knockout selection of southern Italian wines to complete the experience. Italian menu. Dinner. Closed Sun; holidays. Bar. Jacket required. Outdoor seating. **$$$**

[D]

★★★ SHUN LEE PALACE (MAP F)

155 E 55th St (10022)
Phone 212/371-8844
Fax 212/752-1936

The lovely, swirling décor of the Adam Tihany-designed dining room should tell you that something special awaits you at Shun Lee Palace. The large space is perfect for business luncheons or family get-togethers. Restaurateur Michael Tong's extensive haute Chinese menu makes this spot a New York favorite—so much so that a second location has opened on the West Side. Guest chefs visit frequently from Hong Kong, and the special prix fixe lunch is a deal. Chinese menu. Lunch, dinner, late-night. Closed Thanksgiving. Bar. Casual attire. Reservations recommended. **$$$**

★★★ SMITH & WOLLENSKY (MAP F)

797 Third Ave (10022)
Phone 212/753-1530
Fax 212/751-5446
www.smithandwollensky.com

The original after which the national chain was modeled, this 390-seat, wood-paneled dining room is known for sirloin steaks and filet mignon, but also offers lamb and veal chops. Sides are huge and straightforward, with the likes of creamed spinach and hash browns. Good wines and personable service complete the experience. American menu. Dinner. Closed holidays. Bar. Casual attire. **$$$**

★★★ SPARKS STEAK HOUSE (MAP F)

210 E 46th St (10017)
Phone 212/687-4855
Fax 212/557-7409

This temple of beef is one of the standard spots for meat-seekers in New York City. The cavernous dining room has a classic old-world charm to it, with oil paintings, etched glass, and dark wood paneling, and the large bar feels like home as soon as you wrap your fingers around the stem of your martini glass. Sparks is a serious American chophouse, and only serious appetites need apply for entry. There are no dainty portions here, so come ready to feast on thick, juicy steaks, burgers, roasts, racks, and fish (if you must). Steak menu. Dinner. Closed Sun; holidays. Bar. Casual attire. Reservations recommended. **$$$**

★ ★ STEAK FRITES (MAP E)

9 E 16th St (10003)
Phone 212/463-7101
Fax 212/627-2760
www.steakfritesnyc.com

Located down the block from the Union Square Greenmarket, Steak Frites is the perfect rest stop after shopping for the season's best produce. Open for Saturday and Sunday brunch, it is popular on weekends, when locals grab outdoor tables and people-watch. At night, the restaurant is lively and has a rich European flair, decorated with vintage posters and long leather banquettes. This is a fun restaurant to hang out in and just have drinks, but it's also an ideal spot to hunker down over a dinner of the signature steak frites with a bold red wine. The menu also offers a great selection of fish, pastas, and salads. French bistro menu. Lunch, dinner, brunch. Closed Jan 1, Dec 25. Bar. Casual attire. Outdoor seating. **$$**

★ ★ ★ TABLA   258 (MAP E)

11 Madison Ave (10010)
Phone 212/889-0667
Fax 212/889-0914

Tabla is the Indian-inspired culinary star from restaurant tour de force Danny Meyer (Gramercy Tavern, Union Square Cafe—see both). Chef/partner Floyd Cardoz cleverly peppers his menu with the intoxicating flavors of India—sweet and savory spices, chutneys, meats from a tandoor oven, and soft rounds of pillowy, handmade breads. The result is a delicious introduction to the sumptuous flavors of India, not a crash course that hits you over the head. The stunning, bilevel dining room has an almost mystical quality to it, with its muted jewel-toned accents, rich redwood floors, and soaring windows that face Madison Square Park. Indian menu. Dinner. Bar. Reservations recommended. **$$$**

★ ★ ★ TAMARIND   152 (MAP E)

41-43 E 22nd St (10010)
Phone 212/674-7400

The fragrant cuisine of India is served at Tamarind, an elegant restaurant in the Flatiron District with a lively bar and a serene and beautiful dining room. The attraction here is a menu of dishes show-casing perfect-pitch flavors—spicy, sweet, sour, and hot play together wonderfully on the plate. The kitchen serves stunning samosas, naan, pouri, chutneys, and traditional curries, alongside more contemporary dishes that play to the sophisticated New Yorker crowd. Indian menu. Lunch, dinner. Bar. Casual attire. Reservations recommended. **$$$**

★ ★ ★ TOCQUEVILLE (MAP E)

15 E 15th St (10003)
Phone 212/647-1515
www.tocquevillerestaurant.com

Owned by husband Marco Moreira (chef) and wife Jo-Ann Makovitsky (front-of-house manager), Tocqueville is a little slice of paradise in the form of a restaurant. This is the sort of place that will calm you from the moment you walk through the tall blond doors into the petite, elegant room warmed with golden light, butter-yellow walls, and stunningly appointed tabletops. The cuisine is as magical as the space. Chef Moreira offers impeccably prepared, inventive New American fare crafted with care from pristine seasonal ingredients hand-picked from local farmers and the nearby Greenmarket. Intimate and soothing, Tocqueville is a perfect spot for those seeking quiet conversation and luxurious food. American, French menu. Lunch, dinner. Bar. Casual attire. **$$$$**

★ ★ TURKISH KITCHEN (MAP F)

386 Third Ave (10016)
Phone 212/679-1810

Be prepared to enjoy your food at this bustling Murray Hill outpost for authentic Turkish fare. The restaurant specializes in the well-spiced cuisine of this beautiful country, with dishes of tender lamb, beef, and chicken, as well as lots of warm bread for ripping off and dipping in assorted mezze. Stained a deep red, the walls and the Arabic décor give the room a warm feeling. The only drawback is the service, which is very friendly and very knowledgeable, but can be slow. Turkish menu. Lunch, dinner. Children's menu. Casual attire. Reservations recommended. **$$**

★ ★ ★ UNION PACIFIC (MAP F)

111 E 22nd St (10010)
Phone 212/995-8500
Fax 212/460-5881
www.unionpacificrestaurant.com

Rocco DiSpirito is one of New York City's hottest young chefs. A Food Network star (*The Melting Pot*), he looks as though he just walked off the pages of GQ. And he isn't just easy on the eyes. This man can cook—and really well. His culinary domain, Union Pacific, is an elegant oasis for sophisticated New American fare, with an emphasis on the fruits of the sea. The modern dining room, furnished with deep, plush banquettes, is warmed by ultra-flattering lighting. (It takes at least ten years off.) An extensive and carefully chosen wine list, the restaurant's serene waterfall, and operatic food ensure a blissful experience. DiSpirito's talent is balance, contrasting textures, temperatures, and flavors to make the palate sing and swoon. Succulent Taylor Bay scallops, for example, are topped with uni (sea urchin) and set in a bright pool of tomato water dotted with mustard oil. The dish is one of DiSpirito's signatures. After one bite, you'll wonder how you've done without it for this long. *Secret Inspector's Notes: A recent renovation has put Union Pacific back on top in its design elements. The food is still creative and innovative in its use of ingredients and preparations. If you're lucky, you might catch a glimpse of Rocco coming in or out the door!* American menu. Lunch, dinner. Closed Sun. Bar. Casual attire. **$$$$**

★ ★ ★ UNION SQUARE CAFE (MAP E)

21 E 16th St (10003)
Phone 212/243-4020
Fax 212/627-2673

Union Square Cafe is the first restaurant from the man who brought New York Gramercy Tavern, Eleven Madison, Tabla, and Blue Smoke (see all): Danny Meyer. This bright, warm, cheery, bilevel restaurant and bar is still packing in locals and wooing tourists with Meyer's signature hospitality, chef Michael Romano's divine New American fare, and an award-winning wine list. While the menu changes with the seasons and often features produce from the Greenmarket across the way, the chef's succulent signature grilled tuna burger should not be considered optional. If a table doesn't seem possible (reservations are tough to score), a seat at the bar is a fabulous—and more authentic New Yorker—alternative. American menu. Dinner. Closed holidays. Bar. Casual attire. Reservations recommended. **$$$**

★ ★ ★ ★ VERITAS (MAP E)

43 E 20th St (10003)
Phone 212/353-3700
Fax 212/353-1632
www.veritas-nyc.com

If a passion for wine runs through your veins, then a visit to Veritas should be considered mandatory. At this stylish Gramercy Park gem, you'll find a magnificent wine list that, at last count, was 2,700 bottles long. Despite its intimidating length, wine neophytes should not be deterred. There is no fear factor here. The staff is friendly and knowledgeable and all too happy to help you find a suitable wine to match your meal and budget. Bottles range from $20 to $1,300. While wine is the primary draw for Veritas, the food gives the wine a run for its money. It is specifically created with wine in mind and perfectly complements the beverage of focus. The full menu is available at the sleek bar, which is a nice option if you want a quick bite and some (or lots of) wine. Whether you're seated at the bar or tucked into a snug and intimate booth, the restaurant's contemporary American menu is easy to love. Robust flavors, seasonal ingredients, and a light hand in the kitchen make for magical meals. Veritas is a perfect place to explore wine and food alike. *Secret Inspector's Notes: Veritas is an intimate restaurant with warm service. The food is outstanding, and with proper wine assistance, the complete experience is ideal for a special occasion or a romantic meal.* American menu. Dinner. Bar. **$$$$**

★★★ VONG 158 (MAP F)
200 E 54th St (10022)
Phone 212/486-9592
Fax 212/980-3745
www.jean-georges.com
When Jean-Georges Vongerichten, Alsatian-born wonder chef, opened a Thai restaurant called Vong, people weren't sure what to make of it. But doubts were soon dispelled as diners began to experience his exciting and exotic French riffs on fiery Thai classics, incorporating spices and flavors of the East with a New York sensibility. The restaurant feels like a wild and mystical night in the Orient, decorated with long, deep banquettes covered with silk pillows in brilliant jewel tones, walls painted crimson red and accented with gold leaf, and a long table showcasing a Buddha altar. It's a journey for all of the senses. Thai, French menu. Dinner. Closed holidays. Bar. Casual attire. **$$$**

★★ THE WATER CLUB 159 (MAP F)
500 E 30th St (10016)
Phone 212/683-3333
Fax 212/696-4009
www.thewaterclub.com
Special occasions were made for The Water Club, a lovely restaurant with romantic, panoramic views of the East River. The shiplike space features soothing, nightly live piano and an intimate, clubby lounge, perfect for relaxing before or after dinner. While poultry and beef are

on the menu, The Water Club is known for its seafood. In addition to a gigantic raw bar, you'll find an impressive selection of lobster, scallops, cod, tuna, salmon, and whatever else looks good at the fish markets. On a sunny day, you can't beat brunch out on the deck with a fiery Bloody Mary in hand, watching the ships go by, feeling like you're far away from it all. Seafood menu. Lunch, dinner, Sun brunch. Bar. Jacket required. Reservations recommended. Valet parking. Outdoor seating. **$$$**

🄳

★ ★ ZARELA ⬤160 (MAP F)
953 Second Ave (10022)
Phone 212/644-6740
Fax 212/980-1073
www.zarela.com

This colorful and spirited Mexican eatery in Midtown is renowned for its killer margaritas (be careful with these) and delicious regional Mexican fare. Loud and lively, the bar is always packed with a rowdy after-work crowd that lingers well into the evening. Upstairs, in the more intimate yet still boisterous dining room, you'll feast on some of chef/owner Zarela Martinez's vibrant dishes, from rich enchiladas to luxuriously savory moles. Mexican menu. Lunch, dinner. Closed holidays. Bar. Casual attire. **$$**

🄳

Greenwich Village and SoHo

Although New York's fabled bohemian neighborhood has gone seriously upscale and more mainstream in recent decades, evidence of its iconoclastic past can still be found in its many narrow streets, off-Broadway theaters, cozy coffee shops, lively jazz clubs, and tiny bars. Stretching from 14th Street south to Houston Street, and from Broadway west to the Hudson River, **Greenwich Village** remains one of the city's best places for idle wandering, people-watching, boutique browsing, and conversing over glasses of cabernet or cups of cappuccino.

Washington Square Park anchors the neighborhood to the east and, though it's nothing special to look at, is still the heart of the Village. On a sunny afternoon, everyone comes here: kids hot-dogging on skateboards, students strumming guitars, old men playing chess, and lovers entwined in each other's arms. Bordering the edges of the park are a mix of elegant townhouses and New York University buildings.

Just south and west of Washington Square, find Bleecker and MacDougal streets, home to coffee shops and bars once frequented by the likes of James Baldwin, Jack Kerouac, Allen Ginsberg, and James Agee. Le Figaro (corner of Bleecker and MacDougal) and the San Remo (93 MacDougal) were favorites back then and still attract crowds today, albeit mostly made up of tourists.

A bit farther west is Seventh Avenue South, where you'll find the Village Vanguard (178 Seventh Ave S, at 11th St)—the oldest and most venerable jazz club in the city. Also nearby are the Blue Note (131 W 3rd St, near Sixth Ave), New York's premier jazz supper club, and Smalls (183 W 10th St, near Seventh Ave S), one of the best places to catch up-and-coming talent.

At the corner of Seventh Avenue South and Christopher Street stands Christopher Park, where a George Segal sculpture of two gay couples commemorates the Stonewall Riots, which marked the advent of the gay-rights movement. The Stonewall Inn, where the demonstration began in 1969, once stood directly across from the park at 51 Christopher, and Christopher Street itself is still lined with many gay establishments.

At the corner of Sixth Avenue and West 10th Street reigns the gothic towers and turrets of Jefferson Market Library, a stunning maroon-

and-white building that dates to 1876. Across the street from the library is Balducci's (424 Sixth Ave), a famed gourmet food shop.

Short for South of Houston (HOW-stun), **SoHo** is New York's trendiest neighborhood, filled with an impossible number of upscale eateries, fancy boutiques, of-the-moment bars, and, most recently, a few astronomically expensive hotels. Contained in just 25 blocks bounded by Houston and Canal streets, Lafayette, and West Broadway, SoHo attracts trend followers and tourists by the thousands, especially on weekend afternoons, when the place sometimes feels like one giant open-air bazaar.

From the late 1800s to the mid-1900s, SoHo was primarily a light manufacturing district, but starting in the 1960s, most of the factories moved out and artists—attracted by the area's low rents and loft spaces—began moving in. Soon thereafter, the art galleries arrived, and then the shops and restaurants. Almost overnight, SoHo became too expensive for the artists—and, more recently, the art galleries—who had originally settled the place, and became a mecca for big-bucks shoppers from all over the world.

Nonetheless, SoHo still has plenty to offer art lovers. Broadway is lined with one first-rate museum after another, while Mercer and Greene streets, especially, boast a large number of galleries. Some top spots on Broadway include the Museum for African Art (593 Broadway), presenting an excellent array of changing exhibits; the New Museum for Contemporary Art (583 Broadway), one of the oldest, best-known, and most controversial art spaces in SoHo; and the Guggenheim Museum SoHo (575 Broadway), a branch of the uptown institution. To find out who's exhibiting what and where in SoHo, pick up a copy of the *Art Now Gallery Guide*, available at many bookstores and galleries.

SoHo is also home to an extraordinary number of luscious cast-iron buildings. Originally meant to serve as a cheap substitute for stone buildings, the cast-iron façades were an American invention, prefabricated in a variety of styles—from Italian Renaissance to Classical Greek—and bolted onto the front of iron-frame structures. Most of SoHo's best cast-iron gems can be found along Broadway; keep an eye out for the Haughwout Building (488 Broadway), the Singer Building (561 Broadway), and the Guggenheim Museum SoHo.

Top thoroughfares for shopping include Prince and Spring streets,
Broadway, and West Broadway. Numerous clothing and accessory
boutiques are located along all these streets; West Broadway also
offers several interesting bookstores. For antiques and furnishings,
check out Lafayette Street; for craft and toy stores, try Greene and
Mercer streets.

Restaurants and bars line almost every street in SoHo, but one
especially lively nexus is the intersection of Grand Street and West
Broadway. West Broadway itself is also home to a large number of
eateries, some of which offer outdoor dining in the summer.

Restaurants in Greenwich Village and SoHo

★★ ALFAMA (MAP G)
551 Hudson St (10014)
Phone 212/645-2500
The wonderful seaside cuisine of Alfama, an ancient village in
Portugal, is on the menu at this namesake bistro decorated with
authentic blue and white Portuguese tiles in Manhattan's West
Village. Bacalau (salt cod) is one of the most common ingredients
in Portuguese cooking, and it shows up here mixed in a dish with
potatoes and peppers that is alive with robust flavors. Cooking in a
cataplana—a sort of open-mouth clamshell pot made from copper—
is another tradition in Portugal. The cataplana is filled with fish,
scallops, and shrimp and studded with chorizo, potatoes, and tomatoes—a Hungry Man-style bouillabaisse that is complemented by an
incredible selection of Portuguese wines. To keep things like they are
in the old country, soulful Fado singers perform on Wednesday nights.
Portuguese menu. Lunch, dinner. Bar. Casual attire. Reservations
recommended. Outdoor seating. **$$$**

★★★ ANNISA (MAP G)
13 Barrow St (10014)
Phone 212/741-6699
At Annisa, a cozy, off-the-beaten-path gem in Greenwich Village,
chef/partner Anita Lo and partner Jennifer Scism (who runs the front
of the house) bring a bit of Asia and a lot of flavor and savvy style to
the contemporary American table. With the restaurant's golden glow
and elegant, sheer-white curtains draped along the tall walls, it's
easy to feel like you're dining somewhere very close to heaven. The
simple, approachable menu helps keep you in the celestial mood. An

array of wines by the glass and a strong sommelier make pairing wine with dinner a no-brainer. American menu. Dinner. Closed Sun. Casual attire. Reservations recommended. **$$$**
🍽

★★ AOC BEDFORD (MAP G)
14 Bedford St (10014)
Phone 212/414-4764
Located on a quiet, tree-lined street in the West Village, AOC Bedford is a stylish yet rustic retreat that welcomes you in with its exposed brick walls and wood-beamed ceilings. The restaurant derives its name from the term *appellation d'origine contrôlée,* the official French designation for food products of the highest quality. The menu is not exclusively French though. In fact, much of it has a Spanish flare, like the house specialty of suckling pig, served Iberian style (with the bone-in) and accompanied by a pile of dates, or the grand paella, stocked with cockles, clams, shrimp, and squid—all ingredients that shine easily. Italian, Spanish menu. Dinner. Closed Mon. Bar. Casual attire. **$$**
🍽

★★★ AQUAGRILL (MAP G)
210 Spring St (10012)
Phone 212/274-0505
Fax 212/274-0587
When the sun is out and a warm breeze is in the air, you'll find the city's hip locals lounging outside at Aquagrill, a perennial favorite for swimmingly fresh seafood (and great dry-aged steak). With its tall French doors sprung open to the street, Aquagrill has a European elegance and calm to it that makes it an irresistible spot to settle in, even if only for a glass of sparkling wine and a dozen (or two) shimmering oysters. Although the warmer months are the most fun, when there is a nip in the air, the dining room wraps you up, making you

bb sandwich bar

At this hole-in-the-wall sandwich shop in the Village, there is one thing and one thing only on the menu: cheese steaks. And not just any cheese steaks, these are hefty, messy, slight spicy, five-napkin heroes that may not be the authentic Philadelphia article, but nonetheless garner long lines of dedicated fans. For a fast, cheap, heavenly, and tasty bite on the fly, BB Sandwich Bar is tough to beat. *120 W 3rd St (10012). Phone 212/473-7500.*

feel cozy in an instant. Seafood menu. Dinner, brunch. Closed Mon; holidays; also the first week in July. Bar. Casual attire. Reservations recommended. Outdoor seating. **$$$**

★ ★ ★ BABBO   **165** (MAP G)

110 Waverly Pl (10011)
Phone 212/777-0303
Fax 212/777-3365
www.babbonyc.com

Dressed in his signature orange clogs and shorts, Mario Batali is the king of rustic authentic Italian cuisine on television's Food Network. But before he was a star of the small screen, he was a cook—and he is one celebrity chef who still is. Here in New York, you'll find him at Babbo, a charming Greenwich Village carriage house turned stylish duplex hotspot where celebrities, foodies, VIPs, and supermodels fill tables (and every nook of space) for the chance to feast on Batali's unique brand of robust and risky Italian fare. The man is known for serving braised pigs' feet, warm lamb tongue, and testa (head cheese). Cult-status signature pastas like beef cheek ravioli and mint love letters—spicy lamb sausage ragu soothed with mint and wrapped in envelopes of fresh pasta—are lick-lipping delicious and demonstrate that some culinary risks are worth taking. Italian menu. Dinner. Bar. Casual attire. **$$$**

★ ★ ★ BALTHAZAR   **166** (MAP H)

80 Spring St (10012)
Phone 212/965-1414
Fax 212/966-2502
www.balthazarny.com

If you don't know what all the hype surrounding Balthazar is about, you most certainly should. Keith McNally's super-fabulous replica of a Parisian brasserie is one of those rare spots that actually deserves the buzz. From the attractive crowds at the bar to the stunning folks who squeeze into the restaurant's tiny tables (you'll be seated as close to a stranger as is possible without becoming intimate), Balthazar is a dazzling, dizzying, wonderfully chaotic destination that sports a perfect menu of delicious brasserie standards like frisée au lardons, pan bagnat, steak frites, and a glistening raw bar built for royalty, not to mention the fresh-baked bread from the Balthazar bakery next door. To feel like a true New Yorker, pick up a bag of croissants, a couple of baguettes, and a dozen tarts on your way out for breakfast or lunch the next day. Balthazar is fun and loud and, in its own electric way, flawless. French menu. Dinner, brunch. Bar. Casual attire. Reservations recommended. **$$$$**

★ ★ ★ BLUE HILL (MAP G)
75 Washington Pl (10011)
Phone 212/539-1776
Blue Hill is a rare and lovely restaurant offering gracious hospitality, extraordinary seasonal American fare, and a stellar wine list in a warm, cozy, contemporary space that feels just right, like a page out of an upscale Pottery Barn catalog. Chocolate tones, soft lighting, and serene service make this restaurant a luxurious experience perfect for special occasions, and the truly wonderful menu by chef/owner Dan Barber ensures a delicious evening. American menu. Dinner. Bar. Casual attire. Reservations recommended. Outdoor seating. **$$$**
🄳

★ ★ BLUE RIBBON (MAP G)
97 Sullivan St (10012)
Phone 212/274-0404
Brothers Bruce and Eric Bromberg opened Blue Ribbon on a quiet block in SoHo some ten years ago, and it is as packed today as it was on day one. The tiny, low-lit bistro oozes fabulousness (models, moguls, and musicians are regulars) and features an eclectic menu of New York and French staples, like an icy raw bar stocked with oysters, deliriously good fried chicken (served with honey), and a perfect, meaty, and intensely flavored steak tartare garnished with cornichons, onion, egg, and coarse mustard. Blue Ribbon's notoriety comes from its late-night crowd that inevitably includes superstar chefs unwinding after a night of cooking or a night on the town. American, French menu. Dinner, late-night. Closed holidays. Bar. Casual attire. **$$$**

★ ★ BLUE RIBBON BAKERY (MAP G)
33 Downing St (10014)
Phone 212/337-0404
The brothers Bromberg first brought New Yorkers a taste of their creative culinary genius with Blue Ribbon, their hip late-night bistro. With Blue Ribbon Bakery, a rustic, wood-beamed, windowed corner spot in the West Village, they took on the task of baking bread (delicious bread) and decided to offer a menu of salads, small plates, and fresh seasonal entrées to boot. Whether for lunch, brunch, dinner, or an afternoon pick-me-up, Blue Ribbon Bakery is the perfect spot for a casual and always tasty bite. *Secret Inspector's Notes: Bartender Jim G. makes the best dirty martini in the city at this cozy yet lively outlet of the Blue Ribbon empire. A few of the inspector's favorites from the extensive menu include the Blue Rueben; steak tartare; leeks vinaigrette; chocolate bread pudding; endive, watercress and blue cheese*

salad; and foie gras terrine. Perfect for a snack or an evening, Blue Ribbon Bakery is always jammed for good reason. American menu. Lunch, dinner, brunch. Bar. Children's menu. Casual attire. **$$**

sullivan street

In the heart of Greenwich Village, this adorable street is dotted with shops, cafés, and restaurants that represent the alluring feel of this charming neighborhood. A good place to begin is where Sullivan meets Broome Street, walking uptown a bit to the **Sullivan Street Bakery** (73 Sullivan St, phone 212/334-9435, www.sullivanstreetbakery.com). Here you'll find breads, biscotti, and desserts to take home for later and "pizza" for snacking now. This is not conventional pizza, but a thin, crispy crust with an intensely concentrated single-flavor topping. There are usually four flavors a day that rotate seasonally. The zucchini in the summer is not to be missed, and the mushroom found year-round is a slice of heaven.

Once Upon a Tart (135 Sullivan St, phone 212/387-8869, www. onceuponatart.com) is a lovely little spot to read the paper, meet a friend, or pick up an impressive sweet or savory tart for later. The variety and quantity vary day by day, and there are always a few salads as accompaniments. What started as a cute idea is now so popular that they published a cookbook.

You'll see the line winding down the street outside a tiny green storefront and know you've found **Joe's Dairy** (156 Sullivan St, phone 212/677-8780). If it's fresh mozzarella you need, this is the place. It's incredible how much is sold out of this tiny storefront, and though they carry other Italian cheeses, the quality of their mozzarella, salted, unsalted and smoked, is really what the line is about. Continuing the feast would be a necessary stop at **Pepe Rosso to Go** (149 Sullivan St, phone 212/677-4555) on the corner of Sullivan and Houston Street. It's like a moment in Italy amidst the Italian chatter and cell phone buzz. Foods can be taken out for later or eaten at once on of the few tables. The panini are delicious and easily por-table, especially the bresaola, caprino, arugola and truffle oil, worth the extra dollar on focaccia. The pastas and salads are comforting and representative of any casual meal in Italy with a variety to choose from and all under ten dollars. Of course the requisite beverages are offered; most preferred being the tart carbonated lemon beverage, limonciata, often hard to locate in the US. One of the original sources of gourmet gelato and sorbet in the U.S. is located at **Ciao Bella** (227 Sullivan St, phone 212/505-7100) where flavors range from traditional to exotic and texture of both products is creamy and rich. Blood Orange Sorbetto is an excellent palate cleanser for this stage in the feast or between courses of a lengthy meal. Only near NYU would a restaurant succeed over time being solely devoted to humble, quintessentially American Peanut Butter. **Peanut Butter & Co.** (240 Sullivan St, phone 212/677-3935) grinds their own peanut butter, worth purchasing for the pantry, which is used on a variety of namesake sandwiches served classically on paper plates with a garnish of chips and carrot sticks. If peanut butter isn't your thing, their grilled cheese and tomato is quite tasty.

★ ★ ★ BOND STREET 170 (MAP H)
6 Bond St (10012)
Phone 212/777-2500
High-art sushi and sashimi are the calling cards of Bond Street, a hotspot and hipster hangout disguised as a modern Japanese restaurant. Famous fashionistas, celebrities, and supermodels are the typical guests at the white-washed, airy restaurant, and down in the dark and sexy lower-level bar you'll find more of the same. For all the hype, though, Bond Street serves excellent sushi and sashimi, and the extensive and inventive modern Japanese-influenced menu stands up to the scene with impressive resolve. Japanese, sushi menu. Dinner, late-night. Closed holidays. Bar. Casual attire. **$$$$**
🄳

★ ★ BOOM 171 (MAP G)
152 Spring St (10012)
Phone 212/431-3663
Fax 212/431-3643
Located in the heart of SoHo, Boom is a popular spot for European expats living (and shopping) in New York. The stylish crowds give Boom a hotspot vibe, but it's really just a simple, cozy bistro, with wood floors, candles burning, and, through open windows, a great view of the hipsters strolling by on Spring Street. The kitchen is not breaking any culinary ground but manages to turn out a respectable and eclectic menu of tasty global dishes. International menu. Lunch, dinner, brunch. Bar. **$**

★ CAFÉ HABANA 172 (MAP H)
17 Prince St (10012)
Phone 212/625-2001
It's safe to say that if you don't see a crowd of models, musicians, and assorted other super-fabulous people strewn out on the sidewalk outside Café Habana, it is closed. Indeed, as soon as this Cuban diner opens, the crowds are there, like metal to a magnet. The space is decked out in vintage chrome, with a food bar and way-cool retro booths, but the draw here is the flawless menu of cheap, straight-up Cuban grub, like rice and beans, terrific hangover-curing egg dishes, fried plantains, and divine plates of classic ropa vieja. Cuban menu. Breakfast, lunch, dinner, late-night. Casual attire. **$**

★★ CAFÉ LOUP 173 (MAP G)
105 W 13th St (10011)
Phone 212/255-4746
Fax 212/255-2022
Café Loup is a neighborhood favorite for simple but stylish French fare. This spacious, airy restaurant has a soothing vibe and is adorned with fresh flowers, lithographs, and photographs. If you are in the mood for attitude and a scene, head somewhere else, as this is an easy place to feel comfortable and to enjoy dinner. French bistro menu. Lunch, dinner, Sun brunch. Bar. Casual attire. **$$**
🅳

★★ CANTEEN 174 (MAP G)
142 Mercer St (10012)
Phone 212/431-7676
www.canteennyc.com
The creation of restaurateur John MacDonald (Merc Bar), Canteen is a bright, mod, super-hip playground for scensters and their fearless fashionista leaders. Decked out in day-glo orange, this subterranean cafeteria-style space is located underneath the flagship Prada store in SoHo, which does much to explain the super-tall, super-thin, super-fabulous folks pretending to eat here. The contemporary American menu, though, is truly worth digging into with zeal. Dishes like salmon with a fiery wasabi crust and pork chops with roasted corn pudding and bacon ragout are spirited and approachable. American menu. Lunch, dinner. Bar. Casual attire. **$$**
🅳

historic greenwich village

Although no longer the leading edge of the art world and radicalism, Greenwich Village remains a uniquely dynamic neighborhood. Start in Washington Square Park, lined by New York University buildings and the site of the famous arch. The park normally buzzes with street performers, in-line skaters, and families at play. Leave the park from the south side. Judson Memorial Church stands on the corner of West 4th Street and Thompson Street. Designed by Stanford White, the church is noted for its stained-glass windows and front marble work. Thompson Street is lined with chess clubs. At Bleecker Street, turn right. Look for Le Figaro Café (186 Bleecker St) and Café Borgia (185 Bleecker St), a pair of old-time coffeehouses.

Turn right onto MacDougal Street. Here stand two landmark cafés: Caffé Reggio (119 MacDougal St) and Café Wha? (115 MacDougal St), as well as Minetta Tavern (113 MacDougal St), an old standby that serves good Italian food. Make a U-turn, turn right onto Minetta Lane, and then turn right onto Minetta Street, both lined with classic Village townhouses. Cross Sixth Avenue and enter the heart of Bleecker's "neighborhood" shopping—including some of the finest Italian bake shops in the city. Continue across Seventh Avenue and turn left onto Barrow Street. This block features a number of classic red-brick row houses (49 and 51 Barrow St are Federal style) and Chumley's Bar (86 Barrow St), once a speakeasy and a famous writers' hangout. Look for 75 Barrow Street, a strange, narrow house where Edna St. Vincent Millay once lived, and 77 Barrow Street, which was built in 1799, making it the Village's oldest house. Turn right on Bedford, passing a late 19th-century horse stable (95 Bedford), an early 19th-century home with a pair of Tudor-style towers aptly named Twin Peaks (102 Bedford), and a mid-19th-century home built in the Greek Revival style (113 Bedford).

Turn right onto Christopher Street, a throbbing, busy street that's the heart of Village gay life. Go right onto Bleecker, then left onto Seventh Avenue. Sweet Basil (414 Seventh Ave) is a famed jazz club, as is Village Vanguard (178 Seventh Ave S). Turn right on Grove Street and right again on Waverly Place. At 165 Waverly Place stands the Northern Dispensary, built during the 1831 cholera epidemic. Turn left onto Sixth Avenue. The circa-1876, castlelike, Gothic-style Jefferson Market Library is located on 10th Street. Also of note on Sixth Avenue are Balducci's (424 Sixth Ave), a legendary gourmet food shop, and Bigalow's (414 Sixth Ave), the city's oldest continuously operating pharmacy. Continue north and turn right onto 11th Street to minuscule Second Cemetery of the Spanish and Portuguese Synagogue, or return south and turn left onto 8th Street, another major shopping street.

At Fifth Avenue, turn right. Just before Washington Square Park is the picturesque cul-de-sac Washington Square Mews. For more shopping, continue east on 8th Street and then turn south on Broadway. These blocks, not long ago a forsaken neighborhood of old warehouses and sweatshop factory buildings, now thrive with major retail chains like Tower Records and Gap.

★ CORNER BISTRO (MAP G)
331 W 4th St (10014)
Phone 212/242-9502

Corner Bistro is known far and wide for one thing and one thing only: burgers. They are good, but the hype is a bit out of control these days. The place, a run-down little tavern with quite a bit of "character," is located, as its name suggests, on a nice little corner of the West Village, and the space is far from glamorous. In a word, it's a dive, but a friendly one, that serves tasty burgers on cardboard plates topped with cheese, bacon, or, if you're splurging on the Bistro Burger, bacon, raw onions, lettuce, tomato and cheese. The Corner Bistro formula is simple: it's beer, burgers, and if you're lucky, some napkins. If you want anything more, you'd better go elsewhere. American menu, hamburgers. Lunch, dinner, late-night. Bar. Casual attire. No credit cards accepted. **$**

★★ CRISPO 176 (MAP E)
240 W 14th St (10011)
Phone 212/229-1818

Named after its chef/owner Frank Crispo, this newcomer to West 14th Street is already considered a staple for fans of rustic, Italian-accented cuisine, like plates of delicious hand-sliced prosciutto di Parma, simple yet stellar pastas, grilled chops, and seasonal salads. The warm, exposed-brick room gets crowded early on, so plan to reserve a table ahead of time or wait at the bar (not a bad option at all, although the bar area is small) for one of the coveted tables to open up. Italian, Mediterranean menu. Dinner. Closed Sun. Bar. Casual attire. Reservations recommended. Outdoor seating. **$$**

★ ★ ★ DA SILVANO (MAP G)
260 Sixth Ave (10014)
Phone 212/982-2343

If one thing is certain about a meal at Da Silvano, it is that before you finish your Tuscan dinner, you will have spotted at least one actor, model, musician, or other such celebrity. Da Silvano is a scene, and a great one at that. With such a loyal and fabulous following, the food could be mediocre, but the kitchen does not rest on its star-infested laurels. This kitchen offers wonderful, robust, regional Italian fare, like homemade pasta, meat, fish, and salad. The sliver of a wine bar next door, Da Silvano Cantinetta, offers Italian-style tapas paired with a wide selection of wines by the glass. But perhaps the best way to experience Da Silvano is on a warm day, where a seat at the wide, European-style sidewalk café offers prime people-watching. Italian menu. Lunch, dinner. Closed Dec 25. Casual attire. Outdoor seating. **$$$**

★ ★ DO HWA (MAP G)
55 Carmine St (10014)
Phone 212/414-1224

Do Hwa is always crowded with Village trendsetters. It's one of those perpetually hot restaurants, mostly due to the menu, which features spicy, authentic Korean food at reasonable prices. Sure, there are more elegant, refined places to dine in the city, but Do Hwa is not trying to be anything other than what it is—a warm and lively restaurant that focuses on food and does it very well. Korean menu. Dinner, late-night. Bar. Casual attire. Reservations recommended. **$$**

★ ELEPHANT AND CASTLE (MAP G)
68 Greenwich Ave (10011)
Phone 212/243-1400
Fax 212/989-9294

Elephant and Castle feels like a bit of London here in the Big Apple. This pub, styled like those found in rainy England, is low-lit and narrow, with dark wood paneling that gives the place a warm vibe that feels welcoming and cozy. The menu is straightforward and includes easy-to-love New York-style fare like Caesar salads, omelets, burgers, and top-notch sandwiches. The beer list is impressive as well. American menu. Breakfast, lunch, dinner. Casual attire. **$**

★ FANELLI'S CAFÉ (MAP G)
94 Prince St (10012)
Phone 212/431-5744

This classic SoHo eatery dressed in dark wood, with a long, tavern-style bar up front, has been around for a dog's age (since 1872). It remains one of the neighborhood's best hideaways for honest and hearty American meals like mac and cheese, big bowls of hot chili, juicy burgers, and thick steaks. Some things are better for not changing with the times; Fanelli's is one of them. American menu. Lunch, dinner, late-night. Bar. Casual attire. **$$**

★ ★ FELIX (MAP G)
340 W Broadway (10013)
Phone 212/431-0021

Located on a busy stretch of West Broadway in SoHo (more of a mall these days than its former renegade artsy self), Felix is one of those perfect French bistros for moules frites, steak frites, or just about anything with frites. At this beautiful people scene, you'll find statuesque lovelies sipping cocktails and nibbling on salad greens while chiseled men recline and admire them. Felix is really more about the scene than the food, but if you need a place to rest after shopping, you'll do just fine with this menu of decent bistro standards. French bistro menu. Lunch, dinner. Casual attire. Outdoor seating. **$$**

★ ★ ★ FIAMMA OSTERIA (MAP G)
206 Spring St (10012)
Phone 212/653-0100

This upscale and stylish spot for refined Italian fare in SoHo is the first chef-driven restaurant from Stephen Hanson, the owner of hip, casual eateries like Blue Water Grill and Dos Caminos (see both). For this project, Hanson pulled out all the stops, creating one of the best Italian dining experiences in New York City. From homemade pastas to silky fish and tender grilled meats to the all-Italian cheese course to the massive wine list, this is a place to mark for impressing business associates and loved ones alike. Italian menu. Lunch, dinner. Bar. Casual attire. Reservations recommended. **$$$**

★ ★ FLORENT 183 (MAP G)
69 Gansevoort St (10014)
Phone 212/989-5779
Fax 212/645-2498
www.restaurantflorent.com

Florent is a late-night reveler's institution. Located in the now-hip Meatpacking District, Florent has been there for decades. It opened way back in the day when the neighborhood was filled with seedy, unsavory characters, not haute, savory meals. It is still a hotspot, serving its menu of simple, brasserie-style French fare 24-7. You can feast on boudin with caramelized onions, steak frites, eggs, and fat, juicy burgers. The best part of Florent is strolling in after a long night of partying and sitting down to a cup of coffee, a good hot meal, and a whole lot of people-watching. You'll see drag queens, truckers, supermodels, Chelsea boys, and just about every other walk of life sitting side by side, smiling, and enjoying the wonderful world that is New York. French, American menu. Breakfast, lunch, dinner, late-night. Closed Dec 25. Bar. Children's menu. Casual attire. **$$**

★ ★ GHENET RESTAURANT   (MAP H)
284 Mulberry St (10012)
Phone 212/343-1888
www.ghenet.com

Featuring the fragrant dishes of Ethiopia, Ghenet is a charming spot to explore a new and delicious cuisine. The menu reads like a wonderful textbook, with great explanations of all the menu items, many of which are savory rice dishes and lamb or beef stews to be mopped up with Frisbee-size rounds of homemade flatbread. Owned by a husband-and-wife team, this family-run establishment is all about hospitality, and you will feel like family when you leave. Ethiopian menu. Lunch, dinner. Bar. Casual attire. **$$**

★ ★ ★ ★ GOTHAM BAR & GRILL   (MAP G)
12 E 12th St (10003)
Phone 212/620-4020
Fax 212/627-7810

Alfred Portale, the chef and owner of Gotham Bar & Grill, is an icon in New York's hallowed culinary circles. The leader of the tall-food movement and a passionate advocate of seasonal Greenmarket ingredients, he has been a gastronomic force from behind the stoves at his swanky, vaulted-ceilinged Gotham Bar & Grill for more than a decade. The room is loud, energetic, and packed with a very stylish crowd at both lunch and dinner. The lively bar also draws a regular crowd of black-clad after-work revelers. You'll have no problem finding a dish with your name on it at Gotham. The menu offers something for everyone—salad, fish, pasta, poultry, beef, and game—and each dish is prepared with a bold dose of sophistication. Portale is an icon for a reason. Under his care, simple dishes are taken to new heights. And while the food isn't as tall as it used to be, size really doesn't matter. His food is just terrific. American menu. Lunch, dinner. Bar. Casual attire. **$$$$**

★ THE HOG PIT   186 (MAP G)
22 Ninth Ave (10014)
Phone 212/604-0092

Located in the Meatpacking District, the Hog Pit is a down-home barbecue spot with a roadside dive flare. This is the sort of place where licking your fingers is a must, and manners are not necessary. The menu at this rough-and-tumble watering hole includes soul food and barbecue dishes like baby-back pork ribs, and meatloaf served with sides of hush puppies, black-eyed peas, collard greens, and creamy mac and cheese. Barbecue menu. Dinner. Bar. Casual attire. **$**

★★ HOME   187 (MAP G)
20 Cornelia St (10014)
Phone 212/243-9579
Fax 212/647-9393

Owned by husband/wife team David Page (he is also executive chef) and Barbara Shin, Home is one of those rare and wonderful restaurants that wraps you in warmth, hospitality, grace, and delicious cuisine. Tucked away on a sleepy block of the West Village, Home offers diners home-style American meals made from the season's best ingredients. The restaurant has a charming outdoor garden (heated in winter) and boasts one of the most extensive all-New York State wine lists around town. (The couple's own wine, Shin Merlot, made in the North Fork of Long Island was added to the list in 2004.) This gem of a restaurant should be shared with someone as special as it is. American menu. Breakfast, lunch, dinner, brunch. Closed Dec 25. Casual attire. Outdoor seating. **$$**

★★★ HONMURA AN   188 (MAP G)
170 Mercer St (10012)
Phone 212/334-5253

New Yorkers who are over the lines at Nobu and the crowds at Yama flock to Honmura An, a delightful, serene escape in SoHo where spectacular just-made soba and udon noodles are the house specialty. Bring an appetite, because aside from the noodles, the kitchen has an in for some of the most delicious fish in the city—sashimi, sushi, and maki rolls that will force you to order more even if you have reached maximum food capacity. Japanese menu. Lunch, dinner. Closed Mon. Casual attire. **$$$**

★★ HUE ⓐ189 (MAP G)
91 Charles St (10014)
Phone 212/691-4170

Hue (pronounced "hway"), a Vietnamese-inspired Zen den for trend-setters and foodies alike, is a sexy lounge that blends elements of earth, wind, water, and fire in its sultry and serene design. The menu, emblematic of the fare served in this region of Vietnam, is spicy and spirited, heavy on chiles, lemongrass, mint, and sugar cane. The cocktail list is impressive as well, so make sure to imbibe a bit before, during, and after dinner. Vietnamese menu. Dinner. Bar. Casual attire. **$$$**

★★ IL BUCO ⓐ238 (MAP H)
47 Bond St (10012)
Phone 212/533-1932
Fax 212/533-3502

While the Italian food here is some of the most honest and well executed of its kind in the city, Il Buco is all about atmosphere. The place is low-lit and warm, filled with antiques (many for sale) and sturdy farmhouse tables that give the restaurant the soft, inviting charm of an out-of-the-way farmhouse somewhere in the mountains. Romance is always a big draw, but even if you aren't in love, go with friends. You'll have a great meal, and you'll leave feeling all warm and fuzzy inside. Italian, Mediterranean menu. Dinner. Bar. Casual attire. **$$$**

★★★ IL MULINO ⓐ190 (MAP G)
86 W 3rd St (10012)
Phone 212/673-3783
Fax 212/673-9875
www.ilmulinonewyork.com

If Tony Soprano were having dinner out in New York City, chances are he'd love Il Mulino. It's a dark relic of an Italian spot where the service is excellent and the rich, heavy food is read from long lists of specials and served in huge portions (the herb-crusted lamb chops are built for Fred Flintstone). Tableside theatrics like making a Caesar salad and filleting a whole fish give guests even more of a show. Il Mulino is a boys' club with lots of loud, brash eaters who tend to drink one too many bottles of wine. Italian menu. Lunch, dinner. Closed Sun. Bar. Reservations recommended. **$$$$**

the big apple's best chefs

Manhattan is home to extraordinary restaurants—from tiny neighborhood places with cult followings, like Lupa and Five Points; to upscale dens of haute cuisine, like Daniel, Aquavit, and Craft; to sultry hotspots like Spice Market and Pastis in the Meatpacking District. Dining out in New York is, more than ever, exhaustingly fabulous. Every day, chefs fill the city with miraculous food, blazing a mouthwatering path into the future of American cuisine.

With the opening of the Time Warner Center, New Yorkers are officially in a culinary frenzy. **Gray Kunz,** who turned seafood into high art and left diners breathless with awe at Lespinasse, is back after many false starts on his own restaurant projects. Café Gray, a luxurious shrine to seafood, features dishes that incorporate his travels across Southeast Asia with his impeccable classical French training. Joining him in the Time Warner Center are **Jean-Georges Vongerichten** of Spice Market, 66, and, of course, Jean Georges, with his latest restaurant—V Steakhouse—and West Coast culinary master **Thomas Keller** of The French Laundry, whose new restaurant, Per Se, is already on the short list of every gourmand in the city.

These patriarchs of modern American cuisine are joined by pioneers like **Mario Batali,** who started out on his mission of bringing simple, seasonal Italian cuisine to the masses with Po and grew his empire to include glorious Italian eateries like Babbo, Lupa, and Esca. With Casa Mono and Bar Jamon, he brings the same sense of adventure and passion to Spanish cuisine. The spotlight also shines on **Bobby Flay** of Mesa Grill and Bolo, **Rick Moonen** of RM, **Wayne Nish** of March, and **Charlie Palmer,** whose restaurant Aureole remains one of the city's most elegant places to dine. And how could we leave out **Daniel Boulud** (Daniel, DB Bistro), **David Bouley** (Bouley), **Jonathan Waxman** (still going strong after Jams and Washington Park with the recently opened Barbuto), and **Alfred Portale** (who just celebrated 20 years at Gotham Bar and Grill)?

But these old-timers have some serious competition. A groundswell of youthful energy and creativity is bubbling up downtown, where baby-faced chefs (many age 30 and under) are turning up the heat.

The rising star spotlight shines on **Josh DeChellis** of Sumile, who serves a thrilling brand of Japanese-inspired cuisine, including mad dishes like miso-cured brook trout with blood orange pickles. Also challenging the old guard is **Galen Zamarra,** a protégé of David Bouley. Zamarra is the chef/partner of Mas, where he showcases locally farmed seasonal ingredients in exquisite dishes like medallions of Cooperstown lamb wrapped in ramps with eggplant moussaka and a vibrant swoosh of tomato harissa.

Women are also getting in the game. **Sue Torres** owns the deliciously authentic regional Mexican restaurant Suenos. **Alison Vines Rushing,** the wildly talented chef at Jack's Luxury Oyster Bar, blends her spry Southern roots with classic French training to produce feisty dishes like braised pig cheeks served with collards finished with a lip-licking pepper vinegar and her signature New Orleans-style barbecued lobster. At the Spotted Pig, a West Village gastro-pub with a cult following, chef/partner **April Bloomfield**—plucked from London's lauded River Café by Spotted Pig owners Mario Batali and Ken Friedman—has crowds lining the sidewalks for her ricotta gnudi with brown butter and sage and beautifully blistered pork sausages with arugula and lentils.

The list of talent, young and old, is always growing. The best way to keep track of the culinary goods is to get out there and dine.

★ **INO** 191 (MAP G)
21 Bedford St (10014)
Phone 212/989-5769
Jason Denton honed his skills at Mario Batali's first hit restaurant, Po, and decided to branch off on his own and open a little nook of a wine and panini bar in the West Village. Lucky for us. His itty-bitty Italian wine bar is open from breakfast until late at night, serving a mouthwatering selection of pressed sandwiches and an extensive and reasonably priced list of Italian wines by the glass. Don't miss the signature truffled egg toast, a delicious snack anytime of the day. Deli menu. Breakfast, lunch, dinner, late-night. Bar. Casual attire. **$**

★ JOHN'S PIZZERIA (MAP G)

278 Bleecker St (10014)
Phone 212/935-2895

For many pizza aficionados, John's is the beginning, the middle, and the end. There simply is no other. This decades-old standard, located on a congested block of Bleecker Street in Greenwich Village, is almost a dive in terms of décor, but no matter; the pizza—gorgeous, piping hot, bubbling mozzarella-topped pies—is divine. To wash it down, there are carafes of wine, pitchers of beer, and not much else, but what else do you really need? Pizza. Lunch, dinner. Children's menu. Casual attire. **$**

★ KELLEY & PING (MAP G)

127 Greene St (10012)
Phone 212/228-1212

This trendy pan-Asian eatery has been filling up with slinky hipsters since the day it opened. The menu of fiery fare served at this exposed-brick, wood-paneled teashop, noodle bar, and Asian grocery reflects many regions of Asia, including China, Vietnam, Korea, and Thailand. For those who can't make a decision about what to eat first, the menu offers combination platters that include spring rolls, chicken satay, dumplings, and duck pancakes. Pan-Asian menu. Lunch, dinner. Children's menu. Casual attire. **$$**

★ ★ LA METAIRIE (MAP G)

189 W 10th St (10014)
Phone 212/989-0343
Fax 212/989-0810
www.lametairie.com

So you're looking for a quiet, romantic restaurant without hype or a scene? La Metairie fits the bill perfectly. Aside from a large dose of irresistible charm (the restaurant resembles an old French farmhouse with wood-beamed ceilings, dried flowers, and stacks of firewood), this hospitable bistro tucked into the West Village serves a delicious menu of French-Mediterranean fare with flavorful and satisfying dishes like roasted rack of lamb, a lovely Provençal-style vegetable tart, and a nice selection of wines to match. French menu. Lunch, dinner, brunch. Casual attire. **$$$**

★ LOMBARDI'S (MAP H)

32 Spring St (10012)
Phone 212/941-7994

Arguably the best pizza in the city is served at Lombardi's, a decades-old institution in Little Italy. Straight from the coal-fired oven, these pies are served piping hot and smoky from the coal's char, with thin, crispy crusts and fresh toppings. The service can be lazy but is always friendly, and the tables are tight, but who cares? This is not Mobil Four-Star dining, but Four-Star eating, and when you crave pizza and a bottle of red, nothing is better. Pizza. Lunch, dinner. Casual attire. Outdoor seating. No credit cards accepted. **$**

★★ LUCKY STRIKE (MAP G)
59 Grand St (10013)
Phone 212/941-0479

Lucky Strike was one of the first downtown hotspots from Keith McNally, the king of the distressed Parisian chic brasserie—think Balthazar (see), Pastis, and the latest entry, Schiller's Liquor Bar (see). Filled with smoky mirrors and a dressed-down vintage French vibe, Lucky Strike is still a super-cool spot to slink down into a sexy banquette and feast on perfect bistro standards like steak frites, frisée and goat cheese salad, steamed mussels, and juicy roast chicken. French, American menu. Lunch, dinner, late-night. Bar. Casual attire. **$$**

★★ LUPA (MAP G)
170 Thompson St (10012)
Phone 212/982-5089
Fax 212/982-5490
www.luparestaurant.com

There are several sure things about Lupa, celebrity chef Mario Batali's wonderfully rustic, Roman osteria: The line for a table will wind its way down Thompson Street. The heavenly spaghettini with spicy cauliflower ragout (chef/partner Mark Ladner's signature dish since he opened the place in 1999) will leave you wondering how you ever hated cauliflower. The antipasti board—a massive butcher block piled high with house-made cured meats and sausages—will leave you unable to eat these heavenly pork products anywhere else. For all these reasons and more (like wine, atmosphere, service, and style), Lupa is, hands-down, one of the most beloved spots for earthy and satisfying Roman fare. It's worth the wait. Italian menu. Lunch, dinner. Bar. Casual attire. Outdoor seating. **$$**

★★ MARKT (MAP E)
401 W 14th St (10014)
Phone 212/727-3314

Located in the Meatpacking District, the new land of the hip and fabulous set, Markt offers a taste of Belgium in a festive brasserie setting. The specialty of the house, as you might expect from a Belgian restaurant, is mussels, served in a variety of ways with crispy vats of golden fries, a nice dish to pair with one of the dozens of international beers on tap. Outdoor seating in the warmer months makes this place sizzle. Belgian, French menu. Lunch, dinner. Bar. Casual attire. Reservations recommended. Outdoor seating. **$$**

★★ MARY'S FISH CAMP (MAP G)
64 Charles St (W 4th St) (10014)
Phone 646/486-2185
Fax 646/486-6703
www.marysfishcamp.com
Mary Redding, chef/owner of this downscale neighborhood seafood shack, is a smart woman. She knows that even people who don't live in New England crave that simple style of food—fat, sweet steamers; meaty lobster rolls; salt-crusted shrimp; and all sorts of daily-catch specials. At her bustling, minimalist, forever-crowded West Village restaurant, the vibe is fun and casual and the fish is swimming-fresh and delicious. Don't mind the wait—it is so worth it. Seafood menu. Lunch, dinner. Closed Sun. Bar. Casual attire. **$$**

★★ MERCER KITCHEN (MAP G)
99 Prince St (10012)
Phone 212/966-5454
Fax 212/965-3855
Located in the ultra-chic Mercer Hotel in SoHo, this exposed-brick, subterranean hotspot is constantly teeming with celebrities and those who believe that they are celebrities merely because they are dining in their glow. The Asian-influenced American menu, under the talented direction of chef/owner Jean-Georges Vongerichten, is as swanky as the crowd, with signatures like raw tuna and wasabi pizza and yellowtail carpaccio with lime, coriander, and mint. If you haven't the slightest appetite, head over to the sexy bar, where hipsters sip martinis with abandon. American menu. Lunch, dinner, brunch. Closed holidays. Bar. Casual attire. **$$**

★★ MI COCINA (MAP G)
57 Jane St (10014)
Phone 212/627-8273
Fax 212/627-0174
www.micocinanyc.com
Authentic regional Mexican cuisine is featured at Mi Cocina, a cozy, colorful, and lively West Village favorite for outstanding dishes of our neighbor to the south. The menu offers easy-to-love dishes like crisp,

savory quesadillas and soft tacos fashioned from fresh corn tortillas filled with ancho-rubbed pulled pork, as well as vibrant regional specialties like the rich, chocolate moles of Oaxaca and the lime- and chile-marinated fish from the seaside region of Veracruz. Margaritas are wonderfully tart with lots of fresh lime juice and, of course, quite a bit of tequila. This restaurant is all about fun. Mexican menu. Lunch, dinner, brunch. Closed Dec 24-25; also two weeks in Aug. Bar. Children's menu. Casual attire. Outdoor seating. **$$**

★ ★ ★ ONE IF BY LAND, TWO IF BY SEA 204 (MAP G)
17 Barrow St (10014)
Phone 212/228-0822
www.oneifbyland.com
This classic French restaurant, set in a restored, turn-of-the-century carriage house in Greenwich Village that was once owned by Aaron Burr, is one of New York's most cherished spots for romance and other love-related special occasion dining: anniversaries, engagements, and the like. Dark and elegant, the hushed, candlelit, two-story dining room is richly appointed with antique sconces, heavy velvet drapes, oriental carpets, and blazing fireplaces. The menu here is straight-ahead French, with seasonal accompaniments and modern flourishes that add sparkle to the plate. French menu. Dinner. Closed holidays. Bar. Casual attire. Reservations recommended. **$$$$**

★ ★ OTTO 205 (MAP G)
1 Fifth Ave (10003)
Phone 212/995-9559
With Otto, celebrity chef Mario Batali has veered into casual territory, offering New Yorkers a taste of an authentic Italian pizzeria in the style of an old-fashioned European train station. Decorated with tall marble bars and dark wainscoting, this high-energy eatery is always filled with a stylish crowd that comes in for wonderful antipasti (the mussels with chile flakes is delish), can't-stop-at-one-slice prosciutto di Parma, and an amazing array of magnificent thin-crust pizzas. Gelatos are extra-special, especially the one made from olive oil that tastes like a very creamy version of heaven. Pizza. Lunch, dinner. Bar. Casual attire. **$$**

greenwich village nightlife

Greenwich Village and the surrounding areas teem with life day and night. Here are a few recommended spots for after-hours fun:

- **Blue Note.** *131 W 3rd St (10012). Phone 212/475-8592. www. bluenote.net.* For some of the world's best names in jazz, head downtown to Greenwich Village to the Blue Note. This bastion of fine jazz has played host over the years to many well-known jazz performers, as well as rising stars. Although the cover charge is higher here than at many other venues, the acts are worth it. Monday nights can be had for around $10, when the record companies promote new releases by their artists. The club also serves a variety of food and drinks if you want to grab dinner while listening to some cool tunes.

- **Hogs and Heifers Saloon.** *858 Washington St (10014). Phone 212/929-0655. www.hogsandheifers.com.* A biker bar with celebrities' bras hanging off deer antlers? Only in Manhattan. Located in the Meatpacking District (just north of Greenwich Village), this bar has hosted celebs like Julia Roberts and Drew Barrymore—who decided to leave their bras behind as eye candy for patrons. You never know who you'll run into on any given night at this wild place. In addition to downing cheap beer, you'll be treated to music and bar-top dancing. The bar also has a less-famous uptown location at 1843 First Ave, phone 212/722-8635.

- **SOB's.** *204 Varick St (10014). Phone 212/243-4940. www. sobs.com.* Lovers of the Brazilian beat, as well as hip-hop, reggae, salsa, African music, and other kinds of international sounds, have flocked since 1982 to this venerable SoHo nightclub. SOB's (Sounds of Brazil) features new performers and well-known stars who always get the crowd up and dancing. Monday nights are famous for Latin dance lessons, with an entrance fee of just $5 before 7 pm. Novices are most welcome to try out their dancing shoes during these classes. Saturday Night Samba features dancers and Brazilian performers. Every evening has a different theme and varied performers. For your dining pleasure, Latin and Brazilian cuisine are on the menu. While other clubs are quiet for the weekdays, SOB's continues to come alive.

★ PEARL OYSTER BAR (MAP G)

18 Cornelia St (10014)
Phone 212/691-8211
www.pearloysterbar.com

Rebecca Charles, who cooked for many years in New England, offers up the steamy, rustic ocean cuisine of the Atlantic Coast to New Yorkers at her newly expanded restaurant, Pearl Oyster Bar. Named for Charles's grandmother, Pearl is known for its luscious lobster rolls, fat steamers, and fresh fried fish sandwiches. While this warm, upscale New England diner-style place is always packed, it is worth the madness. If tables are taken, the warm and friendly bar is a super place to grab a fresh fish bite with a cold ale. Seafood menu. Lunch, dinner. Closed Sun. Casual attire. **$$**

★ PENANG MALAYSIAN (207) (MAP G)

109 Spring St (10012)
Phone 212/274-8883
Fax 212/925-8530
www.penangnyc.com

Crowds flock to Penang like ants to a picnic, so if you are not up for the masses, go elsewhere. Then again, the hordes of people dining here have to be coming for something, and it's not the atmosphere, which is dim and a bit cramped. It is the food, which is authentic Malaysian and spectacular. Expect bright, invigorating flavors in dishes like Kari Ayam (chicken and potatoes seasoned with red curry in a coconut milk) and Masak Nenas (chicken or beef sautéed with fresh pineapple chunks, lemongrass, mint, and red onion in a fiery curry served in a pineapple shell). Malaysian menu. Lunch, dinner. Bar. Casual attire. **$$**

★ ★ PRAVDA (208) (MAP H)

281 Lafayette St (10012)
Phone 212/226-4944

Vodka is the main theme at Pravda, a sexy, subterranean bar and lounge in SoHo. As for the menu, it pretty much matches what might be served at a Russian vodka bar: caviar, blinis, assorted smoked fish, and black bread—perfect nibbles for late-night revelers of the waif, supermodel, or straight-ahead European expatriate variety. Pravda is dark and luxuriously decadent, and it's all about the vodka. Russian menu. Dinner, late-night. Bar. Casual attire. **$$**

★ ★ PROVENCE 209 (MAP G)

38 MacDougal St (10012)
Phone 212/475-7500
Fax 212/674-7876

Located on a sleepy block in SoHo, Provence offers a taste of this sunny French region right here in the concrete jungle. It is a wonderfully charming restaurant, decorated with antiques and fresh flowers and warmed by delicate, soft lighting. In summer, don't miss out on the charming garden. Even in winter, this place is a simple delight, offering homey French dishes like steak au poivre, bouillabaisse, and bourrides. The menu is authentic Provençal, and all meals start with warm, crusty bread and are complemented by a terrific wine list. French menu. Lunch, dinner, Sat brunch. Closed holidays. Casual attire. **$$**

★ ★ RAOUL'S 210 (MAP G)

180 Prince St (10012)
Phone 212/966-3518
Fax 212/966-0205
www.raoulsrestaurant.com

Raoul's is one of the most French and most romantic restaurants in the city. Opened in the mid-1970s, this intimate little bistro has managed to retain its popularity, meaning that it is constantly packed, so reservations are a must. (Specify which room you'd like to be seated in—the downstairs main dining room is dark and sultry, while the upstairs has a bit more light and feels more civilized.) Seafood dishes are especially good here, although peppercorn steak frites will not disappoint carnivores. House pâté and frisée with cambozola cheese are also lovely menu items. French menu. Dinner, late-night. Bar. Casual attire. Reservations recommended. Outdoor seating. **$$$**
🅳

★ ★ RHONE 212 (MAP G)

63 Ganesvoort St (10014)
Phone 212/367-8440
www.rhonenyc.com

Located in the city's hipster haven known as the Meatpacking District, Rhone is an airy, chic restaurant, lounge, and wine bar that features the wines of its namesake region in France. Sitting in Rhone, with its wide, floor-to-ceiling windows thrown open to the street, you'll feel transported. With about 100 bottles and 30 glasses of Rhone varietals on the list, you'll have no problem finding a match for the ambitious French menu, which includes dishes like potato-crusted seabass and braised lamb shank. Those craving lighter fare may pair

winter and summer restaurant weeks

For one week in January and one week in June, many of the city's finest restaurants offer two- or three-course fixed-price lunches at the bargain price of $20 per person. (Yes, for New York, that is a bargain.) The exact price, if you want to get technical, corresponds to the year ($20.04 in 2004, $20.05 in 2005, etc.). Natives can't wait to get their hands on this wildly popular promotion. Check the local newspapers to see which restaurants are participating and make a reservation ASAP. This is a great way to experience top dining at great prices.

their vino with a cheese plate or caviar. French menu. Dinner. Closed Sun. Casual attire. **$$$**

★★ SAVORE ⬤213 (MAP G)
200 Spring St (10012)
Phone 212/431-1212
Fax 212/343-2605
Located on a lovely block in SoHo, Savore is a quiet little gem that offers Tuscan dining in a relaxed and authentic countryside setting. At Savore, you'll feel like you are dining in Europe. Meals are not rushed, service is leisurely, and the food is simple and delicious—the menu features earthy pastas, grilled whole fish, braised meats, and fresh salads. All you crave after dinner is a ticket to Italy. Italian menu. Lunch, dinner. Closed Dec 25. Bar. Casual attire. Outdoor seating. **$$$**

★★★ SAVOY ⬤214 (MAP H)
70 Prince St (10012)
Phone 212/219-8570
Fax 212/334-4868
Peter Hoffman, the chef and an owner of Savoy, a comfortable, urban dining spot in SoHo, has been a proponent of Greenmarket cooking for more than ten years. You'll find him with his tricycle-pulled wagon at the local farmers' markets several times a week, picking produce for his inspired menu of global fare—dishes taken from Spain, Latin America, France, Morocco, and Greece, as well as America's various regions—brought to life with simple, brilliant ingredients. The intimate dining room upstairs features an open fire-place where many of Hoffman's rustic dishes are cooked right before your eyes in the blazing hearth. French, Mediterranean menu. Lunch, dinner. Closed holidays. Bar. Casual attire. **$$$**

★ SNACK TAVERNA (MAP G)

63 Bedford St (10014)
Phone 212/920-3499

This West Village clone of Snack in SoHo offers the same authentic Greek cuisine in a cozy corner eatery decorated with hardwood floors, wide-open windows, soft candlelight, bistro tables, and vintage tin ceilings. The menu offers great pita, mezze, and lots of wonderful lamb dishes. For those who want to taste something new, different, and delicious, the wine list is all Greek. Greek menu. Lunch, dinner. Bar. Casual attire. **$**

★ ★ SOHO STEAK 216 (MAP G)

90 Thompson St (10012)
Phone 212/226-0602

This longtime standard in SoHo is a classic neighborhood bistro. Tables are crowded together, waiters are charming, wine flows from old-fashioned glass carafes, and the food consists of easy-to-devour diner fare like steak frites, moules, cassoulet, and omelettes. In the summer, the French doors open up to the street, and in winter it feels just as lively, like a warm and bustling Paris bistro. French bistro menu. Lunch, dinner, brunch. Closed holidays. Bar. Casual attire. Outdoor seating. **$$**

★ ★ SPICE MARKET 217 (MAP G)

403 W 13th St (10014)
Phone 212/675-2322
Fax 212/675-4551

Spice Market, the first project from dynamic chef duo Jean-Georges Vongerichten and Gray Kunz, is like something out of the Kasbah—an authentic jewel-toned Moroccan wonderland with raw, color-stained wood panels and benches flown in from India and waitresses decked out in saris and backless silk halter tops. As for the fare, you are in for magic on the plate. Out of the 60-foot-long open kitchen (complete with its own sultry food bar) comes fragrant, exotically spiced, family-style dishes inspired by Morocco and the Far East—satays and summer rolls, dosa and pho, and fragrant pulled-oxtail hot pots with coriander chutney and kumquats. Filled with the most fabulous crowds reclining on stunning banquettes in the amber glow of candles and lanterns, Spice Market is easily a contender for New York's hottest and tastiest scene. International menu. Lunch, dinner. Business casual attire. **$$$**

★ ★ ★ STRIP HOUSE (MAP G)
13 E 12th St (10003)
Phone 212/328-0000
www.theglaziergroup.com
If you can get over the fact that you're eating in a restaurant called Strip House (no dollar bills needed here other than to tip the folks in coat check), you will be in for some of the best beef in the city. The low-lit restaurant, swathed in deep red fabric and decorated with old black-and-white photos of burlesque stars, has a great vibe in a bordello-chic sort of way. It is sexy; tawdry it is not. The kitchen does a great job with its selection of steakhouse favorites (a half-dozen steaks and chops cooked to chin-wiping perfection) and adds some inspired sides, like truffle-scented creamed spinach, goosefat potatoes, and mixed heirloom tomatoes in season. Steak menu. Dinner. Bar. Casual attire. **$$$$**

★ ★ ★ SUMILE 219 (MAP G)
154 W 13th St (10011)
Phone 212/989-7699
There are some restaurants that try to please everyone, and then there are restaurants that dance to the beat of their own drum. Sumile, a spare, windowless, and soothing Zen space, is of the latter category. Filled with leggy lovelies reclining on pillowed banquettes next to assorted men in waiting, Sumile feels like a space out of a movie set with star-quality guests to match. The menu is a celebration of Japanese ingredients and contrasting textures, temperatures, and flavors. Josh DeChellis, the young avant-garde chef, dares to be true to his own culinary vision in the face of populist trends. His menu features innovative plates like sweet braised gulf shrimp in horseradish consommé, poached hamachi with pickled melon and nori salt, and seared duck in a frothy foie gras mousse blended with aged sake. This is not a place for timid eaters. Bring your sense of adventure, or stay home. Japanese, pan-Asian menu. Dinner. Closed Sun. Bar. Casual attire. Reservations recommended. **$$$**

★ ★ SURYA 220 (MAP G)
302 Bleecker St (10014)
Phone 212/807-7770
Surya is a sleek, low-lit restaurant and boîte that offers the most stylish setting in the city for contemporary Indian cuisine. The lounge is a chic place to stop in for a cocktail, like the house tajmapolitan (a cosmopolitan with cinnamon). After that drink, you might want to

move into the sultry dining room for dinner (beef-free), featuring a wonderful list of inspired vegetable dishes like birianyi—basmati rice perfumed with sweet spices and served with raita—and urulakilangu katrika koze, spiced potatoes and eggplant served with paratha (griddle-fried bread). In warm weather, you can dine outside in the restaurant's lovely leafy garden. Indian menu. Dinner. Bar. Casual attire. Reservations recommended. Outdoor seating. **$$**

★ ★ ★ WALLSE **221** (MAP G)

344 W 11th St (10014)
Phone 212/352-2300
www.wallserestaurant.com

Enter this charming restaurant, tucked in a sleepy corner of the West Village, and you are instantly transported to Vienna. Decorated with contemporary art and filled with close, square tables; antique furnishings; deep blue banquettes; and a long, romantic stretch of rich mahogany bar (where the cocktails are stellar), chef Kurt Gutenbrunner's Wallse is a personal and delicious ode to the hearty yet delicate cuisine of his homeland, Austria. The thin, golden-crusted Wiener schnitzel should not be missed. A terrific selection of Austrian wines complements the meal, and a nice slice of strudel will send you off on a sweet note. Austrian menu. Dinner. Bar. Casual attire. Reservations recommended. **$$$**

★ ★ ★ WOO LAE OAK **222** (MAP G)

148 Mercer St (10012)
Phone 212/925-8200
www.woolaeoaksoho.com

If you're searching for a lively spot to gather a large group for some very tasty and authentic Korean food, Woo Lae Oak is the place. This sleek, cavernous multiplex-style space offers some of the best Korean barbecue in the city. Guests grill marinated meats and seafood to a savory char on wicked-cool smokeless grill tables. The food is traditional; novices in the arena of Korean fare should seek assistance from one of the restaurant's très chic yet very friendly waiters. Meltingly creamy black cod simmered in a sweet-hot, garlicky soy sauce is a one of the restaurant's most famous plates, but there isn't a bad choice on the menu. Korean menu. Lunch, dinner. Bar. Casual attire. **$$$$**

★★ ZOË ㉓ (MAP G)

90 Prince St (10012)
Phone 212/966-6722
Fax 212/966-6718
www.zoerest.com

Thalia and Stephen Loffredo opened Zoë smack in the heart of SoHo more than ten years ago, and they have managed to maintain its chic yet comfortable American bistro vibe and, better yet, to keep the kitchen inspired. The menu is still in sync with the demanding and fickle New York palate, offering creative, sophisticated American standards painted with global accents and seasonal flourishes and an extensive, heavily American wine list. There is also a terrific cocktail list and a tempting menu of bar snacks to match, all of which makes Zoë an ideal restaurant for brunch, lunch, dinner, or just wine and a bite at the inviting bar. American menu. Lunch, dinner, brunch. Closed Mon; also July 4, Dec 25. Bar. Casual attire. **$$$**

food tasting and cultural walking tours

These two all-inclusive tours offer you a chance to sample a variety of food and drink while seeing historical sites and soaking up the city's atmosphere. The tour of the Chelsea Food Market and the Far West Village (also known as the Meatpacking District) includes tastings from Chelsea's nearly one-block-long indoor food market. This complex includes five bakeries and the largest produce shop in New York. Sample fresh milk from Hudson Valley dairies, buffalo mozzarella cheese flown in from Italy, homemade preserves, and seeded country French sourdough bread. The second tour of Greenwich Village's off-the-beaten-track sites includes stops at 15 unique food establishments, a 1920s speakeasy, and the narrowest house in the area. Tastings on this tour include homemade chocolates, Italian rice balls, Turkish falafel, and wine. All tastings are done on the go. Wear comfortable shoes and check the weather forecast before reserving a spot. *95 Christopher St (10014). Phone 212/239-1124. www.foodsofny.com.*

East Village and Lower East Side

Once considered part of the Lower East Side, the East Village is
considerably scruffier and more rambunctious than its better-known
sister to the west. For years, it was the refuge of immigrants and the
working class, but in the 1950s, struggling writers, actors, and artists—forced out of Greenwich Village by rising rents—began moving
in. First came such well-known names as Willem de Kooning and
W. H. Auden, followed by the beatniks, the hippies, the yippies, the
rock groups, the punk musicians, and the fashion designers.

Only in the 1980s did the neighborhood start to gentrify, as young
professionals moved in, bringing with them upscale restaurants and
smart shops. Ever since, New York's continuously rising rents have
forced out many of the younger, poorer, and more creative types that
the East Village was known for just two decades ago. Nonetheless,
the neighborhood has not completely succumbed and offers an
interesting mix between the cutting edge and the mainstream.

The heart of the East Village is St. Mark's Place, an always-thronging
thoroughfare where you'll find everything from punked-out musicians
to well-heeled business types, leather shops to sleek bistros. Many of the
street's noisiest addresses are between Third and Second avenues; many
of its most appealing, farther east. At the eastern end of St. Mark's Place
stretches Tompkins Square Park, once known for its drug dealers, now
for its families and jungle gyms. Some of the best of the many interesting little shops that fill the East Village can be found on Avenue A near
the park; others line 7th and 9th streets east of Second Avenue.

The neighborhood's second major thoroughfare, Second Avenue, was
home to many lively Yiddish theaters early in the 20th century. All are
gone now, but the landmark Second Avenue Deli (at 10th St)—known
for its over-stuffed sandwiches—commemorates the street's past with
stars in the sidewalk. At Second Avenue and East 10th Street is St.
Mark's-in-the-Bowery, a historic church where Peter Stuyvesant—the
last of the Dutch governors who ruled Manhattan in the 1600s—is
buried. The church is also known for its poetry readings, performance
art, and leftist politics.

On the western edge of the East Village sprawls Astor Place, home
to Cooper Union—the city's first free educational institution, now
a design school—and a huge cube sculpture oddly balanced on one
corner. On Lafayette Street at the southern end of Astor Place reigns
the Joseph Papp Public Theater, housed in an imposing columned
building that was once the Astor Library. The theater is renowned

for its first-run productions and for Shakespeare in the Park, a free festival that it produces every summer in Central Park.

Restaurants in the East Village and on the Lower East Side

★ 'INOTECA 224 (MAP H)
98 Rivington St (10002)
Phone 212/614-0473

From Jason and Joe Denton, the owners of the tiny and irresistible wine bar 'ino comes 'inoteca, a rustic, wood-beamed Italian wine bar in the super-hip Lower East Side. The wine list is all Italian, all the time—and the wonderful staff is ready, willing, and able to help walk you through it. The simply delicious menu of Italian snacks includes platters of cured meats and cheeses, panini, antipasti, and the house signature truffled egg toast. Although the fashionable crowds gather here in full force on a regular basis, the place is surprisingly attitude free. Be sure to bring your patience, because the waiting is the hardest part. Italian menu. Lunch, dinner, late-night. Bar. Casual attire. **$$**

★ 2ND AVENUE DELI 225 (MAP H)
156 Second Ave (10003)
Phone 212/677-0606
Fax 212/353-1836
www.2ndavedeli.com

Pastrami, chopped liver, and matzo brie are the kinds of things you'll find on the menu at this classic kosher delicatessen, which has been serving traditional Jewish delicacies since 1954. Tongue and corned beef are cured on the premises. If you'd like to re-create the experience after you leave New York, you can order by mail (phone toll-free 800/692-3354). Deli menu. Breakfast, lunch, dinner, late-night. Closed Jewish holidays. Casual attire. **$$**

★ ★ ALPHABET KITCHEN 226 (MAP H)
171 Avenue A (10009)
Phone 212/982-3838

Located on a now bustling block of Avenue A, Alphabet Kitchen is a warm, cozy respite from the grind of city life. This intimate restaurant is all aglow with candles and gets its rustic warmth from wooden tables, a long dark-wood bar, an open kitchen, and a serene garden with a waterfall trickling down a stone wall. The menu has a Spanish flair to it and features inspired tapas and Iberian dishes like paella, chorizo, grilled shrimp, and a succulent and bold braised lamb shank with grilled polenta. To wash it all down, Alphabet Kitchen serves a mean sangria. Fruity yet balanced, this is one beverage that should be ordered by the pitcher. Spanish, tapas menu. Dinner, late-night. Casual attire. Outdoor seating. **$$**

★★ AZUL BISTRO (MAP H)
152 Stanton St (10002)
Phone 646/602-2004
Located on a sleepy corner of Stanton Street in the now hip 'hood known as the Lower East Side, Azul Bistro is a seductive corner spot with raw wood accents and low lighting. Serving South American fare to the soft rhythms of tango music, Azul makes a nice substitute for a trip to Buenos Aires. While the menu focuses on Argentinean cuisine, you'll also find Latin American dishes like ceviche and empanadas. Grilled meats are a specialty, like the lamb and the juicy steak dotted with chimichurri sauce (think garlicky pesto). The watermelon sangria should get the night going on the right foot, no matter what you order. Latin American menu. Dinner, late-night. Bar. Casual attire. **$$**

★★ BAO 111 (MAP H)
111 Avenue C (10009)
Phone 212/254-7773
This sleek little spot on Avenue C gets major snaps for its contemporary brand of Vietnamese fare. Drawing an eclectic crowd of stilettoed babes and overly coiffed men, as well as those without a care about fashion, Bao 111 is an alluring space, marked by amber lighting and wood banquettes littered with embroidered pillows. The menu is authentic Vietnamese, tweaked for a trendy New York palate. Expect dishes like the signature short ribs skewered with lemongrass, spring rolls with mint and basil, five-spice quail, and crab and shrimp soup with noodles. Vietnamese menu. Dinner, late-night. Bar. Casual attire. **$$**

★★ BRICK LANE CURRY HOUSE (MAP H)
342 E 6th St (10003)
Phone 212/979-2900
Brick Lane Curry House is a standout in Curry Row, a stretch of East 6th Street in the East Village that's lined with Indian restaurants. Named for London's Little India dining district, Brick Lane opened to instant raves for its stunning well-spiced Indian cuisine and stylish, hip setting. Some of the dishes, like the phaal curry, are so fiery that

the house will buy you a beer if you can finish it. May the force be with you. Indian menu. Lunch, dinner, late-night. Bar. Casual attire. Reservations recommended. Outdoor seating. **$$**

🅳

★ CHIKALICIOUS (MAP H)
203 E 10th St (10003)
Phone 212/995-9511
Children are always fantasizing about skipping supper and just having dessert for dinner, and secretly, adults crave the same indulgence. With Chikalicious, the dream of an all-dessert-all-the-time meal has come true. At this quaint and sweetly decorated East Village cake, cupcake, cookie, brownie, and muffin depot, you can enjoy haute treats while watching the pastry chefs in action. Chikalicious opens at 3 pm, the perfect time for an afternoon snack, or for breaking the ultimate rule—having dessert before dinner. American menu. Dinner. Children's menu. Casual attire. **$**

🅳

★ ★ THE ELEPHANT (MAP H)
58 E 1st St (10003)
Phone 212/505-7739
Located on the burgeoning restaurant row known as 1st Street in the East Village, The Elephant is a local hipster's hangout, perpetually crowded with trendy twenty- and thirtysomethings who pile in to fill this sexy bistro's cramped tables and experience the cool, dressed-down vibe as well as the Thai-French bistro fare. The Elephant is loud, it has a great buzz, and everyone is fashionably underweight. You get the picture. Thai, French menu. Lunch, dinner. Bar. Casual attire. **$$**

★ ★ ESSEX RESTAURANT (MAP H)
120 Essex St (10002)
Phone 212/533-9616
Located on the Lower East Side, one of Manhattan's hippest 'hoods, Essex is a warm, inviting, minimalist space marked by skylights, white-washed brick, and sleek black tables. This is a perfect place for cocktails or a dinner date. The menu is as eclectic as the neighbor-hood, with dishes that pay tribute to the diverse local popula-tion—like a potato cake napoleon (a haute version of the knish), the Essex cubano sandwich, a scallop and mango ceviche, and kasha varnishkes. Late-night, the place turns into a loud and lively DJ party, the perfect prelude to the $12 brunch with all-you-can-drink Bloody Marys, mimosas, or screwdrivers. Eclectic/International menu. Dinner, late-night, brunch. Closed Mon. Bar. Casual attire. **$$**

bowlmor lanes

A New York landmark since 1938, this 42-lane, two-level "more than a bowling alley" features a restored retro bar and lounge with red booths, a yellow ceiling, and a DJ on Monday nights. Richard Nixon, Cameron Diaz, and the Rolling Stones have all bowled at these lanes, where a colorful Village crowd frequents the place until all hours. Munch on anything from nachos and hamburgers to fried calamari and grilled filet mignon in the restaurant, or have your meal brought straight to your lane. It's a funky, fun hangout, even if you don't bowl. Note that no one under 21 is admitted after 6 pm. *110 University Pl (10003). Phone 212/255-8188. www.bowlmor.com.*

★ FRANK ● 236 (MAP H)

88 Second Ave (10003)
Phone 212/420-0202
www.frankrestaurant.com

Do you love simple, rustic Italian food? Do you love reasonable prices and a cool downtown vibe? If you answered yes to these questions, you will fall in love with Frank in an instant, for the same reason that throngs of East Villagers are already swooning over this cramped, thrift-store-furnished spot for southern Italian cuisine. You'll find great food, cheap prices, and a happening crowd that doesn't mind waiting over an hour to get inside and sit elbow to elbow. Italian menu. Lunch, dinner. Bar. Casual attire. Outdoor seating. No credit cards accepted. **$$**

★ ★ ★ JEWEL BAKO ● 239 (MAP H)

239 E 5th St (10003)
Phone 212/979-1012

This is one restaurant that sounds like its name—it is a shoebox-sized jewel of a place, serving precious, glorious sushi and sashimi as well as more traditional Japanese meals. The tiny, intimate, and chic East Village sliver of a space is owned by a husband/wife team who make it their mission to ensure that your experience is marked by warm service and gracious hospitality. The restaurant's small size and popular following make reserving a table ahead of time a good plan. Japanese menu. Dinner. Closed Sun; also one week in Aug. Casual attire. Reservations recommended. **$$$**

★★ KOMODO 240 (MAP H)
186 Avenue A (10009)
Phone 212/529-2658

Located on a busy stretch of Avenue A, Komodo offers smart, flavorful Asian fusion cuisine in a chic, low-lit, Zenlike space. Expect a sexy crowd and inspired dishes—heavy on the fish—accented with Asian and Latin ingredients like soy, chiles, ginger, cilantro, garlic, and miso. Sake is a wise choice for pairing. Mexican, Asian menu. **$$**

★★ LA PAELLA 241 (MAP H)
214 E 9th St (10003)
Phone 212/598-4321

La Paella is a lively Iberian hotspot that seems tailor made for large, loud groups of friends who are on a budget. While the room could seem claustrophobic to some, with gaggles of couples and hordes of singles sitting at candlelit tables, somehow it seems cozy and quaint. The specialty is—shocker—paella, and it is offered in five different varieties, in addition to a dozen or so hot and cold tapas. Spanish, tapas menu. Dinner. Casual attire. **$$**

★★ LA PALAPA 242 (MAP H)
77 St. Marks Pl (10003)
Phone 212/777-2537

In Mexico, when the blazing afternoon sun beats down on the beach, locals flock to palapas—palm-thatched shelters where icy cervezas wash down spicy fish tacos. The seaside palapa now exists in New York City, thanks to chef/owner Barbara Sibley and her partner Margaritte Malfy, who opened La Palapa, a hacienda-style urban shelter in the East Village featuring tearfully good authentic Mexican home cooking. Expect strong, tart margaritas and plates piled high with chile-rich regional signatures like masa pockets stuffed with chicken in chipotle and grilled muscovy duck breast in a wild raspberry and ancho chile mole. Mexican menu. Lunch, dinner. Bar. Children's menu. Casual attire. Outdoor seating. **$$**

★★ LE SOUK 243 (MAP H)
47 Avenue B (10009)
Phone 212/777-5454

The fragrant and seductive foods of Morocco and Egypt are served with warm hospitality at this East Village hideaway. Amber lighting and hookah pipes lend an opium den quality to the dining room that doubles as a stage for belly dancers. The menu includes Moroccan specialties like chicken cooked in a tagine, moulekaya—a rich and savory Egyptian stew—and toasty pita bread with assorted mezze (think Middle Eastern tapas like stuffed grape leaves, hummus, baba ghanoush, and the like). A tray of deserts arrives in show-and-tell style, and the selection includes everything from chocolate mousse cake to baklava. Moroccan menu. Dinner. Bar. Casual attire. Outdoor seating. **$$**

★★ LESHKO'S **(MAP H)**
111 Avenue A (10009)
Phone 212/777-2111

This diner in the East Village is home to some of the best pierogies and Eastern European comfort food in town. Blintzes, borsht, goulash, dumplings, and the like fill out the authentic menu. The space, which feels like a fancy, sleek diner, fills up quickly with a trendy crowd that craves the restaurant's simple, warm, home-style fare. Eastern European menu. **$**

★★★ MAMLOUK **245** **(MAP H)**
211 E 4th St (10009)
Phone 212/529-3477

At Mamlouk, a cozy Middle Eastern spot in the East Village, you are taken away to an Arabic land filled with sitar music and warm, fragrant spiced meals of Middle Eastern fare. Mamlouk is an experience, from the gentle rhythmic music to the tables named "Beirut" and "Jerusalem," to the hostess who addresses everyone as "darling." While hookah smoking is now banned by New York City law, Mamlouk still manages to spirit you off to a star-filled night by the Nile. Dinner at Mamlouk is always six courses, with dishes like zatter, a flat bread topped with a paste of sesame seeds, olive oil, and thyme; vegetarian moussaka; and mjadarra, a sweet spice-flecked lentil purée served with tender grilled chicken. Middle Eastern menu. Dinner. Closed Mon. Bar. Casual attire. Outdoor seating. **$$**

★ MAX **246** **(MAP H)**
51 Avenue B (10009)
Phone 212/539-0111

Delicious and cheap are two words commonly used to describe Max, a no-frills joint for terrific red sauce, pasta, lasagna, and all sorts of dishes whose names end in parmagiana. Other words you might be tempted to throw into the mix include crowded, loud, and no-reservations, all of which means that you'd better be prepared to wait, and to shout to be heard. But that's part of Max's charm, and the food makes it worthwhile. Pizza. Lunch, dinner. Casual attire. Outdoor seating. No credit cards accepted. **$**

★★ MERMAID INN (MAP H)
96 Second Ave (10003)
Phone 212/674-5870

Jimmy Bradley (of The Red Cat and The Harrison—see both) has opened another easy-to-love restaurant with The Mermaid Inn, located in the East Village. The restaurant will take you away to the bluffs of a windswept seashore with its dark wainscoting, hurricane lamps, vintage nautical maps, and big, icy raw bar. The menu here is all seafood, all the time. The signature lobster sandwich—a sort of lobster roll gone burger—is a mess of sweet, fat, juicy lobster meat, held together by just the right bit of mayo, that is served on a wide, puffy, golden brioche bun with a mountain of skinny, crispy fries dusted with Old Bay seasoning. Bradley also offers more global takes on seafood, like a flaky, moist skate, sautéed until golden and set in a nutty puddle of white gazpacho sauce made from almonds. Mermaid has a great neighborhood vibe that makes it perfect for a first date, a last date, or dinner with the girls, the guys, your parents, or heck, even your enemies. Seafood menu. Dinner, late-night. Bar. Casual attire. Outdoor seating. **$$**

★ PAT PONG 249 (MAP H)
97 E 7th St (10009)
Phone 212/505-6454

Located in the East Village, Pat Pong serves a need in the local community for reasonably priced and very tasty Thai cuisine. The restaurant is spare and bright, with a variety of authentic dishes on the menu, including beef, pork, shrimp, and many vegetarian options. Thai menu. Lunch, dinner. Casual attire. **$**

★ PIE BY THE POUND 250 (MAP H)
124 Fourth Ave (10003)
Phone 212/475-4977

At Pie, a slick little pizza joint in the East Village, pizza by the slice is taboo. Ditto for pizza by the round pie. The pizzas at Pie are long and rectangular, with scissors used to slice off just the amount you want. You can have your very own pizza party by selecting a variety of pizzas topped with fresh and tasty ingredients like crispy potato, tallegio, and walnuts or pillowy mozzarella, tomato, and basil. Once you make your selections, your slices are weighed, and you pay by the pound, not by the slice. Pizza. Lunch, dinner. Children's menu. Casual attire. Outdoor seating. No credit cards accepted. **$**

★★ PRUNE   251 (MAP H)
54 E 1st St (10003)
Phone 212/677-6221

Prune is one of those neighborhood restaurants that immediately
seduces you. The distressed décor—very Left Bank chic—is irresistible.
The American bistro menu, devised by chef/owner Gabrielle Hamilton,
is a list of guilty pleasures, from her signature Triscuit and canned
sardine appetizer to more labor-intensive dishes like slow-cooked
lamb shanks to her leftover dish of bread heels and pulled chicken.
This is one of the most popular restaurants in New York for a reason.
Although the tables are too close together and the waits are too
long, the food is delicious, and the vibe is casual but fierce. Brunch
on Sundays is a must, even if you go just for the Bloody Marys.
Eclectic/International menu. Lunch, dinner, brunch. Bar. Casual attire.
Reservations recommended. **$$**

★★ RADIO PERFECTO   (MAP H)
190 Avenue B (10009)
Phone 212/477-3366
Fax 212/477-4336

This hip, retro eatery in the East Village is known for its terrific juicy
rotisserie chicken, but it also keeps hordes of locals happy with its
spicy blend of Mexican fusion cuisine like steak with tequila mush-
room sauce and kickin' chile-rubbed pulled pork. This is a lively joint
to hang with friends. Lines can get long, so be prepared to wait—with
a killer margarita in hand. American, Mexican menu. Dinner, Sun
brunch. Bar. Casual attire. Outdoor seating. **$$**

★★ RAGA   253 (MAP H)
433 E 6th St (10009)
Phone 212/388-0957

Located on Curry Row in the East Village, Raga sets itself apart
with its dark, sexy décor and truly innovative Indian menu. While
you'll find straight-ahead classics, the kitchen serves a few more
contemporary plates as well. Vegetable curries share menu space
with ambitious dishes like roasted lamb sirloin with cranberry beans,
mussels steeped in lemongrass, and wildly flavorful house samosas.
The kitchen is not afraid of being fresh and innovative, making eating here an exciting and delicious experience. Indian menu. Dinner.
Closed Mon. Casual attire. **$$$**

the slipper room

This club features a mix of offbeat shows and music. From quiz show nights to bawdy burlesque performances to up-and-coming bands, the Slipper Room is a fun, inexpensive place to act silly and party with your friends. The club gets a mixed late-night crowd and is the kind of place that attracts fun-loving night owls who like to party until dawn. *167 Orchard St (10002). Phone 212/253-7246. www.slipperroom.com.*

★★ **SCHILLER'S LIQUOR BAR** (MAP H)
131 Rivington St (10002)
Phone 212/260-4555
The latest hipster haunt from Keith McNally, the king of the distressed vintage Parisian brasserie, Schiller's Liquor Bar is already bursting at its authentic subway-tiled seams with the most up-to-the-minute stars and scene-seekers. It's safe to say that this formerly grungy corner of Rivington and Norfolk has never seen so much Prada and Paul Smith. American, Mediterranean menu. Breakfast, lunch, dinner, brunch. Bar. Casual attire. **$$**
🄳

★★ **SOBA-YA** 256 (MAP H)
229 E 9th St (10003)
Phone 212/533-6966
Located in the East Village, Soba-Ya is a tiny, serene space that is the neighborhood's perennial favorite for Japanese noodle dishes. Noodles come both hot and cold, plus you can watch the soba and udon noodles being cut and hung to dry like in an old laundry house. Although the noodles make the best impression, the rest of the menu deserves attention as well, like tempura vegetables with spicy curry sauce and an excellent assortment of sakes, organized on the menu to pair up with the food. Japanese menu. Lunch, dinner. Closed holidays. Casual attire. **$$**
🄳

★ ★ THE TASTING ROOM   259 (MAP H)

77 E 1st St (10003)
Phone 212/358-7831

The Tasting Room, a charming shoebox-sized East Village restaurant, features a seasonal American menu with dishes in two sizes—tasting (appetizer size) and sharing (entrée size), allowing you to sample many of the gifted chef's wonderful seasonal dishes. Chef/owner, Colin Alevras, is dedicated to shopping from local organic producers, and his passion for local products extends to the all-American, 300-bottle wine list. Colin's wife, Renee, runs the petite dining room, making you feel like you are at home in an instant. The Tasting Room is truly a jewel of a spot, perfect for intimate evenings. American menu. Dinner. Closed Sun. Casual attire. **$$$**
𝔻

★ UNITED NOODLES   260 (MAP H)

349 E 12th St (10003)
Phone 212/614-0155

At this narrow, modestly priced, ultramodern noodle house in the East Village, the menu is all about noodles—think soba and udon—spiced with an assortment of pan-Asian accents. The room, a bit space-aged in design, feels like it belongs aboard the *Starship Enterprise*, and it fills up fast with regulars who love the terrific cheap eats. Thai menu. Breakfast, lunch, dinner, brunch. Casual attire. **$**
𝔻

yonah schimmel knish bakery

Yonah Schimmel is one of the last places left in the city (Mrs. Stahl's in Brighton Beach being one of the others) to get your hands on delicious homemade knishes. Located next to the brand-new Landmark Sunshine Movie Theater (a great art house spot), Yonah's is a sweet takeout joint with old-world charm (it's a bit beat up) that will satisfy your knish craving—whether cherry cheese or plain old potato—in no time. *137 E Houston St (10002). Phone 212/477-2858. www. yonahschimmel.com.*

Lower Manhattan

Lower Manhattan consists of three diverse neighborhoods: TriBeCa, Chinatown, and the Financial District, with Little Italy sitting just to the north. Non-New Yorkers may think of this area only in relation to its most famous street, Wall Street, but much goes on in Lower Manhattan after the markets close.

Short for *Triangle Below Canal*, **TriBeCa** is a former industrial district encompassing about 40 blocks between Canal, Chambers, and West streets, and Broadway. Like SoHo, its more fashionable cousin to the north, the neighborhood discarded its working-class roots years ago and now has its share of expensive restaurants and boutiques. Upper-middle-class residents have replaced factory workers, and avant-garde establishments have replaced sweatshops.

Nonetheless, TriBeCa is much quieter than SoHo—and many other sections of Manhattan—and, in parts, still retains its 19th-century feel, complete with cobblestone streets and dusty façades. After dark, especially, much of the area seems close to deserted.

TriBeCa's main thoroughfares are Broadway, West Broadway, and Church Street, three wide roads comfortable for strolling. West Broadway was originally built to relieve the congestion of Broadway and is home to a few art galleries, including the SoHo Photo Gallery (15 White St at W Broadway), a cooperative gallery featuring the work of 100-plus members. At Church and Walker streets reigns the sleek new TriBeCa Grand, the neighborhood's first upscale hotel.

Also well known is the TriBeCa Film Center, housed in the landmark Martinson Coffee Company warehouse (375 Greenwich St at Franklin St). The center was started in 1989 by actor Robert DeNiro, who wanted to create a site where filmmakers could talk business, screen films, and socialize. Today, the center houses the offices of several major producers and the TriBeCa Grill, a chic eatery usually filled with more celebrity-watchers than celebrities. At Greenwich and Harrison streets stand the Harrison Houses, a group of nine restored Federal-style homes. Several were designed by John McComb, Jr., New York's first architect. East of the houses, at the northwest corner of Harrison and Hudson streets, find the former New York Mercantile Exchange. In this five-story building, complete with gables and a tower, $15,000 worth of eggs would change hands in an hour around the turn of the century. Today, TriBeCa is still the city's distribution center for eggs, cheese, and butter; a few remaining wholesalers cluster around Duane Park, one block south of the former exchange, between Hudson and Greenwich streets.

At the southern end of TriBeCa is Chambers Street, where you'll find the Borough of Manhattan Community College (199 Chambers St, near West St). At the western end of Chambers, cross over West Street via the TriBeCa Bridge to reach a public recreation center called Pier 25.

The only truly ethnic neighborhood still thriving in Manhattan, **Chinatown** is filled with teeming streets, jostling crowds, bustling restaurants, exotic markets, and prosperous shops. Once limited to a small enclave contained in the six blocks between the Bowery and Mulberry, Canal and Worth streets (now known as "traditional Chinatown"), it has burst these boundaries in recent years to spread north of Canal Street into Little Italy and east into the Lower East Side.

Chinatown is the perfect neighborhood for haphazard wandering. In traditional Chinatown, especially, every twist or turn of the small, winding streets brings mounds of shiny fish—live carp, eels, and crabs—piles of fresh produce—cabbage, ginger root, Chinese broccoli—or displays of pretty, colorful objects—toys, handbags, knickknacks. Bakeries selling everything from moon cakes and almond cookies to "cow ears" (chips of fried dough) and pork buns are everywhere, along with the justifiably famous Chinatown Ice Cream Factory (65 Bayard St, near Mott), selling every flavor of ice cream from ginger to mango.

Chinese men, accompanied by only a handful of women, began arriving in New York in the late 1870s. Many were former transcontinental railroad workers who came to escape the persecution they were experiencing on the West Coast. But they weren't especially welcomed on the East Coast either, and soon thereafter, the violent "tong wars" between criminal Chinese gangs helped lead to the Exclusion Acts of 1882, 1888, 1902, and 1924, forbidding further Chinese immigration. Chinatown became a "bachelor society," almost devoid of women and children—a situation that continued until the lifting of immigration quotas in 1965.

Today, Chinatown's estimated population of 100,000 is made up of two especially large groups—the well-established Cantonese community, who have been in New York for over a century, and the Fujianese community, a much newer and poorer immigration group who come from the Fujian Province on the southern coast of mainland China. The Cantonese own many of the prosperous shops and restaurants in traditional Chinatown, whereas the Fujianese have set up rice-noodle shops, herbal medicine shops, and outdoor markets along Broadway and neighboring streets between Canal Street and the Manhattan Bridge.

To learn more about the history of Chinatown, visit the Museum of Chinese in the Americas (70 Mulberry St at Bayard). To get a good meal, explore almost any street, with Mott Street—the neighborhood's main thoroughfare—holding an especially large number. Pell Street is especially known for its barber and beauty shops and for its Buddhist Temple (4 Pell St). The neighborhood's biggest festival is the Chinese New Year, celebrated between mid-January and early February; then, the streets come even more alive than usual with dragon dances, lion dances, and fireworks.

Restaurants in Lower Manhattan

★ 88 PALACE (MAP H)
88 E Broadway (10002)
Phone 212/941-8886
If you are craving dim sum, or a perfect Chinese tea luncheon, consider stopping at 88 Palace, a bustling Chinese restaurant featuring a delicious and authentic selection of dim sum and house-made soups, fish, meats, and rice dishes. The restaurant is a favorite among Chinatown's locals, and many of the staff don't speak much English, but no matter. The point-to-order method works well. Chinese menu. **$**

★ ★ ★ BAYARD'S (MAP H)
1 Hanover Sq (10004)
Phone 212/514-9454
www.bayards.com
Fresh flowers, a rare Buddha collection, crafted ship models, stately antiques, fine china, mahogany double staircases, and hand-carved working fireplaces are just some of the charming details you will encounter at Bayard's—an exquisite French-American restaurant located in the India House, a historic landmark building located at One Hanover Square, near Wall Street. To match the surroundings,

executive chef Eberhard Müller delivers a magnificent menu that showcases the seasons. Indeed, most of the menu's fruits and vegetables are hand-harvested from Satur Farms—the 50-acre family farm chef Müller and his wife own in the North Fork of Long Island—making every bite a delicious discovery of the land. Signatures include Fisher's Island oysters, served warm with champagne sauce and osetra caviar, Maine lobster with black trumpet mushrooms and pea shoots, and dry-aged New York strip steak with cipolini onions, creamed spinach, and fingerling potatoes. American menu. Dinner. Bar. Casual attire. **$$$**

★★★★ BOULEY 263 (MAP G)
120 W Broadway (10013)
Phone 212/964-2525
www.bouley.net

After a hiatus following the terrorist attacks of 9/11, acclaimed chef David Bouley is back behind the stoves at his temple of haute French gastronomy. Housed in the newly renovated and impeccably decorated space that was once his more casual bistro, Bouley Bakery, the new Bouley is taking a stab at winning back Manhattan's most discerning and divine diners—and succeeding. The elegant and oh-so-civilized place is packed with well-heeled foodies, fashionistas, political pundits, and celebs who understand that a night in Bouley's care is nothing short of miraculous. Bouley delivers on every front: the service is charming, the seasonal ingredients are stunning, the French technique is impeccable, and his kitchen magic is nothing short of brilliant. American menu. Lunch, dinner. Closed the first week of Sept. Casual attire. **$$$$**

★★★ CAPSOUTO FRERES 264 (MAP G)
451 Washington St (10013)
Phone 212/966-4900
Fax 212/925-5296
www.capsoutofreres.com

As its name suggests, Capsouto Freres is owned by the Capsouto brothers. What you may not get from its name is that this is a lovely choice for a special night on the town. Set in a restored 1891 factory in TriBeCa, it has an understated elegance, with original beam floors, exposed brick walls, magnificent open windows, and sunny floral arrangements. The restaurant is a neighborhood institution, having survived for years in this once deserted and now hip part of town. The eclectic menu features an impressive variety of choices, from calf's liver in sherry vinegar sauce to cassoulet, salmon with green herb sauce, and wild Scottish venison. If you are wandering around downtown on a Sunday, the brunch here is a great choice, with omelets and excellent French toast at reasonable prices. Contemporary French menu. Lunch, dinner, brunch. Bar. Casual attire. Outdoor seating. **$$$**

★ ★ ★ CHANTERELLE FRENCH RESTAURANT (MAP G)

2 Harrison St (10013)
Phone 212/966-6960
www.chanterellenyc.com

Long hailed as one of the most romantic restaurants in New York City, Chanterelle has been the scene of many bent-knee, velvet-box-in-hand proposals. Indeed, this restaurant is a New York dining icon. But Chanterelle, located on a sleepy corner in TriBeCa, offers much more than romance. Husband-and-wife owners David and Karen Waltuck (he is the chef, she works the room) have been serving brilliant, unfussy, modern French fare for more than 20 years. The menu, handwritten each week, reflects the best products available from local greenmarkets and regional farmers, and the award-winning wine list makes meals here even more memorable. French menu. Lunch, dinner. Closed Sun; holidays; also the first week in July. Reservations recommended. **$$$$**

★ ★ ★ ★ DANUBE 266 (MAP G)

30 Hudson St (10013)
Phone 212/791-3771
Fax 212/267-1526
www.bouley.net

Danube is the creation of David Bouley, the inspired and famed chef who has created many notable New York establishments. It is a stunning place to spend an evening. It has the feel of an old Austrian castle, with dark wood; deep, plush banquettes; and soft, warm lighting. It repeatedly draws a glamorous crowd that craves Bouley's masterful technique and creativity. Bouley's regal, majestic restaurant celebrates the cuisine of Austria within the framework of a New York restaurant. On the menu, you'll find a couple of Austrian-inspired dishes interspersed with lighter, modern, and truly exciting seasonal New American dishes. Bouley has a rare talent, and his food is spectacular, though not for those who are fearful of taking some risks at dinner. This is not a creamed-corn-and-roast-chicken place. The staff offers refined service, and the wine list is eclectic and extensive. As you would expect, it includes some gems from Austria. The cocktail lounge at Danube is a perfect spot to relax and get cozy before or after dinner. It is low-lit and romantic, and the bartenders serve delicious, perfectly balanced cocktails. American, Austrian menu. Dinner. Bar. Casual attire. Reservations recommended. **$$$$**

★ DIM SUM GO GO **(MAP H)**
5 E Broadway (10038)
Phone 212/732-0796

Looking for a chic little spot to have a quick bite of inventive Chinese fare? Dim Sum Go Go is your place. This super-mod, super-hip, minimalist spot sports a terrific menu of Chinese snacks like fresh soybeans with pickled vegetables, as well as homemade noodles and bigger dishes like the Garlicky Go Go roast chicken, with a taut golden skin. On weekends, you can sample fresh steamed dumplings with fillings like shark fin and crunchy white sea fungus. Come on, live a little. Dim Sum, Chinese menu. Lunch, dinner. Casual attire. **$**

★ ★ GIGINO TRATTORIA **(MAP G)**
323 Greenwich St (10013)
Phone 212/431-1112
Fax 212/226-3855
www.giginony.com

Gigino Trattoria has been a local favorite for Italian fare since 1983. Owned by Phil Suarez and Bob Giraldi (partners in Patria and Jean-Georges), this TriBeCa gem offers casual, comfortable dining and the tasty, home-style cooking of an authentic Italian trattoria. Generous bowls of pasta, brick-oven pizzas, seasonal produce, game, fish, and meats round out the appealing menu. Italian menu. Lunch, dinner. Closed Jan 1, Memorial Day, Dec 25. Bar. Casual attire. Outdoor seating. **$$$**

★ GREAT NY NOODLETOWN **(MAP H)**
28 1/2 Bowery (10013)
Phone 212/349-0923

It would be impossible to pass NY Noodletown off as your own private discovery. Anointed years ago by rave reviews, this bright corner spot continues to draw crowds all day and late into the night. Press in and enjoy the bustle. This is not the place for complicated dishes. Treat NY Noodletown like a Chinese version of your local coffee shop: avoid preparations that have more than two ingredients and you'll do well. The roast meats are top-notch, particularly the crisp-skinned baby pig. Greens are basic and fresh, and perfectly cooked noodles, naturally, are a strong point. When summer comes, the salt-baked soft-shell crab is a must, juicy and tasting of the sea, as much of a New York ritual as a trip to Coney Island. Chinese menu. Lunch, dinner. Casual attire. No credit cards accepted. **$**

★ ★ ★ THE HARRISON 270 (MAP G)
355 Greenwich St (10013)
Phone 212/274-9310
www.theharrison.com
With its amber lighting, hardwood floors, wainscoting, and inviting bar, The Harrison is one of those restaurants that makes you feel like never leaving. Owned by Jimmy Bradley and Danny Abrams, the savvy team behind The Red Cat and the Mermaid Inn (see both), this Mediterranean-accented restaurant is a charming neighborhood hotspot with a chic clientele. The signature fried clams with fried slivered rounds of lemon are a must have, whether seated at the happening bar or at one of the well-spaced, linen-topped tables. American menu. Dinner. Bar. Casual attire. Outdoor seating. **$$$**

★ ★ IL CORTILE 271 (MAP H)
125 Mulberry St (10013)
Phone 212/226-6060
Fax 212/431-7283
www.ilcortile.com
Il Cortile has been a pillar of Italian cuisine in Little Italy since 1975. This neighborhood tratorria, located amid the bustling streets of Little Italy and Chinatown, offers heaps of authentic Italian fare—antipasti, pasta, fish, poultry, and beef, prepared with love and with a nod to the traditions of the old country. The restaurant has a sunny indoor garden room that makes you feel like you are dining somewhere on the Mediterranean. Italian menu. Lunch, dinner. Bar. Closed Thanksgiving, Dec 24-25. Casual attire. Reservations recommended. **$$$**

★ JING FONG 272 (MAP H)
20 Elizabeth St (10013)
Phone 212/964-5256
Jing Fong is a dim sum lover's paradise. This vast banquet hall offers mountains of delicious dim sum from carts, but also allows those too hungry to wait for a cart to hover by the kitchen to snatch up plates of fresh morsels—dumplings, buns, rolls—as they are cooked. In addition, you can opt for a feast from a buffet of raw seafood and have it cooked to order. Don't leave without sampling one of the tiny

white mochi desserts—coconut shells filled with black sesame paste that tastes like peanut butter. Asian menu. Breakfast, lunch, dinner. Casual attire. **$**

---

the feast of san gennaro

More than 75 years old, this giant street festival in Little Italy salutes the patron saint of Naples with a celebratory Mass and a candlelit procession of the Statue of the Saint. More than a million people descend on Little Italy over 11 days in mid-September to feast on food from the old country, watch the parades, enjoy the live music, and compete for the title of cannoli-eating champion. *Mulberry St between Canal and Houston sts (10013). Phone 212/768-9320. www.sangennaro.org.*

★ ★ ★ LAYLA **(MAP G)**
211 W Broadway (10013)
Phone 212/431-0700
Fax 212/431-0920
www.myriadrestaurantgroup.com
The foods of the Mediterranean and Middle East are the focus at Layla, Drew Nieporent's sultry, Arabian Nights-style restaurant that offers belly dancing nightly, with wickedly good cocktails to inspire diners to join in. (You might discover a new talent.) In between swilling and dancing, you can feast on soft, puffy, tandoor-oven-baked breads to dip into the restaurant's delicious signature mezze like hummus, muhammara, and tzatziki. The menu keeps the taste buds' interest piqued with a wide selection of robust, aromatic-spiced dishes like tagine of duck and harissa-marinated baby chicken kabobs with sweet, jeweled rice and toasted almonds. Mediterranean, Middle Eastern menu. Lunch, dinner. Closed Sun; holidays. Bar. Outdoor seating. **$$**

★ ★ ★ MONTRACHET 274 **(MAP G)**
239 W Broadway (10013)
Phone 212/219-2777
Fax 212/274-9508
www.myriadrestaurantgroup.com
Montrachet is the first restaurant from restaurateur Drew Nieporent. (He also owns Nobu and TriBeCa Grill, among others.) While the restaurant is pushing 20, it is still one of the most prized and romantic dining experiences to be had in New York City. The seasonal, modern French-

American menu and the warm, attentive service remain as fresh and inspired as they were on day one. Montrachet's wine list has been met with critical acclaim and marries well with the sophisticated fare, making for delightful dining. French, American menu. Lunch, dinner. Closed Sun; holidays. Bar. Casual attire. Reservations recommended. **$$$**
Ⓓ

★★ NAM 275 (MAP G)
110 Reade St (10013)
Phone 212/267-1777
The fresh, spicy flavors of Vietnam are on the menu at Nam, a chic, breezy, bamboo-accented restaurant in TriBeCa. Giving a city-slicker kick to this Asian cuisine, Nam offers Vietnamese classics like noodle dishes, soups, spring rolls, green papaya salads, and simply magnificent seafood dishes. The crispy whole red snapper is slathered in chile and lime and served with steamed jasmine rice, while the steamed sea bass is a fleshy, sweet dish, accompanied by stewed tomatoes. Vietnamese menu. Lunch, dinner. Bar. Casual attire. **$$**

★ NHA TRANG CENTRE 276 (MAP H)
148 Centre St (10013)
Phone 212/941-9292
New Yorkers who are forced to serve jury duty look forward to it for one reason and one reason only—not their chance to serve their community, but because the courthouses are near Nha Trang, a frenetic, fast-paced, cafeteria-style spot serving some of the best authentic Vietnamese fare going. The place is generally chaotic, especially at lunch (be prepared to share your table with people you don't know), but the experience is a great one nonetheless, considering that you can feast on excellent bowls of pho, spicy spring rolls stuffed with basil and shrimp, and delicious dishes like banh xeo, crispy yellow rice-flower pancakes wrapped around sautéed mushrooms, shrimp, and sprouts. Vietnamese menu. Lunch, dinner. Casual attire. **$**

★ NICE 277 (MAP H)
35 E Broadway (10002)
Phone 212/406-9510
In classic Chinatown form, Nice, a Cantonese restaurant with a following, serves loads of delicious steaming dim sum out of traditional trolley carts. The crowds come out in numbers on the weekends, making this massive place feel a tad scary, so try to sneak in during the week or be prepared to feel claustrophobic. Chinese menu. Lunch, dinner. Casual attire. **$**

★ ★ ★ NOBU `278` (MAP G)

105 Hudson St (10013)
Phone 212/219-0500
Fax 212/219-1441

There is a place in New York where folks have been known to cry when they eat because the food is so good. That place is Nobu. The lively room is decorated with seaweed-like wall coverings and bamboo poles and has a serene vibe despite the high-energy, high-fashion crowd that packs in nightly for some of famed chef Nobu Matsuhisa's simply spectacular sushi and unique brand of Asian-Latin-inspired seafood. Lime, soy, chiles, miso, cilantro, and ginger are flavors frequently employed to accent many of the chef's succulent creations. A signature dish is black cod with miso, and it's a signature for good reason. The fish is coated in a sweet miso glaze, and once it enters your mouth, it slowly vaporizes, melting away like ice over a flame. The omakase ("chef's choice") menu is an option for those with an adventurous palate. If you can't get a reservation (call well in advance and be prepared for many busy signals), you can always try to sneak in at the sushi bar. Be warned, though; once you eat sushi here, it's hard to eat it anywhere else. *Secret Inspector's Notes: Due to Nobu's popularity, a simpler version that does not take reservations was opened nearby. Next Door Nobu is a great alternative if you can't get through on Nobu's reservations line. They don't take reservations but will call you on your cell phone as you endure the wait at a nearby watering hole.* Japanese menu. Lunch, dinner. Closed holidays. Casual attire. Reservations recommended. **$$$$**

south street seaport

This 12-block area was restored to display the city's maritime history, with an emphasis on South Street in the days of sailing vessels. The South Street Museum piers at South and Fulton streets now moor the *Ambrose*, a lightship (1908); the *Lettie G. Howard*, a Gloucester fishing schooner (1893); the fully-rigged *Wavertree* (1885); the *Peking*, a German four-masted barque (1911); and the *Pioneer*, a schooner (1885). Permanent and changing maritime exhibits include models, prints, photos, and artifacts. If history isn't your thing, this festival marketplace has more than 100 souvenir and mall-type stores, like Abercrombie & Fitch and the Body Shop, as well as 35 mostly casual restaurants. Don't miss the three-story glass and steel Pier 17 Pavilion, which extends into the East River and offers great views of the Brooklyn Bridge and New York Harbor. *Fulton and Water sts, at the East River. Phone 212/732-7678. www.southstreetseaport.com.*

★ NYONYA 279 (MAP H)
194 Grand St (10013)
Phone 212/334-3669

Serving some of the best Malaysian fare in town, Nyonya is a slightly chaotic spot with a vibrant and authentic menu. While the atmosphere is not exactly elegant (it feels like a diner), this restaurant is an ideal place for a group of friends to sit down to dinner and taste the variety of refreshing Malaysian dishes on the menu. But be sure to come on an empty stomach, as the food is too good not to lick plates clean. Malaysian menu. Lunch, dinner. Casual attire. Reservations recommended. No credit cards accepted. **$**

★★ ODEON 280 (MAP G)
145 W Broadway (10013)
Phone 212/233-0507
Fax 212/406-1962

Odeon is the original hipster diner. This sleek, retro space, located in TriBeCa, has been serving delicious brasserie fare like perfect frisée au lardons, thick and juicy burgers, and steak frites to the masses of fabulous locals for almost two decades. Brunch is a must, but if you are in the area late at night, it is also a hotspot to grab a bite to tide you over until morning. Celebrities of the Robert DeNiro caliber are bound to be tucked into booths, so keep an eye out. American, French menu. Lunch, dinner, Sun brunch, late-night. Bar. Children's menu. Casual attire. Outdoor seating. **$$**

★★ PING'S 281 (MAP H)
22 Mott St (10013)
Phone 212/602-9988

Be sure to pack your sense of culinary adventure when you go to Ping's, a Chinatown favorite for dim sum and gorgeous live seafood cooked up to order. The room is usually filled to capacity with Chinese families and lawyers on break from arguing at the nearby courthouses, but do not be deterred by the crowds. The steamed pork buns alone make Ping's worth the wait. Chinese menu. Lunch, dinner. Casual attire. **$$**

★ SWEET AND TART 282 (MAP H)
20 Mott St (10013)
Phone 212/964-0380
Fax 212/571-7696
www.sweetandtart.com

In the heart of Chinatown, you will find Sweet and Tart, an authentic Hong Kong-style Chinese restaurant that offers enough variety to please an army of eaters. The space has three levels: the upper level is crowded with families, while the ground floor soda-fountain diner is more for Gen Xers. The menu sticks to impeccably prepared Cantonese classics and delicious dim sum, and also offers dishes from Thailand and Japan. Chinese menu. Lunch, dinner, late-night. Casual attire. Reservations recommended. **$**

🅳

★ ★ ★ TRIBECA GRILL   **(MAP G)**
375 Greenwich St (10013)
Phone 212/941-3900
Fax 212/941-3915
This New York icon from super-restaurateur Drew Nieporent (Nobu, Montrachet—see both) and partner Robert DeNiro is a shining example of what a restaurant should offer. First, hospitality—the service is warm, attentive, and knowledgeable without an ounce of pretension. Second, atmosphere—the Grill is a comfortable, urban dining room with exposed brick walls, oil paintings by Robert DeNiro, Sr., and a magnificent cherry wood, wraparound bar that looks like it fell off the set of *Cheers*. Third, food—the kitchen features an approachable, contemporary, seasonal American menu with dishes for every type of diner, from wild foodies to simple roast chicken eaters. Finally, wine—TriBeCa Grill offers an impressive and diverse wine program led by David Gordon, who has earned the restaurant much praise and admiration near and far. TriBeCa Grill, which is more than ten years old, remains a winner on all counts. American menu. Dinner, Sun brunch. Bar. Casual attire. **$$$**

murray's cheese

For the best gourmet cheese selection in the city, pop into this 63-year-old New York institution. The shop will entice any discerning palate with its 250 varieties of domestic and imported cheeses, as well as a selection of breads, olives, antipasti, and personalized gift baskets. Murray's also has a second, newer location in Midtown at 73 Grand Central Terminal. *257 Bleecker St (10014). At Cornelia St between Sixth and Seventh aves. Phone toll-free 888/692-4339. www.murrayscheese.com.*

Bronx

Jonas Bronck, a Swedish settler, bought 500 acres of land from the Dutch in 1639, lending his name to the future borough. Locally it is always referred to as "the Bronx," never simply "Bronx." It is the only borough in New York City on the North American continent (the others are all on islands).

Restaurants in the Bronx

★ CHARLIE'S INN 284 (MAP B)
2711 Harding Ave (10465)
Phone 718/931-9727
This classic old-timer has been around since the 1930s and is still serving authentic German fare and one of the heartiest all-you-can-eat Sunday brunches in the Bronx, if not the entire city. While the menu includes stomach-filling fare like sauerbraten, Wiener schnitzel, and sausages, it is also stocked with lighter continental dishes like pasta, baked clams, fish, and chicken. In the summer, the restaurant opens its outdoor beer garden on Sundays, giving you the perfect excuse to be lazy all day long. American, German menu. Lunch, dinner, Sun brunch. Closed Mon. Bar. Children's menu. Casual attire. Outdoor seating. **$$**

★ ★ EMILIA'S 285 (MAP A)
2331 Arthur Ave (10458)
Phone 718/367-5915
Fax 718/367-1483
arthuravenuebronx.com/emilia's.htm
The Bronx is certainly not short on Italian food, but Emilia's takes traditional fare and makes it shine, without breaking the bank. Lunch specials are the reason many locals flock here, but dinner is also a sure thing, with a generous menu of pastas, fish, and meat. Emilia's serves a killer tiramisu with a healthy dose of alcohol in the sponge cake that will make you want to return and have dessert for dinner. Italian menu. Lunch, dinner. Closed Mon; Dec 25. Bar. **$$**

★ FEEDING TREE (MAP A)

892 Gerard Ave (10452)
Phone 718/293-5025

Feeding Tree is one of New York's most beloved Jamaican restaurants, located within a home run's distance of Yankee Stadium. At this friendly and lively joint, a steel drum plays in the background, and you can almost feel the Caribbean sun on your face. This is the sort of spot to tuck a napkin into your collar and fill up on jerk chicken, stewed kingfish, oxtail, curried goat, and crisp golden patties filled with spiced meat—the perfect snack to grab before a game. Caribbean menu. Breakfast, lunch, dinner. Children's menu. Casual attire. **$**

★ ★ JIMMY'S BRONX CAFE (MAP A)

281 W Fordham Rd (10468)
Phone 718/329-2000

This legendary Bronx restaurant and bar from the venerable Jimmy Rodriguez has a cult following, and is especially nutty when the Yankees are playing. This is one of the few velvet rope joints in the Bronx, with a boisterous bar and a cavernous 450-seat restaurant jammed with sports, music, and celebrities. The Caribbean-Latin menu is an ode to Rodriguez's Latin-American heritage, and the kitchen turns out impressively tasty and flavorful food. Don't expect a peaceful night here; aside from the din of the crowds and the thumping beat of the music, the place is also a sports bar and boasts more than 15 televisions. Caribbean, Latin menu. Lunch, dinner, late-night. Bar. Casual attire. **$$**

arthur avenue

Old-world charm abounds in this charming section of the Bronx, which has been the home of generations of Italian families. Seven square blocks make up the **Arthur Avenue Retail Market,** an Italian-American food oasis. One of the last indoor markets in New York, opened by Mayor Fiorello LaGuardia in the 1940s, it thrives to this day as a bustling cacophony of sights, sounds, and smells. Shoppers entering through the rickety doors can only think of the possibilities lined up before them as they begin to scan the stands. It is a mecca for serious cooks. The crowded storefronts of mom-and-pop shops sell everything from fine Italian wines and homemade pastas to imported cheeses and meats to gifts and cookware.

And then there are the mouthwatering restaurants, pizza parlors, and pastry shops—some dating to the 1920s—to entice your palate. Have a blast with the two greengrocer brothers whose stand dominates the southern end of the market. Their knowledge of produce and preparation techniques equals any high-priced culinary education. If you are lucky enough to have a garden and are looking for heirloom seed varieties, see **Joe Liberatore's** *Garden of Plenty* (2344 Arthur Ave, phone 718/733-7960) located inside the market. They carry seeds ideal for the Italian kitchen, difficult to find elsewhere. Do not miss the fresh, locally made (farm and production in Pennsylvania) cheeses and velvety ricotta at **S. Calandra & Sons** (2314 Arthur Ave, phone 718/365-7572), or the pungent scent that welcomes you at **Calabria Pork Store** (2338 Arthur Ave, phone 718/367-5145). Be sure to look up at the gems hanging from the ceiling! The bread sold at **Terranova Bakery** (691 E 187th St, phone 718/733-3827) is a feast in itself. **Marie's Roasted Coffee** (2378 Arthur Ave, phone 718/295-0514) will make you disdain any other espresso blend. Get a pound, put it in the car, and no matter how long it takes you to get home, that fresh-ground coffee smell will be overwhelming.

Forget calories when shopping here, as the Mediterranean diet offers excellent health benefits, and you won't break the bank in these reasonably priced eateries and shops. Many of the nearly 200 shops around this densely packed area do not take credit cards, so have plenty of cash on hand. If all the shopping and snooping has made you hungry, one of the best restaurants to enjoy an Italian-American meal is **Roberto's** (632 E 186th St, phone 718/733-9503). And if you desire a little culture with your stuffed tummy, there's even a small repertory theater, the **Belmont Playhouse,** dedicated to works by Italian writers. Additionally, the **Italian Cultural Center,** part of the New York Library, has an amazing collection of Italian books, newspapers, and films.

What is most fascinating about the evolution of this historic market is that although the products sold and the dishes served are primarily consumed by Americans of Italian descent, the area serves a nondistinct community. Fordham University students prowl at all hours for sustenance; families coming from or going to the nearby Bronx Zoo or Botanical Garden come by to stock up on tasty morsels for their picnics or for their dining tables back in Manhattan. And any foodie in the area worth his or her salt makes a regular pilgrimage.

★ ★ ★ LE REFUGE INN (MAP B)

620 City Island Ave (10464)
Phone 718/885-2478

Le Refuge Inn is, as its name suggests, a refuge. This 19th-century Victorian manor house on historic City Island is a cozy chalet of warmth, peace, and romance, perfect for melting away stress. Surrounded by the waters of the Long Island Sound, you will instantly be transported to the French countryside once tucked inside the elegant antique-filled dining room and treated to a menu of wonderful classics like bouillabaisse and duck à l'orange. French menu. Dinner. Closed Mon. Bar. Children's menu. Jacket required. Reservations recommended. Outdoor seating. **$$**

🄳

★ ★ LOBSTER BOX (MAP B)

34 City Island Ave (10464)
Phone 718/885-1952
Fax 718/885-3232
www.lobsterbox.com

The Lobster Box is a historic City Island landmark that, true to its name, offers its specialty, fresh lobster, any way you like it. Choices include broiled, steamed, stuffed, fra diavolo, or marinara, and every preparation is delicious. Pasta is also on the menu, many laden with meaty bits of lobster meat, like the lobster ravioli with sun-dried tomatoes and basil cream sauce. The Lobster Box is an easy-to-love place where the portions are generous and the expansive river views are mesmerizing. Seafood menu. Lunch, dinner. Bar. Casual attire. Valet parking. **$$**

★ ★ ROBERTO'S TRATTORIA (MAP A)

632 Crescent Ave (10458)
Phone 718/733-9503

Set in the Italian enclave of the Bronx, Roberto's Trattoria is not high on décor or elegant atmosphere, but it is filled with terrific food prepared in the Positano style. The kitchen is sure-handed and sends out home-style dishes like grilled calamari and assorted pastas, as well as heartier fare like tender short ribs. For a real treat, ask the kitchen to prepare the house specialty, a four-course meal with dishes from Roberto's native Amalfi coast that will bring applause to your table. Italian menu. Lunch, dinner. Closed Mon. Casual attire. Outdoor seating. **$$**

★ VENICE RESTAURANT AND PIZZERIA 291 (MAP A)

772 E 149th St (10466)
Phone 718/585-5164

Old-school pizza and pasta are what you'll find at Venice, a little short on décor but long on value and honest Italian-American food. Founded more than 50 years ago, this restaurant has a menu that focuses on seafood but also offers whole thin-crust pies. Italian menu, pizza. Lunch, dinner. Children's menu. Casual attire. **$**

★ VERNON'S NEW JERK HOUSE 292 (MAP B)

987 E 223rd St (10466)
Phone 718/655-8348

As the name suggests, Caribbean fare is the specialty of the house at Vernon's New Jerk House, a lively spot in the Bronx with an easy vibe and a loyal community following. Dinner here can mean a ginger beer and a bowl of curried goat, or a plate of sweet-spiced jerk chicken with rice and beans. Take this advice: if you have never tried jerk, make a special trip; it doesn't get much better than this, at least without a plane ticket. Caribbean menu. Lunch, dinner. Bar. Casual attire. No credit cards accepted. **$**

Brooklyn

Many of the novels, plays, films, and television shows about New York City—ranging from *Death of a Salesman* to *The Honeymooners*—are set in Brooklyn rather than Manhattan, perhaps because of the widely differing characters of these two boroughs. While Manhattan is world-class in sophistication and influence, Brooklyn is famous for such things as the hot dogs on Coney Island, and always has been quintessentially American.

Yet there is much more to Brooklyn than the popular stereotype. Manhattanites flock to performances at the renowned Brooklyn Academy of Music, and the Egyptology collection at the Brooklyn Museum compares with those in London and Cairo. Brooklyn's beautiful Prospect Park was designed by Olmsted and Vaux, who considered it more beautiful than another park they designed—Central Park in Manhattan.

As the most heavily populated borough, Brooklyn handles about 40 percent of New York City's vast shipping industry. It was pieced together from 25 independent villages and fought valiantly before allowing itself to be taken into New York City in 1898.

Restaurants in Brooklyn

★★ 360   293 (MAP J)
360 Van Brunt St (11231)
Phone 718/246-0360
360 is an off-the-beaten-path neighborhood spot that may take a bit of effort to find, but those who persevere will be rewarded. The dining room is marked by artisan woodwork as well as by partner Arnaud Erhart's charming ways that welcome you inside, help you make a wine selection from the mostly organic list, and ensure that your night here is memorable. But the charm doesn't just come from the dining room; the kitchen also doles out the goods in the form of a three-course prix fixe menu that changes daily, with dishes like roasted scallops with leek fondue, hanger steak, and à la carte, wine-friendly bites like oysters and charcuterie. French menu. Dinner. Closed Mon-Wed. Bar. Casual attire. Reservations recommended. Outdoor seating. No credit cards accepted. **$$**

★ A TABLE 294 (MAP K)
171 Lafayette Ave (11238)
Phone 718/935-9121

A Table offers a charming slice of the Mediterranean just a stone's throw from the Brooklyn Academy of Music in the heart of Fort Greene. Sunny, sponge-painted walls and wide windows (with nooks to curl up in and have a morning snack) give the place breezy warmth, and the communal farmhouse table lends a charming, convivial feel. The menu offers something for everyone, like Argentine shell steak, slow-roasted lamb shank, foie gras, a raw bar, and fish dishes like sea bass. Mediterranean menu. Breakfast, lunch, dinner. Closed Mon. Bar. Casual attire. Reservations recommended. **$$**

★ ★ AL DI LA TRATTORIA 295 (MAP J)
248 Fifth St (11215)
Phone 718/636-8888

Al Di La is a charming neighborhood trattoria decorated with antiques and crowded with candlelit tables of locals laughing and inhaling the delicious Venetian cuisine. It is owned by a husband-and-wife team (he runs the room, she is in the kitchen) who have amassed a strong fan base, making lines inevitable. But patience will pay off, as the daily changing menu from chef Anna Klinger (Lespinasse and San Francisco's La Folie) includes stunning antipasti like grilled sardines with fennel; magnificent pastas like poppy-seeded sweet beet ravioli; and savory main courses like braised rabbit over polenta and roasted monkfish with lemon-rosemary escarole. Italian menu. Dinner. Closed Sun. Bar. Casual attire. Reservations recommended. Valet parking. **$$$**

★ ★ ALMA 296 (MAP J)
187 Columbia St (11231)
Phone 718/643-5400

After many years as chef at Zarela (see), one of Manhattan's most popular authentic Mexican restaurants, chef Gary Jacobson decided to take his soulful chile-laden fare to Brooklyn. At Alma, a bilevel restaurant and bar with a stunning lantern-lit roof deck for dining by skyline, you will find his food has remained as good as it was on Second Avenue. Guacamole; tortillas filled with braised duck; sweet, warm tamales; and tender seafood ceviche make up some of the best appetizers while generous entrées include dishes like ancho chile rellenos stuffed with shredded pork, raisins, and green olives. Mexican menu. Dinner, brunch. Bar. Business casual attire. Reservations recommended. Valet parking. Outdoor seating. **$$**

★ ★ BLUE RIBBON BROOKLYN (MAP J)

280 Fifth Ave (11215)
Phone 718/840-0404

Set in a former grocery store in Park Slope, Blue Ribbon Brooklyn is a sleek, bustling and expansive, brick-colored bistro with a well-stocked raw bar—just like its next door sibling, Blue Ribbon Sushi (see). But in addition, this branch also offers the owners' (brothers Bruce and Eric Bromberg) signature overly ambitious menu filled with all sorts of deliciously comforting dishes—marrow bones, chicken liver, variations on surf and turf, famous fried chicken, and plates of golden fries piled sky-high. Like the New York branch, the restaurant is open until 4 am to satisfy all those late-night hunger pangs. American menu. Breakfast (Sun), dinner, late-night. Children's menu. Casual attire. **$$**

★ ★ BLUE RIBBON SUSHI 298 (MAP J)

278 Fifth Ave (11215)
Phone 718/840-0408

Blue Ribbon Sushi is the beloved Brooklyn sibling of the brothers Bromberg's Blue Ribbon Sushi in the city. Located on a thriving strip of Fifth Avenue in Park Slope, this lively wood-accented restaurant and sushi bar offers the same winning formula the Bromberg's offer in Manhattan—just to larger crowds, thanks to easier access to real estate. Expect the best raw fish in town, warm and knowledgeable service, and a tremendous selection of sake—but not a table after 7 pm without a wait. Japanese, sushi menu. Dinner, late-night. Closed Mon. Children's menu. Casual attire. **$$$**

★ ★ BONITA 299 (MAP K)

338 Bedford Ave, Williamsburg (11211)
Phone 718/384-9500

Although Bonita can get very crowded, you will still be happy you came to this happenin' little eatery that serves top-notch authentic Mexican fare in a lively diner-esque setting. Owned by the folks who own Diner (see), also in the youthful hipster land of Williamsburg, Bonita serves spot-on tapas-style Mexican fare including a vibrant, chile-studded guacamole, a hefty torta, and a mean mole. The vibe is cool and slick yet the service is friendly and efficient with no 'tude. Mexican menu. Lunch, dinner. Closed Mon. Bar. Casual attire. Valet parking. **$$**

🄳

★★ CHESTNUT **300** (MAP J)
271 Smith St (11231)
Phone 718/243-0049

Chestnut, a cozy newcomer to Cobble Hill's restaurant row (Smith Street), is already winning fans from the 'hood and from Manhattan. With its wide French doors, high blond chestnut-beamed ceilings, and raw slate-tiled walls, the restaurant is a warm, lively gathering place that makes you feel like staying a long while. The talented kitchen turns out a menu of honest and delicious food with ingredients that shine, and plates that are filled with smart, creative, and well-articulated flavors. The menu features rustic dishes like chicken liver and apple toast as well as more elegant dishes like tea-smoked scallops with fingerling potatoes and sweet-hot mustard, and comforting plates like roasted organic chicken with artichokes and soft polenta. American menu. Dinner. Closed Mon. Bar. Casual attire. Reservations recommended. Outdoor seating. **$$**

★★ CHICKENBONE CAFÉ **301** (MAP K)
177 S 4th St, Williamsburg (11211)
Phone 718/302-2663

Chickenbone Café, a slickly rustic, inviting, wood-paneled hang in Williamsburg is constantly buzzing from the moment it opens early in the evening to the minute it closes in the early hours of the morning (when it is still bursting at the seams with young, sexy, and hip locals). The reason for its mass appeal is the irresistible, modestly priced, international menu of small plates, sandwiches, salads, soups, and sweets made from sustainably-grown, local ingredients. This is the sort of tasty fare that you'll want to feast on every day. There's a Vietnamese sausage sandwich that gives sweet and hot taste buds a thrilling twister ride, a tartiflette that clogs arteries with delight, and a slab of cashmere-like foie gras tourchon that brings a calm sense of bliss to the whole body. American menu. Dinner, late-night. Bar. Casual attire. Valet parking. **$$**

★★ CONVIVIUM OSTERIA **302** (MAP J)
68 Fifth Ave (11217)
Phone 718/857-1833

Convivium Osteria is a local gem serving some of the most soul-satisfying Mediterranean fare in the borough, if not all of New York City. With a setting straight out of a hillside in Tuscany, the restaurant is all aglow in candlelight and a rustic, distressed vintage design that makes you feel like its been here forever. The menu is stocked with country-style dishes from Spain, Portugal, and Italy that focus on robust flavors in casseroles, as well as earthy pastas, slow-cooked meats, and plentiful amounts of preserved, cured, and smoked ingredients—think salt cod and lots of delicious pig parts. Mediterranean menu. Dinner. Casual attire. Outdoor seating. **$$**

★★★ CUCINA (MAP J)
256 Fifth Ave (11215)
Phone 718/230-0711
Fax 718/230-0124
www.cucinarestaurant.com
Cucina was one of the first restaurants to brave the Brooklyn neighborhood of Park Slope, and years later it is still wooing neighborhood regulars and Manhattanites alike with its warm and elegant setting and refined menu of sumptuous Italian fare. The restaurant is decorated with old-world tapestries and warm ocher walls, giving it a sort of Italian Renaissance-styled elegance. While the menu features outstanding pasta, the kitchen is also savvy with seafood—like salt cod and salmon—and features a lengthy and wonderful list of antipasti to make the wait for the main courses quite enjoyable, indeed. Italian menu. Dinner. Closed Mon; Thanksgiving, Dec 25. Bar. Children's menu. **$$$**

★ DIFARA'S PIZZERIA (MAP A)
1424 Avenue J (11230)
Phone 718/392-1222
Heading out to the recesses of Brooklyn may not be on your list of things to do for something as seemingly ordinary as a slice of pizza, but DiFara's pizza is the one of those handmade slices that warrants a visit. Tucked into a residential stretch of Avenue J, you'll find pizza-man Dominick DeMarco flipping his signature Neapolitan pies as he has been for decades. He tops his pies with basil grown in the window, a drizzle of extra-virgin olive oil, tomato sauce, and gooey lumps of mozzarella. A dusting of hand-grated Parmesan is the final touch on the masterpiece that is DiFara's Pizza. Pizza. Lunch, dinner. Bar. Casual attire. **$**

★ DINER (MAP K)
85 Broadway, Williamsburg (11211)
Phone 718/486-3077
Williamsburg hipsters flock to Diner like ants to a picnic. Indeed, this place often feels like a zoo for young, thrift-store clad locals. Set in a

loungy, refurbished dining car, this bar and restaurant is a mess hall for struggling writers, actors, musicians, and the like. The menu is a fun selection of contemporary American dishes including juicy burgers, platters of charcuterie, fresh salads, crisp and golden fries, and hearty sandwiches stuffed with seasonal ingredients. American menu. Lunch, dinner, late-night, brunch. Casual attire. **$$**

★ GRIMALDI'S PIZZERIA (MAP H)

19 Old Fulton St (11201)
Phone 718/858-4300
In Brooklyn, Grimaldi's is synonymous with pizza. And not just any old pizza by the slice, but thin-crusted, piping hot pizza pies layered with milky house-made mozzarella, bright tomato sauce, and vibrant strips of zingy basil. The restaurant is decorated in casual pizzeria style with gingham-printed tablecloths and the requisite Sinatra soundtrack playing in the background. Aside from the basic tomato, mozzarella, and basil pies, you can choose your own mess of toppings from a wide list that includes spicy sausage, house-roasted peppers, spinach, and mushrooms. Pizza. Lunch, dinner. Bar. Children's menu. Casual attire. **$**

★ ★ ★ THE GROCERY (MAP J)

288 Smith St (11231)
Phone 718/596-3335
When husband/wife team Charlie Kiely and Sharon Patcher—chef-veterans of the New York restaurant scene—opened The Grocery, an intimate spot on Smith Street with a leafy back patio and yard,

coney island

Although it's become a bit frayed, you can still experience a bit of old New York along Coney Island's beachfront boardwalk. Take a ride on the legendary Cyclone roller coaster at Astroland Amusement Park (1000 Surf Ave, 718/372-0275, www.astroland.com; open on weekends in April, seven days a week June-Labor Day). Afterward, grab the perfect hot dog, waffle fries, and a lemonade at Nathan's Famous. For some really cheesy thrills, experience the nearby circus sideshow shown on weekends in summer. *1208 Surf Ave (11224). Phone 718/372-5159. www.coneyisland.com.*

they had no idea that they would inspire a cult following. This stylish, earth-toned dining room has a serene vibe, and the delicious food coming out of the tiny kitchen makes the 13-table space all the more exquisite, with dishes that mirror the seasons. There's not a plate on the menu that won't make your mouth water. Seasons dictate the menu, but star dishes include brook trout with spinach and bacon-flecked spaetzle, ratatouille-stuffed squid, roasted beets with goat cheese ravioli, duck confit with roasted quince sauce, and pork loin with sweet potatoes and roasted pears. Get ready to fall in love with dining in Brooklyn. American menu. Dinner. Closed Sun. Bar. Casual attire. Outdoor seating. **$$$**

★ ★ M SHANGHAI BISTRO & DEN 308 (MAP K)
138 Havenmeyer St (11211)
Phone 718/384-9300

M Shanghai is not your average Chinese restaurant. Decorated in a slinky style, with chocolate brown banquet tables, brick walls, and a moody soundtrack, M is a lovely den of design and food, graciously presided over by owner May Liu. The menu also sets itself apart from the fray with vibrant dishes of steamed dumplings and puffy pork buns, and deliciously flavored main courses like shredded pork with bean curd and salmon with smooth and well-seasoned tofu sauce. Once you are through with dinner, head down to the hopping downstairs lounge. Chinese menu. Dinner, late-night. Closed Mon. Bar. Casual attire. **$$**

★ ★ MISS WILLIAMSBURG DINER 309 (MAP K)
206 Kent Ave, Williamsburg (11211)
Phone 718/963-0802

This vintage 1940s boxcar diner is a charming old-timer with brushed aluminum siding, distressed leather banquettes, and swivel stools under a Formica counter. The place feels like something out of an old movie and transports you back in time. The menu takes its cues from Italy, and owner Max Bartoli presents a reasonably priced, market-driven menu of Mediterranean-inspired small plates like fontina bruschetta with zucchini purée, as well as hearty plates like grilled pork chops, and gorgeous pastas like beet ravioli with lemon sauce and lasagna oozing with a sinfully hearty ragu. Italian menu. Dinner. Closed Mon. Bar. Casual attire. Reservations recommended. **$$**

★★ PATOIS 310 (MAP J)

255 Smith St (11231)
Phone 718/855-1535

Restaurant Row in Cobble Hill is Smith Street, and Patois is one of this hopping street's original destinations for flavorful French fare served in a warm bistro setting. Patois overflows with charm from its saffron-colored walls, open kitchen, and delightful Provençal-style garden. The menu is classic French (think steak frites), with a little bit of Morocco thrown in for good measure in dishes like lamb sausage with couscous and nectarine chutney. The weekend brunch is a zoo, so grab a mimosa or an espresso and get ready to wait in line. French menu. Dinner, Sun brunch. Closed Mon. Casual attire. Outdoor seating. **$$**

★★★ PETER LUGER STEAK HOUSE 311 (MAP K)

178 Broadway (11211)
Phone 718/387-7400
Fax 718/387-3523
www.peterluger.com

Peter Luger Steak House is the stuff legends are made of. This landmark restaurant has been serving juicy porterhouse steaks since 1887 and is still one of the city's top tables. Don't expect elegant surroundings with your expertly charred dry-aged slab of beef, though. This place is bare bones, with exposed beamed ceilings, worn tables and chairs, and waiters that are as well seasoned as the beef. In addition to the gorgeously marbled steaks, you can dig into sides like German-fried potatoes and creamed spinach. If you make it over for lunch you can wrap your hands around New York's best burger, made from fresh ground beef and served with slices of tearjerker raw onion and a thick beefsteak tomato. Steak menu. Lunch, dinner. Bar. Casual attire. Reservations recommended. **$$$$**

★ PIER 116 312 (MAP J)

116 Smith St (11201)
Phone 718/260-8900

Pier 116 is a great neighborhood seafood pub that instantly transports you to the windswept New England Coast. Come inside and you'll feel immediately at home amongst the crowds of happy families sitting elbow to elbow with vintage-clad locals. The menu serves up that sand-in-your-toes feeling all year long, with fat, sea-salty steamers served in pails; succulent, meaty lobster rolls; crunchy buttermilk fried chicken; and meaty, flavorful baby-back ribs. To prevent choking on all this lip-licking seashore grub, the Pier keeps a terrific selection of ice-cold brews on tap like Dogfish Head Indian Brown

Ale, Old Speckled Hen, and Stone Smoked Porter. American, seafood menu. Lunch, dinner. Bar. Casual attire. Outdoor seating. **$$**

★ ★ RELISH   ③⑬ (MAP K)
225 Wythe Ave (11211)
Phone 718/963-4546
At Relish, a sleek, refurbished railcar diner, you can dig into contemporary Southern fare in style. This former dining car is now a bright, stylish, windowed hang, offering regional comfort food like macaroni and cheese, hearty cheeseburgers, and rich, smoked pork loin with spiced mango chutney. Relish is also quite the popular spot on weekends, when the crowds line up for the eggs with Serrano ham and cheddar grits. American menu. Lunch, dinner. Bar. Casual attire. **$$**

★ ★ ★ RIVER CAFÉ   ③⑭ (MAP H)
1 Water St (11201)
Phone 718/522-5200
Fax 718/875-0037
www.rivercafe.com
If romance is on the evening's agenda, The River Café should be as well. Located on the Brooklyn waterfront, with the an unmatched view of the East River and the twinkling Manhattan skyline, this elegant old-timer has always been a favorite for celebrating special occasions and for creating reasons to celebrate new ones. The kitchen is skilled at sophisticated New American fare like lobster, rack of lamb, and duck, artistically plated so as to inspire oohs and aaahs. The wine list is award winning, the service is graceful and unobtrusive, and is practiced at staying away when not needed, so as to let the romance bloom. American menu. Lunch, dinner. Bar. Jacket required. Reservations recommended. Valet parking. Outdoor seating. **$$$$**

★ ★ SAUL   ③⑮ (MAP J)
140 Smith St (11201)
Phone 718/935-9844
Restaurant Saul is one of those truly inviting spots that every neighborhood craves. Known for its terrific New American fare—courtesy of chef/owner Saul Bolton—Saul is urbane in décor, with warm, sandy tones and exposed brick walls. The modest menu reflects Bolton's training at Le Bernardin (see); expect plates adorned with stunning seasonal ingredients and simple, flavorful preparations of everything from diver scallops, to leg of lamb, duck confit, and foie gras. Don't forget to have dessert; Saul is known for its sweets, especially the classic baked Alaska. American menu. Dinner, Sun brunch. Bar. Casual attire. **$$**

★ ★ **SEA** (MAP K)
114 N 6th St (11211)
Phone 718/384-8850
www.spicenyc.com
Sea is known just as much for its wild Zen-inspired disco décor
(complete with an in-ground pool watched over by a golden Buddha)
as it is for its fiery Thai fare. Often crowded and loud, with fast
servers who are interested in turning tables, Sea is not a peaceful
place to dine, but it is a tasty one. The menu includes dishes like
whole red snapper, rice paper-wrapped spring rolls, and a fun list of
desserts like the crispy banana with green tea ice cream. The cocktail
list guarantees a hangover with easy-to-imbibe drinks like the spicy
pineapple-ginger martini. Thai menu. Lunch, dinner, late-night. Bar.
Casual attire. Reservations recommended. **$$**

★ ★ **SMITH STREET KITCHEN** (MAP J)
174 Smith St (11201)
Phone 718/858-5359
www.smithkitchen.com
At this casual Smith Street restaurant, neighbors gather for winning
meals made with a careful and skilled hand. The dining room has an
easy, warm vibe, set with white-linen tablecloths and moody votive
candles. The modest menu changes seasonally and always features
a fresh fish of the day, as well as a wonderful selection of oysters
in addition to pasta, salads, game, and chicken. In the summertime,
dining outside in the charming brick-walled garden is a nice treat.
Seafood menu. Dinner. Bar. Reservations recommended. Outdoor
seating. **$$$**

★ ★ **SUPERFINE** 318 (MAP H)
126 Front St (11201)
Phone 718/243-9005
Located in DUBMO, Superfine is a casual neighborhood eatery with
a warm, earthy vibe marked by brick walls, high ceilings, stunning
flower arrangements, and views of the Manhattan Bridge. The kitchen
boasts some serious skills, turning out robust Texas-style fare like
seared duck breast with rutabaga and sliced shiitake mushrooms, and
grilled pork chops with mashed potatoes and bitter greens The menu
of easy-to-love eats has the place packed with kids and families and
the hot crop of locals. On Sundays, brunch gets a pick-me-up from a
bluegrass band and burritos laced with eggs, refried beans, and zesty
salsa. American menu. Lunch, dinner, Sun brunch. Closed Mon. Bar.
Casual attire. **$$**

atlantic avenue

New York has a vibrant and diverse Middle Eastern community spread throughout a number of neighborhoods. Manhattan alone has an incredible array of restaurants offering cuisines from the distinct nations of the Middle East, but Brooklyn's Atlantic Avenue is one of the best, most affordable, and most approachable areas to sample foods and purchase ingredients.

Two of the best restaurants to feast like royalty for a reasonable sum are **Bedouin Tent** (405 Atlantic Ave, phone 718/852-5555) and **Fountain Café** (183 Atlantic Ave, phone 718/624-6764). The staff at both restaurants are traditionally hospitable, and the food is flavorful and abundant.

For stocking a pantry, **Sahadi** (187 Atlantic Ave, phone 718/624-4550) is the stop to make. Filled with nuts, spices, flavorings, candies, and anything else you could imagine, it's a popular weekend stop for families, so try to visit on a weekday. After stocking up there, **Damascus Bakery** (195 Atlantic Ave, phone 718/625-7070) is a must-visit for the best pita bread in New York. In addition to the light and fluffy pita, the za'tar bread—pita with a vibrant spice-blend topping—makes a flavorful snack or hors d'oeuvre. Pita isn't the only highlight here; you'll also find a wonderful selection of both sweet and savory baked goods, the best of which is a spinach and cheese pie in flaky pastry, and of course succulent baklava.

If you're putting together an evening of entertaining or if you're just famished and looking for an easy snack, **Mélange** (444 Atlantic Ave, phone 718/935-1220) is a fine stop. The shop is filled with a collection of prepared foods, salads, cheeses, and other compulsory items. After you've removed the food from its packages and placed it on your lovely wedding china, no one will ever know that you aren't the maestro behind the meal.

Queens

By far the largest borough geographically, Queens occupies 121 square miles of Long Island. Like Brooklyn, it was assembled from a number of small towns, and each of these neighborhoods has retained a strong sense of identity. Parts of the borough are less densely settled than Brooklyn, and the majority of Queens's population are homeowners. Many manufacturing plants, warehouses, and shipping facilities are in the portion called Long Island City, near the East River. Forest Hills, with its West Side Tennis Club, at Tennis Place and Burns Street, is a world-famous center for tennis. Flushing Meadows Corona Park has been the site of two world's fairs; many facilities still stand.

Restaurants in Queens

★★ CAVO (MAP I)
4218 31st Ave, Astoria (11103)
Phone 718/721-1001
Joining the ranks of the non-Greek restaurants in Astoria, Cavo is a sprawling Mediterranean spot with a stone patio and a wonderful, wide garden that will leave you wanting to set up camp in the backyard and never leave. The menu features all the wonders of the Mediterranean, from assorted savory pastas to whole fish with lemon and herbs, rack of lamb, and assorted mezze to start. Cavo attracts a local crowd but also pulls in guests from the city, giving new meaning to Bridge and Tunnel. Mediterranean menu. Dinner, late-night. Bar. Casual attire. Reservations recommended. Outdoor seating. **$$**

★★ CHRISTOS HASAPO-TAVERNA (MAP I)
41-08 23rd Ave, Astoria (11105)
Phone 718/726-5195
www.christossteakhouse.com
Christos Hasapo is a restaurant with dual personalities, and both are wonderful. By day, locals crowd into this butcher shop to purchase their day's beef. But at night, the shop turns into a Greek steakhouse, serving Astoria's finest selection of beef, prepared simply and perfectly every time. This lovely Greek taverna makes you feel like you are in Athens, and the wine list is surprisingly terrific, making a trip from the city a great idea. Greek menu. Lunch, dinner. Bar. Casual attire. Outdoor seating. **$$$**

★★ CINA 321 (MAP I)

45-17 28th Ave, Astoria (11103)
Phone 718/956-0372

If you've ever wondered what sort of dinners people have in Romania, this Romanian bistro, with a lively staff and a convivial vibe, will answer all your questions. First on the menu would be steak—and lots of it—grilled to juicy perfection. Then there might be some polenta topped with sour cream and perhaps some grated feta. Cina features both of these dishes and more, like sausages, spicy stuffed cabbage, and, for fearless eaters, a deep-fried Cornish hen. And if you thought American donuts were good, try the papanasi—fried lumps of yeasty dough topped with, you guessed it, sour cream. Romanian menu. Lunch, dinner. Casual attire. Reservations recommended. **$$**

★★ COOKING WITH JAZZ 322 (MAP B)

12-01 154th St, Whitestone (11357)
Phone 718/767-6979
www.cwj.net

Cooking with Jazz is a spirited restaurant that brings a bit of New Orleans to the modest hamlet known as Queens. From the vibrant and festive décor to the enthusiastic and well-informed staff to the creative Cajun menu, this homey freestanding restaurant is bursting with energy and robust cooking. The chef/owner is a Paul Prudhomme protégé, and his training shows in classics like chicken jambalaya, a rich and smoky stew stocked with blackened chicken and meaty Andouille sausage. If you're feeling adventurous, try some alligator, which can be found in fritters or in sausage. Cajun/Creole menu. Dinner. Closed Sun-Mon. Casual attire. No credit cards accepted. **$$**

★ ELIAS CORNER 323 (MAP I)

24-02 31st St, Astoria (11102)
Phone 718/932-1510

Elias Corner is not easy on the eyes. The restaurant, a cult favorite, is a bit garish, decked out in all turquoise, and is far from subtle in the décor department. But the blinding color scheme does not seem to deter the herds of folks who come here to feast on the restaurant's standout Greek fare. If you can stand the wait (the line is usually out the door), you will be treated to a wonderful meal, cooked from whatever is in the refrigerated deli case at the front of the restaurant. Usually, that includes some sort of fish, lamb, and, of course, a selection of mezze with a warm, puffy pita. Greek menu. Dinner. Casual attire. Outdoor seating. No credit cards accepted. **$$**

★ JACKSON DINER (MAP I)
37-47 74th St, Jackson Heights (11372)
Phone 718/672-1232
Bright, open, and airy, the Jackson Diner has been a Queens favorite
for years, serving authentic Indian cuisine in a bright and casual setting. The enormous buffet lunch is a steal, and the à la carte dinner
menu is a terrific taste of the kitchen's talents: yogurt-marinated
lamb chops, assorted dosas, and tasty appetizers to share among
the table, like coconut-flecked chicken, fried fish, and flaky samosas.
Indian menu. Lunch, dinner. Casual attire. No credit cards accepted. **$**

★ KABAB CAFÉ (MAP I)
25-12 Steinway St, Astoria (11103)
Phone 718/728-9858
Kabab Café may not look like much from the outside, but on the
inside, it's a different story. For instance, it takes your basic mezze
trio—baba ganoush, hummus, and tahini—and makes them shine.
Creamy, spicy, zesty, and ridiculously good, the mezze here are truly
remarkable, reaching beyond the ordinary trio to more exotic treats
like eggah (an Egyptian omelette), foul (a white bean salad with
puréed tomatoes, lemon juice, spices, and olive oil), and a crunchy
fava bean falafel. In addition to the stellar spreads (served with
delicious fresh-from-the-oven bread), you can feast on larger dishes
like slow-cooked lamb shank and sautéed calf's liver. Middle Eastern
menu. Lunch, dinner. Closed Mon. Casual attire. No credit cards
accepted. **$**

★ KHAO HOMM (327) (MAP I)
39-28 61st St, Woodside (11377)
Phone 718/205-0080
Fax 718/205-0048
This fresh and fun Thai restaurant comes complete with a spirited
menu, a talented and accommodating kitchen, gracious service,
karaoke machines, and a loyal clientele. What sets Khao Homm apart,
though, is perhaps its willingness to cook dishes that are not on the
menu. But more than likely, you won't have to bother the kitchen,
as the menu offers tasty options like fried whole fish topped with
papaya, roasted cashews, and a sweet-and-sour vinegar sauce and
pad kee mao—broad noodles coated in chiles and basil. Thai menu.
Lunch, dinner. Casual attire. **$**

★ KUM GANG SAN   328 (MAP B)

138-28 Northern Blvd, Flushing (11354)
Phone 718/461-0909

Kum Gang San, a Korean barbecue, sushi, and seafood stalwart, never closes. If you'd like to perform your own Survivor, try to stay for all 24 hours. You could spend part of the day hanging out by the indoor waterfall while having a lunch of blistering barbecue, crisped scallion and seafood pancakes, and pungent kimchi. Then you could move over to the sushi bar for an afternoon snack, and for dinner, take a stab at plates of panchan—Korean-style tapas-like crab claw with hot pepper and soy-marinated shortribs. And in the wee hours, you might join the late-night revelers and watch the fresh fish coming in from the seafood markets. Korean menu. Lunch, dinner, late-night. Casual attire. **$$**

★★ MANDUCATIS   329 (MAP F)

13-27 Jackson Ave, Long Island City (11101)
Phone 718/729-4602
Fax 718/361-0411

Sure, Manhattan boasts some fairly impressive Italian eateries, but one of the best-hidden treasures is located in Queens. Owned by Vicenzo Cerbone, Manducatis is a family-run operation serving the

astoria

Experience your own Big Fat Greek Wedding in this Hellenic community, just 15 minutes from Midtown, which offers the best Greek food this side of Athens. Astoria has an estimated Greek population of 70,000—the largest community outside of Greece—which means that the area is alive with music, culture, and melt-in-your mouth saganaki and baklava. Food markets, gift shops, bakeries, restaurants, and intimate cafés await your shopping and dining pleasure. Finish your excursion by relaxing on a nice, sunny day with a cup of Greek coffee in nearby Astoria Park and take in a great view of upper Manhattan. If you want to combine this Greek experience with other area attractions, the American Museum of the Moving Image (phone 718/784-0077) and the historic Kaufman Astoria Motion Picture Studios (phone 718/392-5600) are located in Astoria. This fun neighborhood proves that there is life in the outer boroughs of New York City. *At the NW tip of Queens. Phone 718/286-2667.*

home-style dishes of Italy's best mamas. The terra-cotta room has an earthy, countryside appeal, as does the menu. Expect delicate home-made pastas topped with soft pillows of milky mozzarella. The kitchen also turns out lovely fish and meat dishes and has an extensive wine list that includes many rare wines from small producers. In the winter, grab a seat by the blazing fireplace and you will be transported to the mountains of Tuscany. Italian menu. Lunch, dinner. Closed holidays; also the last two weeks in Aug. Bar. **$$**

★★ MOMBAR 330 (MAP I)

2522 Steinway St, Astoria (11103)
Phone 718/726-2356

Mombar is a warm, family-owned Egyptian restaurant with a big heart. Owned by artist and chef Moustafa El Sayed and run by his wife and family, the restaurant is decorated with his stunning handmade tile work, mix-and-match wooden tables, and comfy, pillow-filled banquettes. El Sayed is there all the time, to cook, to chat, and to guide you through a meal you will never forget. While his menu changes daily, you can't go wrong with the mezze plate or any of his clay pot stews: Moulekaya, an aromatic stew made from Egyptian greens with braised rabbit or chicken, or the fragrant, soft lamb pulled from a tagine filled with a messy stew of raisins, almonds, and olives. Meals end with tea—served in old-world tea glasses—and dense little powdered sugar-coated nut cookies. Middle Eastern menu. Dinner. Closed Mon. Children's menu. Casual attire. No credit cards accepted. **$$**

★★ PARK SIDE 331 (MAP B)

107-01 Corona Ave, Corona (11368)
Phone 718/271-9274
Fax 718/271-2454

If you try to imagine what *My Big Fat Greek Wedding* would have been like with an Italian family, you'll get an idea of what dinner is like at Park Side, a lively, boisterous restaurant in Queens that serves hearty portions of Italian food. The waiters give the place an old-school vibe, all dressed in black suits, while the dining room feels like an ornate catering hall filled with large parties and the occasional celebrity. The menu is straight-ahead and delicious Italian—think spicy red sauce, big steaks, giant orders of fill-in-the-blank-parmigiana, and heaping bowls of risotto, in addition to a superb hot and cold antipasti selection. Italian menu. Lunch, dinner. Bar. Valet parking. Outdoor seating. **$$**

★ ★ ★ PICCOLA VENEZIA   332 (MAP I)
42-01 28th Ave, Astoria (11103)
Phone 718/721-8470
Fax 718/721-2110
www.piccola-venezia.com

There are only a few reasons to leave the island of Manhattan. One is baseball. (Yankees and Mets games both require a trip through a bridge or tunnel.) Another is Piccola Venezia, an old-world trattoria offering authentic northern Italian fare in the humble borough of Queens. Located in Astoria since 1973, Piccola Venezia is a family-run operation that features delicious homemade pastas and a generous menu of salads, antipasti, seafood, meat, and game prepared with imported ingredients and a strong nod to the wonderful culinary traditions of Italy. Italian menu. Lunch, dinner. Closed Tues; Jan 1, Dec 25; also late July-late Aug. Valet parking. **$$$**

main street, flushing

Main Street in Flushing embodies the thing that draws so many people to live in a city that can be so challenging. Almost immediately after you step off the F train, it's difficult to figure out where to begin to eat and shop, not to mention what country you're in. There are streets of flavor to be found in many parts of Queens: Astoria Boulevard, Jackson Avenue, Roosevelt Avenue, and, most easily accessible, Main Street running through the heart of Flushing. Flushing has gone through many transitions of ethnic compositions, and at no time like the present have more groups been represented, living side by side in this small area.

It is argued that Flushing has far better Chinese restaurants than those found in Manhattan's Chinatown. Famous **Joe's Shangai** (136-21 37th Ave, between Main and Union sts, phone 718/539-3838) of soup dumpling fame has a location in Manhattan, but purists argue that the dumplings are better in Queens. **East Lake** (42-33 Main St, phone 718/539-8532) has a fantastic dim sum selection, and the rest of the mammoth menu should not be disregarded. **Jade Palace** (136-13 38th Ave, just off Main St, phone 718/353-3366) is another dim sum mindblower; the seafood quality and variety are darn good too.

Previously mostly Chinese, the area has become increasingly Korean in population, making it just as much a destination for Korean cuisine. **Kum Gang San** (138-28 Northern Blvd, off Main St, phone 718/461-0909) is often considered the temple of Korean cooking, and although the location in Manhattan is good, the one in Queens is far better. It may take a little spying on your neighbors to figure out what might be worth trying in addition to the standard dishes. The location is a short walk from the subway; parking makes it convenient for a short drive so that you can stock up at all the marvelous Asian supermarkets nearby.

Continuing on the Asian tour, we suggest Vietnamese food, often mediocre in Manhattan but abundant and well represented in this area. **Pho Bang** (41-07 Kissena Blvd, just off Main St, phone 718/939-5520) specializes in its namesake, pho, the stomach-warming and palate-delighting noodle soup that is a national dish of Vietnam. With the restaurant offering a number of versions as well as tasty spring rolls, it's impossible to believe how small the check is when you've enjoyed such a satisfying meal.

★ ★ PING'S SEAFOOD 333 (MAP A)
8302 Queens Blvd, Elmhurst (11373)
Phone 718/396-1238
This old-time favorite for Chinese cuisine is a straightforward spot to dine on fresh fish infused with the bright flavors of Asia. As you might expect, Ping's specializes in fish, but not just any old fish. Bring along a sense of culinary adventure if you decide to dine here, as the restaurant features tanks filled with all sorts of wild sea creatures for you to experiment with at dinner. The restaurant also offers dim sum, including steamed pork buns and shrimp dumplings. Chinese menu. Closed Sun. Lunch, dinner. **$$**

★ ★ RESTAURANT 718 334 (MAP I)
35-01 Ditmars Blvd, Astoria (11105)
Phone 718/204-5553
While Astoria was once all about Greek restaurants, the recent influx of Manhattanites fleeing rent hikes has brought about a shift in the culinary landscape. Restaurant 718 marks the official arrival of the French bistro to the Big Fat Greek scene. This sweet, cozy Parisian

bistro offers standards like duck terrine and steak frites, but also features Spanish-accented plates like grilled tuna with chorizo and soy-cherry sauce, roasted duck with Serrano ham, and, in a respectful nod to the neighborhood, tzatziki with endive. French menu. Dinner, brunch. Bar. Casual attire. Reservations recommended. **$$**

★ S'AGAPO TAVERNA 335 (MAP I)
34-21 34th Ave, Astoria (11106)
Phone 718/626-0303
At this neighborhood taverna, a taste of the Greek Isles is served up with charm every night of the week. The service is warm and welcoming, as you would expect from a local gathering place. The restaurant specializes in swimmingly fresh grilled seafood as well as classic mezze like tangy, garlicky tzatziki. The only potential downside to S'Agapo is that the place can get cramped at times, as tables are snuggled up right next to one another. But if you don't mind cozy dining, you should be fine. Greek menu. Lunch, dinner. Casual attire. **$$**

★ ★ SICHUAN DYNASTY 336 (MAP B)
135-32 40th Rd, Flushing (11354)
Phone 718/961-7500
If you are one of those people who has trouble deciding what to order, do not go to Sichuan Dynasty. The menu contains some 60 items and will stymie even the most decisive of eaters. The key to dining here may be to go with a large group that can handle lots of fiery fare so that no dish will be left off your evening's menu. The selections run the gamut from your basic kung pao chicken and whole fish to more Fear Factor-style dishes like kidney in sesame oil. The setting is bright and comfortable, with colorful tabletops, wide booths, and an upper-deck bar stocked with a decent selection of California wines. Chinese menu. Lunch, dinner. Casual attire. **$$**

★ SRIPRAPHAI 337 (MAP I)
64-13 39th Ave, Woodside (11377)
Phone 718/899-9599
Sripraphai serves the sort of food you might get in Thailand. But instead of hopping a jet plane, all you have to do is grab the number 7 train out to Queens. The only problem is that you may have to wait in the line that stretches out the door to get your table. The menu is filled with authentic Thai dishes like noodle bowls, green papaya salad, chile-rubbed pork, and fire-breathing dishes of green curry that will set your mouth ablaze with spice. If you have issues with heat, make sure to let your waiter know. Thai menu. Lunch, dinner. Closed Wed. Casual attire. Outdoor seating. No credit cards accepted. **$**

★ ★ TOURNESOL 338 (MAP F)

50-12 Vernon Blvd, Long Island City (11109)
Phone 718/472-4355
tournesolny.com

Tournesol is a sunny little French bistro just across the river from Manhattan in Long Island City that could have fallen off any old charming rue in Paris. Filled to the gills with trappings of Paris—romantic music, a sidewalk café, bistro tables and chairs, floor-to-ceiling French doors, and vintage tin ceilings—this cheery local favorite offers up friendly service and a rustic menu of classic French standards like rabbit stew, braised beef cheeks, frisée au lardons, and country pâté. Tournesol is a sweet little gem of a restaurant that offers all the romance of Paris without the hassle of transcontinental travel. French menu. Lunch, dinner, brunch. Casual attire. Reservations recommended. Outdoor seating. **$$**

★ UBOL'S KITCHEN 339 (MAP I)

24-42 Steinway St, Astoria (11103)
Phone 718/545-2874

This neighborhood Thai restaurant gets consistent "Wows" from locals who head over for vibrant fare with a generous amount of heat. The menu includes many standard curry and noodle dishes, but also makes an effort to woo vegetarians with dishes like mock duck. In a neighborhood that is inundated with a slew of ubiquitous Thai restaurants of the same formula, Ubol's remains a spicy favorite. Thai menu. Lunch, dinner. Casual attire. **$**

Groceries and Markets

MEGA-STORES

Agata & Valentina
1505 First Ave at 79th St
Phone 212/452-0690
Specializes in Italian foods with a terrific cheese selection, reasonably priced house-label condiments, and outstanding prepared foods.

Citarella
1313 Third Ave at 75th St
Phone 212/874-0383
www.citarella.com
Also at 2135 Broadway
at 75th St
Phone 212/874-0383
Sells a wide variety of prepared foods, but the strongest department in these tight aisles is the fish.

Dean & Deluca
560 Broadway at Prince St
Phone 212/431-1691
www.deandeluca.com
Everything is just gorgeous at this downtown gourmet market, but you might need to sell your Vespa to shop here very often.

Eli's
1411 Third Ave at 80th/81st St
Phone 212/717-8100
Eli Zabar goes enormous in a much more convenient location. Everything here is perfect from the flowers to the prepared foods but be forewarned, you might not ever recover from your total bill at the end.

Fairway
2127 Broadway at 74th St
Phone 212/234-3883
Fairway Uptown
2328 12th Ave at 132nd St
While Fairway on the Upper West Side is a demolition derby-like shopping experience to access the best and most well-priced produce in town, Uptown Fairway at the right time of day can be better than the suburbs with the same quality items and those neat butcher jackets you get to wear in the meat locker section.

Grace's Marketplace
1237 Third Ave at 71st
Phone 212/737-0600
www.gracesmarketplace.com
Cramped and chaotic, Grace's can test your good will but there's a reason it's always packed considering the local competition.

The Vinegar Factory
431 E 91st St (1st and York)
Phone 212/987-0885
The home of Eli Zabar's stupendous breads is accompanied by everything you could ever imagine not being able to make as well at home. One of the few spots in NYC that offers validated parking at their lot across the street.

Zabar's
2245 Broadway
at 80th/81st sts
Phone 212/787-2000
www.zabars.com
Always crowded because the foods are high-quality, yet the prices aren't wallet-busting.

BAKERIES

Amy's Bread
672 Ninth Ave at 46th/47th sts
Phone 212/977-2670
www.amysbread.com
This yummy bakery opened in 1992 with five employees in a small Hell's Kitchen storefront. It now employs more than 100 people and has expanded to three stores.

Balthazar Bakery
80 Spring St at Broadway/ Crosby
Phone 212/965-1785
www.balthazarbakery.com
French breads, pastries, and sandwiches prepared to perfection.

Buttercup Bake Shop
973 Second Ave
at 51st/52nd sts
Phone 212/350-4144
www.buttercupbakeshop.com
When you need cupcakes, this is the place to go; they carry all flavors and colors with a few customized garnishes to pile on top.

Chelsea Market
75 Ninth Ave at 15th/16th sts
Phone 212/462-4338
Breads, baked goods, and sandwiches with truly big flavors. One of the best grilled cheese sandwiches to be found comes out of this tiny shop.

Cupcake Café
522 Ninth Ave at 39th St
Phone 212/465-1530
www.cupcakecafe.com
There is much dispute as to the quality of cake and quantity of icing on these cakes and cupcakes, but no one disagrees that the designs are incredible.

Damascus Bakery
195 Atlantic Ave, Brooklyn
Phone 718/625-7070
www.damascusbakery.com
Now THIS is pita: warm and fresh out of the oven. The Za'tar bread is addictive and a great party snack.

Glaser's Bake Shop
1670 First Ave
at 87th/88th sts
Phone 212/289-2562
Over all its years in business, this classic bakery has never given in to the trends. Cakes, pies, cupcakes, and other goodies are all made the good old-fashioned way, and we certainly hope it stays around for many more years.

Kossar's Bialys
367 Grand St
Phone 212/473-4810
www.kossarsbialys.com
A bagel is an easy find in the Big Apple, but a good bialy is becoming less and less available.

Little Pie Company
424 W 43rd St at Ninth/
Tenth aves
Phone 212/736-4780
www.littlepiecompany.com
Also in Grand Central
Food Court
Pies in all these flavors are one thing, but little pies in all these flavors—well, that's just adorable.

Magnolia Bakery
401 Bleecker St at 11th St
Phone 212/462-2572
These cupcakes would show up any other mom during the kindergarten birthday madness. They make cakes too.

Once Upon a Tart
135 Sullivan St
Phone 212/387-8869
www.onceuponatart.com
Sweet and savory tarts in all shapes and sizes.

Payard Patisserie
1032 Lexington Ave
at 73rd/74th sts
Phone 212/717-5252
www.payard.com
For a special event, these pristine pastries are worth the spurge. You can sit and enjoy them in the small café and have a fabulous café au lait to go with.

Sullivan Street Bakery
73 Sullivan St
Phone 212/334-9435
Also at 533 W 47th St at
10th/11th sts
Phone 212/265-5580
www.sullivanstreetbakery.com
There's nothing like the pizza squares with seasonal toppings found at this modern bakery. It's difficult to wait out the seasons for your favorite to return. And the bread, biscotti, desserts, and espresso are pretty phenomenal as well.

Tal Bagels
333 E 86th St
Phone 212/427-6811
Not just outstanding bagels but also all the toppings to match.

ETHNIC FOODS

Foods of India
121 Lexington Ave
at 28th/29th sts
Phone 212/683-4419
Next door to Kalustyan's and often overlooked, with friendlier service and less expensive gold leaf.

Kalustyan's
123 Lexington Ave
at 28th/29th sts
Phone 212/685-3451
www.kalustyans.com
An all-inclusive shop for anything South Asian, Middle Eastern, and often in between. After perusing the aisles, you can head upstairs for a tasty snack in the small café.

Two Little Red Hens
1112 Eighth Ave, Brooklyn
Phone 718/499-8108
1652 Second Ave
at 85th/86th sts
Phone 212/452-0476
Fun and tasty, these cakes, pies, and mini-cakes make lovely hostess gifts or holiday surprises.

Veniero's
342 E 11th St at First/
Second aves
Phone 212/674-7070
Traditional Italian-American pastries to eat there or take away. The incredible assortment of sweets seems to attract an incredible assortment of crowds at peak times.

Katagiri
224 E 59th St
at Second/Third aves
Phone 212/755-3566
www.katagiri.com
You may not be able to read the writing on most of the packaging in this Japanese supermarket, but if it's exported, they carry it.

Kitchen Market
218 Eighth Ave
at 21st/22nd sts
Phone 212/243-4433
www.kitchenmarket.com
One of the sunniest shops to buy Mexican ingredients in Manhattan dispersed amongst various tchotchkes and Mexican toys. Include some takeout in your visit, as their food is excellent and easily transported.

Ninth Ave International
543 Ninth Ave
at 40th/41st sts
Phone 212/279-5514
Bare boned in atmosphere, yet warm in service, this is a don't-miss for spices, olives, feta cheese, nuts, and grains. The best-kept secret though is the taramosalata, creamy and salty and sold at four times the price in some of the city's best Greek restaurants.

Sahadi's
187 Atlantic Ave, Brooklyn
Phone 718/624-4550
www.sahadis.com
Although Sahadi's specializes in Middle Eastern ingredients, it's easy to collect a wide variety of Mediterranean and other foods here. Either go on a weekday or brace yourself for the crowds.

CANDY AND CHOCOLATE

Aji Ichiban
153 Centre St
Phone 212/625-1122
www.ajichiban-usa.com
This Japanese chain carries everything imported, from fruit jellies to squid chips. The design is colorful and energetic, and tasting is often allowed.

Economy Candy
108 Rivington St
(Essex/Ludlow)
Phone 212/254-1531
www.economycandy.com
By mail order or in person, this is a super source for bulk candy and nuts.

La Maison du Chocolat
1018 Madison Ave
at 78th/79th sts
Phone 212/744-7117
www.lamaisonduchocolat.com
The best chocolate from France doesn't come cheap, but it's well worth every bite. The hot chocolate is absolutely divine as well, and a much softer sell.

Richart Design et Chocolat
7 E 55th St
(Fifth Ave/Madison)
Phone 212/371-9369
www.chocolats-richart.com
Build your own dresser of chocolate drawers at Richart, where each chocolate looks to be hand-painted and tastes just as good.

Teuscher
25 E 61st St
Phone 212/751-8482
www.teuscher.com
For fans of Swiss chocolate, it gets no better than this.

BUTCHERS

Faicco's Pork Store
260 Bleecker St (6th/7th)
Phone 212/243-1974
Nothing can compare
to the quality, variety,
and friendly, knowledgeable
service at this West Village
pork store, where the arancini
aren't bad and the sandwiches
are even better.

Lobel's
1096 Madison Ave (82nd/83rd)
Phone 212/737-1373
www.lobels.com
You can see your steak aging
in Lobel's private room through
the glass from the sidewalk.
It's definitely better, but it's a
lot more expensive than any
steak you'll ever buy from a
butcher. And to think they have
regulars....

SPECIFIC FOODS

Barney Greengrass
(Smoked Fish)
541 Amsterdam Ave (86th/87th)
Phone 212/724-4707
www.barneygreengrass.com
Sturgeon, nova, whitefish, and
sable have always ruled this
Upper West Side restaurant,
where takeout is a better idea
than the crowded brunch.

Caviarteria
502 Park Ave
Phone 212/759-7410
Toll-free 800/422-8427
www.caviarteria.com
Sit at the caviar bar and be
indulgent, or allow them to ice
your roe for transport to near
or far.

Gus's Pickles
35 Essex St
Phone 212/254-4477
Anything pickled is a standout
at this specialty shop.

Petrossian
911 Seventh Ave (57th/58th sts)
Phone 212/245-2217
www.petrossian.com
The best caviar in Manhattan
when money is no object.

Russ & Daughters
*179 E Houston St (Allen/
Orchard)*
Phone 212/475-4880
www.russanddaughters.com
Arguably Manhattan's most
sacred smoked fish temple, where
nova and sable hold the throne.

Sable's
*1489 Second Ave
at 77th/78th sts*
Phone 212/249-6177
Not much on atmosphere,
but great on quality and
service for not only sable,
but also the usual suspects.

Cheese

Di Palo Dairy
206 Grand St
Phone 212/226-1033
Italian cheeses straight from the boot are featured here. Don't leave without a ball of their homemade mozzarella, salted or unsalted.

Ideal Cheese
1205 Second Ave
at 63rd/64th sts
Phone 212/688-7579
www.idealcheese.com
Inconsistent service but excellent quality and variety can be found behind this unassuming storefront on the Upper East Side.

Joe's Dairy
156 Sullivan St
(Houston/Prince sts)
Phone 212/677-8780
Salted, smoked, or just plain creamy, fresh mozzarella is what Joe's is all about. Don't let the line intimidate you; it's worth the wait.

Murray's Cheese
257 Bleecker St
Phone 212/243-3289
www.murrayscheese.com
Many consider Murray's to be the best cheese shop in Manhattan. Service and selection set this tiny shop apart from the rest.

WINE/LIQUOR

Best Cellars
1291 Lexington Ave
Phone 212/426-4200
You can find great low prices here. Browse the shelves by the wine's characteristics rather than its region.

Burgundy Wine Company
143 W 26th St
Phone 212/691-9092
burgundywinecompany.com
If you want a Burgundy, Rhone, or Oregon wine, this is the place to visit.

Italian Wine Merchants
108 E 16th St
Phone 212/473-2323
www.italianwinemerchants.com
If there ever was a need for a wine specialist, it's for often misunderstood and little appreciated Italian wines. This warm retail store off Union Square can turn all the misconceptions around. It's so cozy you may want to stay for a while.

Neil Rosenthal
318 E 84th St at 1st/2nd
Phone 212/249-6730
Though primarily an importer, Neil Rosenthal opened a retail shop on a quiet residential street on the Upper East Side, and it's wonderful to visit. Always an education and perpetually a success, it seems silly to buy wines from anyone else.

Sherry-Lehman
679 Madison Ave
Phone 212/838-7500
www.sherry-lehman.com
This store specializes in
Champagne, wines, and sparkling
wines, and will store your
purchase in their cellars for up to
a year—free of charge.

TEA/COFFEE

Empire Coffee & Tea
592 Ninth Ave
at 42nd/43rd sts
Phone 212/586-1717
www.empirecoffeetea.com
New Yorkers in the know suffer
the Port Authority for excellent
quality and fair prices at this
specialist.

Takashimaya (The Tea Box)
693 Fifth Ave
at 54th/55th sts
Phone 212/350-0100
Like everything else in
Takashimaya, the tea shop is
enviable in its faultlessness.
Enjoy traditional Japanese tea
service before shopping at the
small café, and the prices will be
easier to swallow.

Ten Ren Tea & Ginseng Co
75 Mott St at Bayard/Canal
Phone 212/349-2286
www.tenrenusa.com
If it's Chinese tea you want,
this is where you must go.
Some of the jars are filled with
liquid gold.

T Salon & Emporium
11 E 20th St at Broadway
and Fifth Ave
Phone 212/358-0506
The owner of this charming
place has dedicated her life
to tea, and it shows. From
exceptional teas hunted down
from around the world to unique
blends created for restaurants
and celebrities, there is nothing
on par with this tea collection.

50 Spots to Have a Drink

Asia de Cuba
237 Madison Ave
Phone 212/762-7755
www.asiadecuba.com
This Cuban-Asian hybrid
is as hip as they come.

Au Bar
41 E 58th St
Phone 212/308-9455
Be prepared for the hefty cover
charge at this ultra-hip spot.

Aubette
119 E 27th St
Phone 212/686-5500
A great date spot
with a smart, trendy
atmosphere.

Auction House
300 E 89th St
Phone 212/427-4458
One of the only spots above
86th Street that doesn't hurt
your ears—or your wallet.

Automatic Slims
733 Washington St
Phone 212/645-8660
A local favorite for its 1980s
jukebox and reasonably priced
drinks.

B Bar (aka Bowery Bar)
40 E 4th St
Phone 212/475-2220
Set in a former gas station,
the Bowery Bar is a tribute to
late '80s style and indulgence.

Barmacy
538 E 14th St
Phone 212/228-2240
The wonderful weirdness of this
"pharmacy" is infectious with
great cocktails and music.

Beauty Bar
231 E 14th St
Phone 212/539-1389
www.beautybar.com
This former salon offers a
manicure and a beer for $10 as
well as great rockabilly.

Blind Tiger Ale House
518 Hudson St at W 10th St
Phone 212/675-3848
www.blindtigeralehouse.com
A beer and microbrew lover's
dream, with a 16-page beer list.

Bond Street Lounge
6 Bond St
Phone 212/777-2500
The ultra-mellow vibe fits
perfectly with the hipster crowd
and interesting Japanese cuisine.

Bowlmor Lanes
110 University Pl
Phone 212/255-8188
www.bowlmor.com
A kitschy homage to Midwestern
bowling alleys. Great place to
bring out-of-towners.

Bubble Lounge
228 W Broadway
Phone 212/431-3433
www.bubblelounge.com
A great Champagne bar that caters to the Wall Street crowd.

Café Noir
32 Grand St
Phone 212/431-7910
This smooth and relaxed café features great Moroccan-inspired food and ample drinks.

The Campbell Apartment
15 Vanderbilt Ave
Phone 212/953-0409
This luxurious space has been restored to its former 1930s glory. A must-see.

Candela
116 E 16th St
Phone 212/254-1600
Dark and cozy with an almost medieval décor.

Church Lounge
2 Sixth Ave
Phone 212/519-6600
This lounge features a wraparound interior balcony to view the bar below.

Coffee Shop
29 Union Sq W
Phone 212/243-7969
This coffee shop is anything but. A great place for people-watching.

Craftbar
47 E 19th St
Phone 212/780-0880
The comfort-food sibling to Tom Colicchio's Craft is a haven of simple pleasures.

Divine Bar
244 E 51st St
Phone 212/319-9463
This trendy hotspot for twentysomethings features a great upstairs tapas room.

Dylan Prime
62 Laight St
Phone 212/334-4783
www.dylanprime.com
Excellent cocktails and terrific food in one of the nicest lounges in TriBeCa.

Evelyn
380 Columbus Ave
Phone 212/724-2363
This dark, multi-roomed bar has a very clublike atmosphere.

Failte Irish Whiskey Bar
531 Second Ave
Phone 212/725-9440
A traditional Irish pub with a not-to-be-missed upstairs fireplace lounge.

Fanelli's Café
94 Prince St
Phone 212/226-9412
This SoHo institution is home to terrific clam chowder and has been around since 1847.

Fiona's Bar and Restaurant
1664 First Ave
Phone 212/348-3783
A wonderfully greasy spoon with the requisite sawdust floor and rugby on the television.

Grand Bar (at the SoHo Grand Hotel)
310 W Broadway
Phone 212/965-3588
A luxurious, if touristy, cavern of decent food and drink.

Hudson Library Bar
356 W 58th St (Hudson Hotel)
Phone 212/554-6317
Located in the ultra-hip Hudson Hotel, this bar offers a subdued oasis from the city outside.

Ike
103 Second Ave
Phone 212/388-0388
www.ikebyc.com
This classic cocktail emporium is full of hip, retro charm.

Le Colonial
149 E 57th St
Phone 212/752-0808
A legendary French-Vietnamese establishment definitely worth a visit.

Lot 61
550 W 21st St
Phone 212/243-6555
This New York watering hole has an incredible interior featuring art by Damien Hirst.

Lotus Club
35 Clinton St
Phone 212/253-1144
A classic neighborhood bar with some of the city's most affordable cocktails.

Markt
401 W 14th St
Phone 212/727-3314
This swanky West Village brasserie serves up tasty mussels and even tastier Belgian beers.

McSorley's Old Ale House
15 E 7th St
Phone 212/473-9148
This classic Irish pub has been a fixture in New York for more than 150 years.

Morgan's Bar
237 Madison Ave
Phone 212/726-7600
A creative cocktail menu, better than average food, and guaranteed celebrity sightings make this trendy spot a must-see.

Opium Den
29 E 3rd St
Phone 212/505-7344
Dimly lit and cozy, upscale yet bohemian, the Opium Den drips with atmosphere.

The Park
118 Tenth Ave
Phone 212/352-3313
www.theparknyc.com
This super-trendy spot continues to be one of the most popular in New York.

Pentop Bar
700 Fifth Ave (Peninsula Hotel)
Phone 212/956-2888
This bar in the Peninsula Hotel offers breathtaking views and an incredible tiramisu martini.

Pravda
281 Lafayette St
Phone 212/334-5015
www.pravdany.com
This happening SoHo spot features a modern Russian vodka list.

Rise
2 West St (Ritz-Carlton)
Phone 917/790-2626
Located on the 14th floor of the Ritz-Carlton, this impressive room can be pricey.

Rodeo Bar
375 Third Ave
Phone 212/683-6500
rodeobar.com
For the urban cowboy in all of us, there is Rodeo Bar.

Russian Vodka Room
265 W 52nd St
Phone 212/307-5835
rvrclub.com
A Midtown destination known for its house-flavored vodkas and imported caviar.

Sakagura
211 E 43rd St
Phone 212/953-7253
www.sakagura.com
Located deep below a Midtown office building, this Japanese drinking den is possibly the best hidden treasure in New York.

Serena
222 W 23rd St
Phone 212/255-4646
This cavernous lounge is located under the infamous Chelsea Hotel.

Suite 16
127 Eighth Ave
Phone 212/627-1680
A fun bar with hotel-themed service. Each of the 16 banquette booths has its own stocked minibar.

Thom's Bar
60 Thompson St
Phone 212/219-2000
This boutique hotel bar has quickly become a SoHo favorite for its incredible décor and well-made libations.

Toad Hall
57 Grand St
Phone 212/431-8145
A sports bar with an incredible Bloody Mary. Who would have thought?

Trinity Public House
229 E 84th St
Phone 212/327-4450
The friendliest of Irish pubs is right here in New York; patrons serve as guest bartenders on Thursdays.

Underbar
201 Park Ave S
(W Hotel Union Square)
Phone 212/358-1560
www.mocbars.com
This Gramercy bar located in the W Hotel Union Square has intimate booths with buzzers to summon the waitstaff.

Von
3 Bleecker St
Phone 212/473-3039
Named after the owner's grandfather, this establishment evokes the charm of an authentic Alsatian wine bar.

Waterfront Ale House
540 Second Ave
Phone 212/686-4104
www.waterfrontalehouse.com
This friendly ale house carries an assortment of homemade liquors and very reasonably priced food and drinks.

The Whiskey
1567 Broadway
(W Times Square Hotel)
Phone 212/930-7444
This hip spot in the W Times Square Hotel is a great place for weekend fun and dancing.

Budget-Friendly Restaurants

Romantic Restaurants

Family-Friendly Restaurants

Restaurants That Are Good for Groups

Quiet Restaurants

Restaurants That Serve Brunch

Restaurants with Outdoor Seating

Restaurants for
<u>Business Meals</u>

Restaurants with Unique Décor

Special-Occasion Restaurants

Hip & Trendy Restaurants

Fun Finds

Index

Index by Cuisine